A Bit on the Side

JASMINE BIRTLES

A Bit on the Side

500 ways to boost your income

PIATKUS

Visit the Piatkus website!

Piatkus publishes a wide range of best-selling fiction and non-fiction, including books on health, mind, body & spirit, sex, self-help, cookery, biography and the paranormal.

If you want to:
- read descriptions of our popular titles
- buy our books over the internet
- take advantage of our special offers
- enter our monthly competition
- learn more about your favourite Piatkus authors

VISIT OUR WEBSITE AT: www.piatkus.co.uk

Copyright © 2004 by Jasmine Birtles

First published in 2004 by
Piatkus Books Ltd
5 Windmill Street
London W1T 2JA
e-mail: info@piatkus.co.uk

The moral right of the author has been asserted

A catalogue record for this book is available from the British Library

ISBN 0 7499 2569 8

This book has been printed on paper manufactured with respect for the environment using wood from managed sustainable resources

Edited by Ian Paten
Text design by Paul Saunders

Typeset by
Action Publishing Technology Ltd, Gloucester
Printed and bound in Italy by
Legoprint Srl, Trento

Contents

Acknowledgements   **vii**

Introduction   **1**

1. Sell Your Body!   **5**
Sell your hair   5
Sperm or egg donation   7
Surrogacy   9
Medical experiments   11
Psychological research   13
Bein g an escort   14
Police line-ups   16
Modelling   17
Life modelling   20
Hand modelling   22
Film/TV extra   24
Be a lookalike!   27

2. Time to Spare?   **30**
Market research   30
Mystery shopping   33
Babysitting   36
The school run   38
Be a doula   41
Dog-walking and pet-minding   43
Gift fund-raising   45
Delivering   47
Invigilating exams   48
Bar and restaurant work   50
Saturday shop work   52
Debt collecting   53
House-sitting and house-minding   55
Cleaning   57
Ironing/laundry   61
Poll clerk   62
Plant car and hire   63

3. Space to Spare?   **67**
Renting out a room   67
Foreign students and visiting lecturers   71
Running a B&B   75
Renting out your home   77
Storage Space   80
Renting out your driveway or garage   81
Your home as a film set   83
Boarding pets in your home   86
Propagating seedlings   89
Growing vegetables and fruit to sell   91
Hiring out your garden as allotments   92
Bee-keeping   94
Horses and dogs   95

4. Got a Car?   **99**
Minicab driving   99
Chauffer work   101

Driving instruction 103
Food home delivery 106
Nappy delivery 107
Ads on your car 109
Car valeting 111
Car repair 113
Car buying and selling 115
Furniture removals 117
Dispatch and courier services 119

5. Home Alone **121**
Childminding 121
Fostering 123
Teleworking 126
Virtual assistant/secretarial 129
Tutoring and therapies 131
Proof-reading 133
Writer's research 135
Answering service 137
Accepting deliveries 139
Indexing 140
Book design and layout 142

6. Got a Hobby? **121**
Antiques dealing 144
Art dealing 147
Collecting 149
Sewing, dressmaking and altering 154
Dress designing 155
Millinery 158
Handbag-making 161
Hampers 163
Sweet-making 166
Pottery 169
Curtains and soft furnishing 171
Catering and cooking 172
Cake-making and decorating, jams 175
Greetings cards 178
Picture framing 180
Toy-making 183
Musical instrument-making 185
Photography 187

7. Are You Practical? **191**
DIY and odd jobs 191
Carpentry 193
Assembling furniture 196
Painting and decorating 198
Gardening 200
Window cleaning 202
Wood-stripping 203
Hedge-trimming 205
Gutter-clearing 206
Drain-unblocking 208
Fence-erecting and treating 209
Door-to-door security 211
Property manager 213
Inventing 214
Work abroad **217**

8. Could You Teach? **220**
   Computer training 220
   Fitness 222
   Tutoring 225
   Adult evening class 227
   Dog-training 229
   English as a Foreign Language 232
   Exam-marking 234

9. Therapies **237**
   Counselling 237
   Beautician 239
   Hairdressing 242
   Massage 244
   Alternative therapies 247

10. Can You Write? **250**
   Articles 250
   Novels 253
   TV or film screenplays 255
   Create a TV game show format 257
   Write a play or a musical 259
   Other types of book 262
   Joke-writing 263
   Copywriting 265
   Competitions 269
   Poetry 271
   Being a reader 273
   Songwriting 275

11. Are You Fun? **278**
   Party planning 278
   Children's entertainer 281
   Tour guide 283
   Entertainer – functions 286
   Master of ceremonies 289
   Busking and street entertaining 291
   Disc jockey 294
   Product demonstrating/selling 296
   Promotional work 298
   Voice-overs 300
   Club nights 301
   Selling stories to newspapers 305

12. Buying and Selling **307**
   Selling on the internet 307
   Car boot sales 312
   Garage Sales 315
   Auctions 316
   Property development 319
   Property finder 323
   Market trading 325
   Bulk buying and selling 328
   Import/export business 329
   Network marketing/direct selling 332
   Private swap shops 336
   Selling your own perfume 337
   Telesales 346

13. Got a Computer?   **342**
CV and letter-writing   343
Online research   345
Desktop publishing   347
Web design   349
Affiliate/partnership schemes   352
Earn while you surf   354
Online auctions   355
E-commerce   355

14. A Bit on the Dumb Side   **359**
Make Money Fast Schemes   359
Home-working schemes   360
Envelope stuffing   361
Medical claims processors   361
SMS and 09011 competitions   362
Internet scams   362
Cyber begging   364
The Lottery (Lotto)   364
Free lotteries   365
Gambling generally   366
Premium bonds   366
Property   367

15. Being a Business   **369**
Is it for you?   369
Make a plan   370
Keeping your books   371
Bank accounts   372
Advertising   372
Marketing   373
PR   373
Insurance   375
Getting paid   375

16. Do I Have to Pay Tax?   **377**
Expenses you can claim   379
What you can't claim   380
National Insurance   380
VAT   380

17. Make Money by Saving Money   **382**
Saving money without changing your lifestyle   383
Cutting back   387
Freebies   388
Saving tax   389
Quick tips   396

18. Making Your *Money* Make Money   **392**
How to do it   393
Investment options   394
Cash   394
Bonds   395
Gilts   396
Shares (also known as equities)   396
Property   398
Pensions   401

Appendix   **403**

Acknowledgements

A big thank-you to my assistant/researcher, Kerry McCarthy, who really helped with the mammoth task of researching this book. Also to my agent, Darin Jewell, who has been unfailingly enthusiastic about the project.

Also, big thanks to all the Motley Fool crew for their continuous help and advice, particularly Cliff D'Arcy, Jane Mack – who even put me in touch with her brother, who propagates seedlings – Bruce Jackson, George Row and Andrew Morris. Big thanks too to my editor at the *Independent on Sunday*, Sam Dunn, for his help and advice.

Huge thanks, of course, to my enthusiastic editor, Alan Brooke, and all the sales, marketing, PR and design teams at Piatkus for their excellent work. Also, thanks to all the friends and friends of friends who agreed to be quoted or 'used' in the book as examples or experts in their various fields. And a word for friends who helped with parts of the book – Annie Davies, Mike Halson, Stephen Thompson and especially Mike Anderiesz, who gave me loads of information on the technology-based sections of the book.

Thanks too to the inspiring example of my mother, who runs her own nanny and doula agencies, and to my best friend, Tom Johnsen, for his continuous support, advice and great goodness.

Introduction

EVERYONE NEEDS TO make a bit on the side once in a while! Whether you're dealing with debt, saving up, investing in your future or just sick of running out of money before the end of every month, on the quiet we all yearn for a bit more cash.

Mind you, it's highly likely that you've already got more than you think you have. For a start, how much money are you wasting? There's no point taking the time and effort to *make* more money if you're throwing it down the drain each week. So make sure you've read and followed Chapter 17 (Make Money by Saving Money) before you go out and try some of the money-making ideas in the book. Don't forget to have a good spring clean around your home too. Go through every room in your house and pull out anything you don't want any more. Sell it on eBay, Amazon or go and do a car boot sale for a day. Do that at least once or twice a year and you will have a clearer home and some useful cash every now and then, just using stuff you have already.

When I've sold things this way – and I do, regularly – it's a useful reminder of what a waste of money so many things were in the first place, particularly if I bought them new. You only have to have the experience of trying to sell a top you know cost you £35 and only getting £2.50 for it to realise that you really need to think through everyday purchases much more. Imagine the junk we accumulate simply because at the time we just *had* to have it!

That so-called 'shopping therapy' is one of the most bogus 'treatments' you can get, particularly if you do it all on credit (by the way, whenever you see the word 'credit', replace it with the word 'debt' in your own mind and then see how you feel about it). So another way of making, and saving, money is to get a new attitude to 'things'. Do you *really* need the thing you think you're desperate for? Do you think it will make your life instantly better if you had it? One of the best money-making and money-saving words in the English language is 'no'. Use it more often when people are trying to sell things to you – or when your 'inner child' is screaming for the latest toy – and you'll feel *so* much better for it!

The other great resources *you already have* are your own abilities and talents (yes, you do have some) and that's a great way to start on your money-making quest. Use your hobbies, the qualifications, training or experience you already have to turn into money. Think laterally too. If you have carpentry skills you could turn them into toy-making or if you are a great cook and you have given birth at least once you could become a doula (birth partner or post-birth partner). Just a long-time interest in something can be a money-maker if you work at it. A gardening fanatic who is totally self-taught can still make money propagating seedlings or doing some gardening or hedge-cutting for people in the neighbourhood.

Any job is more than just a money-making exercise. However much we might moan and groan about having to get up and go out to work, unemployment is usually more boring and stressful. All types of activities give us more than just an income – you can meet people, get a sense of satisfaction, go places you wouldn't normally visit, learn things that are interesting or useful and often stretch yourself and find out things about your abilities and strengths you never knew you had. So if there's something you've always wanted to do – teach English as a foreign language, for example, be a stand-up comedian or run some fun parties, don't let your lack of qualifications or experience stop you. If you can afford it, this is the time to get that training or experience and go for it. Even if you don't make masses of money and you spend more time on it than you meant, at least you will have had a go and you won't get old and grey wishing you'd tried.

Don't just grab at dodgy money-making activities out of desperation, though. We joke that some people will do anything for money, but when you look at some of the more lurid news stories that come up you realise how worryingly true that is. When you're desperate for cash, the bailiffs are knocking at the door, the children are in a state and you feel imprisoned by your situation, it's very easy to stop thinking straight and to do things for money that can do you a lot of harm long-term, or even short-term. The sex industry, for example, is proliferating across the globe, in part thanks to the Internet and there are thousands of women and men involved in it. However, becoming a real or digital sex worker is a career fraught with complications. Certainly there's money to be made, sometimes eye-watering amounts, but the losses, financially, emotionally, health-wise and spiritually – are too great to make it genuinely worth it for most people.

There has also been a lot of news coverage about people, even in the Western world, trying to sell their vital organs over the internet for money. Kidneys, particularly, sell for thousands and for people who need a serious injection of cash it can be a temptation, but a big deep breath, a calm moment and possibly a word with close friends should help them squash that!

When you're looking for a way to earn some extra cash, don't just look at the bottom line. Look at the expenses in terms of the money you will have to invest, the effort and time you will have to take and remember the 'invisibles': how it could harm you physically and what it could steal from your soul – the essential essence of *you* and your ability to love and take joy in life and other people. If you really think this through you may realise that some ways of making money actually take much more from you in the long run than they could ever give.

Oh, and, very importantly, don't limit yourself or allow others or circumstances to limit your opportunities to get active and make money. Even if you can't physically get about, you can make money – see Chapters 2, 3, 5, 10 and 13 for ideas if you're stuck at home. Many women (and it is mostly women) are single parents, feeling stuck at home with the kids and unable to afford childcare. There are many ideas that would be specially good for you in this book, but again, think laterally. Can you get together with other single parents and childmind for each other on alternate days, allowing each other to go and do some work at least part-time? Think round and through obstacles. Too many of us think we can't do things for all kinds of reasons even before we've tried. Don't let that happen to you – there is an infinite number of ideas and opportunities in the world for everyone, right now. It's just that most of us don't believe it so we don't even try to look for them.

It's quite likely that you will end up doing a few different things to make a bit on the side, not just one. Some of my friends seem to make all their money just doing 'bits on the side', particularly writers and performers who make very little at their 'main' job but keep themselves going as film extras, market researchers, mystery shoppers, buskers, waiters, virtual and real secretaries and babysitters. It's an honest living and at least they get variety!

I've picked up all sorts of ideas and tips from these friends and friends of friends and I've tried to include unusual and strange jobs as well as the ones you might expect. However, I'm always interested in any new ideas people have so if you have a fun or different way (make sure it's honest and relatively decent, please) of making money that I haven't included, do let me know. Write to me c/o Piatkus Books, 5 Windmill Street, London W1T 2JA. I'll be *very* interested to hear from you!

Sell Your Body!

EVEN IF YOU think you have no talents, time or expertise, you still have one great asset to use – your body. Everyone has one, so why not make some honest money out of it?

Sell your hair

Extensions, wigs and hairpieces are increasingly popular and many are made out of real hair. European hair is particularly sought after as it is rarer in type than, for example, Asian hair. If you have long flowing locks, and you want to get them cut anyway, why not make money out of them?

HOW TO DO IT

Your hair needs to be at least 6 inches long for it to be of any use in making a wig. It must be clean and must have had no chemical treatments at all – no colouring, perming or tinting. Once it is cut it needs to be put in a ponytail so that it is obvious which is the top and which is the bottom. Hair follicles go in a certain direction and it will be ruined if some of the hair is upside down. The colour of your hair doesn't make any difference to the price as it is all stripped of colour before it is sold.

The main buyer (and therefore seller) of real hair for wigs, extensions and so on is Banbury Postiche (also known as Wigsuk.com). 'People can send us their hair by post and if we want it we'll weigh it and send them a cheque back,' says sales director Nick Allen. 'If it's not right we'll just send it back to them.' He adds that most European hair comes from outside Britain where long hair is more common. European hair is increasingly in demand, however, as more people in this country go for real hair extensions or wigs and need the special texture and qualities of European hair to match their own.

HOW MUCH CAN YOU MAKE?

According to Banbury Postiche, the fees are £3 per ounce if your hair is 6–12 inches long and £5 per ounce if it is more than 12 inches long. They have asked us to point out, though, that no one is going to get rich by selling their hair!

COSTS

Just the cost of having your hair cut – which, one assumes, you would be doing anyway.

TRAINING AND QUALIFICATIONS

You don't need training or qualifications.

PROS

This is an easy way of making money and getting a free haircut at the same time.

CONS

You can only do it once every few years, and do you really want short hair again?

USEFUL CONTACTS

Wigsuk.com (also known as Banbury Postiche), Little Bourton House, Southam Road, Banbury, Oxfordshire OX16 1SR, 01295 750606, www.wigsuk.com

Wig Specialities Ltd, 173 Seymour Place, London W1H 4PL, 020 7262 6565, www.wigspecialities.co.uk

Sperm or egg donation

In this country, sperm and egg donation is supposed to be more of a voluntary activity than a money-making one. You can, however, make a small amount of money which, in the case of men, can really make it worth it. For women, though, you have to really want to do it as a gift to society to make it worth it!

HOW TO DO IT

If you decide to become an egg or sperm donor, you should go to your local fertility clinic or hospital. Get in touch with the Human Fertilisation and Embryology Authority (HFEA) for a list of local approved centres (contact details below).

The relevant treatment centre must ask you for personal details. By law, donors' names and dates of birth have to be given to the HFEA to be held on its confidential information register. At the moment no identifying information about you may be given to children born following treatment with your donated eggs or sperm. The government has said, however, that it may make some information available to children of future sperm or egg donors – so keep that in mind, along with the fact that no identifying information can be given without your consent.

Egg donors have to be healthy and aged between 18 and 35. It's important that your periods are regular as this indicates that your hormone levels are within the normal range. You should not have any personal history of viral sexually transmitted infections, and there must be no personal or family history of inheritable disorders.

You will be given drugs to regulate your menstrual cycle so that it is easier to collect the eggs. Drugs turn a woman's normal menstrual cycle into something like a human egg harvest. After she has been taking the drugs for four weeks, her eggs are ready for harvest and she undergoes a ten-minute operation (yes, operation!) to remove them. The surgery isn't risk free as there is always the danger of injury or infection. Frankly, it is quite an invasive process, and you need to really *want* to help childless people to do this!

For men it is much easier, although it is by no means definite that you will qualify. According to a spokeswoman from the HFEA: 'Many men are turned away by fertility clinics as they don't have good enough quality sperm. An ideal sperm donor needs to have high-quality sperm with good mobility and a high sperm count.' You will also have to go through medical screening, of course, including an HIV test.

Man Not Included, an Internet site aimed at lesbian and single women who want children (not licensed by the HFEA), use fresh sperm, unlike HFEA clinics, which freeze sperm for proper screening, and they often pay more in expenses than standard clinics, though not much more than £40.

HOW MUCH CAN YOU MAKE?

Not a lot, given the effort involved (at least for women). The HFEA keeps the payment low to make sure that people 'donate' out of altruism rather than for the money. Therefore you can only get £15 per donation plus 'reasonable expenses' (travel, childcare, etc.) up to a maximum of £50 per day.

COSTS

There are no real costs involved as your expenses are reimbursed.

TRAINING AND QUALIFICATIONS

You don't need any training or qualifications ... just good concentration if you're a man!

PROS

This is a fairly easy way to make some money if you're a man – in fact it could be seen as a way to make money out of a leisure activity! You also have the satisfaction of knowing that you are helping childless people who desperately want a baby.

CONS

There is very little money in it and a lot of effort, particularly for women, for whom it is a thoroughly invasive and even painful process. If the laws change there is also the possibility that any progeny may be able to trace you later on, although you will be informed of this if you decide to donate.

USEFUL CONTACTS

Human Fertilisation and Embryology Authority, 020 7291 8200, www.hfea.gov.uk. This is the official body regulating sperm and egg donation. Contact details for your local fertility clinics and hospitals are on this site as well as information on your rights as a donor.

Man Not Included, www.mannotincluded.com, a fertility clinic for single and lesbian women

Association of Independent Clinical Research Contractors, 01162 719727

Surrogacy

As with egg and sperm donation, the authorities are very keen to make sure that women are not 'paid' to be surrogate mothers. Rather, a woman can be reimbursed 'reasonable expenses' for acting as a surrogate mother.

HOW TO DO IT

Get in touch with Surrogacy UK and COTS (Childlessness Overcome Through Surrogacy) for information on how to become a surrogate mother and what the rules are.

There are two types of surrogacy. The first is straight surrogacy, also known as traditional surrogacy, which is when the egg of the surrogate mother and the sperm of the intended father are used. This can be performed in an IVF clinic, but more often the technique of artificial insemination is used at home. The second is host surrogacy, also known as gestational surrogacy. This method uses the eggs of the intended mother combined with the sperm of her husband or donor sperm. In this case an IVF clinic is always needed. A baby conceived by this method has no biological connection to the surrogate. This is a far more difficult way of getting pregnant. The chances of it working are low, and it requires a lot more time and energy to complete.

You have to be 100 per cent sure that you are comfortable with the whole situation, as once the pregnancy has started there is no going back – imagine the heartache that can occur when intended parents and surrogate mothers find out that they do not get along after conception has occurred!

Being a surrogate mother is nine months of often gruelling work. You have to endure doctor's appointments, morning sickness, back pain, extra weight, enormous ankles, sleeplessness and the possibility of complications at birth. It is by no means an easy way to make money – in fact, it is probably one of the hardest.

HOW MUCH CAN YOU MAKE?

Carol O'Riley of Surrogacy UK, who has been the surrogate mother of three babies, says that mothers get between £4,000 and £10,000 in expenses. 'You have to take time off work for two years, eating a proper diet doubles your grocery bill and you have extra travelling and childcare costs. No surrogate walks out having made any real money.'

COSTS

You really have to look after yourself when you're pregnant, so do expect to pay more for good food, and of course you will have to put the rest of your life on hold when you become heavily pregnant. Going for regular check-ups and tests will also involve travel expenses.

TRAINING AND QUALIFICATIONS

You don't need any training or qualifications.

PROS

If you enjoy being pregnant and giving birth – and many women do – this can be a good excuse to do it again. You will also have the satisfaction of knowing that you have helped a childless couple have a baby.

CONS

How much more invasive can it be than to have to get pregnant for money? It will have a major effect on your body and could cause all sorts of harm. Also, it is possible that, if your egg is being used, you will not be able to bear to part with the baby when it is born.

USEFUL CONTACTS

Childlessness Overcome Through Surrogacy (COTS), 0844 414 0181, www.cots.org.uk

Surrogacy UK, 01531 821889 or 01933 389294, www.surrogacyuk.org – a website run by two women who have been surrogate mothers

Medical experiments

Drugs, creams, cold remedies – they all need testing on humans, and the money is quite good. If you don't mind swallowing pills for money this can bring in hundreds at a time.

HOW TO DO IT

There are all sorts of agencies and centres that are looking for people to test their medical products. Many advertise in local newspapers and magazines, on the Net or in student halls and hostels used by travellers and foreign students.

You can also find information on where to go on Internet sites such as www.biotrax.co.uk, which has information on medical and other trials all over the UK, including non-invasive activities such as blood testing (£60 a pint) and contact lens testing (up to £200, depending on the length of time). They also produce a directory of medical testing centres and other ways of making money through surveys and market research which you can buy for £20.

You don't have to be in *perfect* health to take part in these trials, although most centres will want you to be healthy. Many have rules on what kind of people they will and won't take for whatever reason. Some, for example, prefer men to women because of the fear that women of child-bearing age could get pregnant, which would invalidate the trial. Quite often the women they use have to be either sterilised or using contraception. There are many trials conducted, however, using people with medical conditions, including asthma and life-threatening diseases.

If you've got a cold and you live near Cardiff – or you don't mind travelling there – you can get free medicines to try out and get paid for it at the Common Cold Centre at the Cardiff School of Biosciences. All volunteers are paid for the time they spend at the centre and for any inconvenience.

HOW MUCH CAN YOU MAKE?

Potentially thousands a year if you do a lot of these. This may not be good for your body, however, and you may be prevented from doing more than a few by the labs themselves.

COSTS

There are no costs involved other than travel.

TRAINING AND QUALIFICATIONS

You don't need any training or qualifications.

PROS

The money is quite good for very little actual work. The non-invasive experiments are particularly easy and will not harm your body.

CONS

Who knows what the long-term, or even short-term, effects of drugs could be on your body? You could be taking your life in your hands by trying out some of these drugs, or at least giving yourself unnecessary health problems.

USEFUL CONTACTS

Biotrax, 0161 736 7312, www.biotrax.co.uk – a very comprehensive website with information and support and a directory for those wanting to get involved in clinical trials

www.gpgp.net – a sister website to Biotrax with information and support for regular medical volunteers

www.hotrecruit.com – a website with many varied clinical trials that you can get paid for

Common Cold Centre, Cardiff School of Biosciences, Cardiff University, Park Place, Cardiff CF10 3US, freephone 0500 655398, www.cf.ac.uk/biosi/associates/cold/home.html

Psychological research

This is a similar deal to physical medical research but much less invasive.

HOW TO DO IT

There are often ads in local papers, on student noticeboards and on the Internet looking for people to take part in psychological tests. The tests are usually pretty easy, involving either brain scans or simple memory exercises. You will be paid cash for your time and to cover travel expenses, although many centres will only recruit in their local area.

For example, Clinical Neuroscience in Kent recruit people for memory tests, brain imaging and cognitive function studies and will pay you for your time and reimburse travel expenses. The Manchester-based School for Psychiatry and Behavioural

Sciences will pay up to £60 a session for brain scanning and imaging studies.

HOW MUCH CAN YOU MAKE?

From about £10 to £60 a session.

COSTS

There are no real costs as your travel expenses are usually reimbursed.

TRAINING AND QUALIFICATIONS

You don't need any training or qualifications.

PROS

This is a nice, easy, non-invasive way of making a bit of cash. The tests can sometimes be fun too.

CONS

You may not consider the money enough to make it worthwhile, and anyway there may not be a centre close enough for you to visit.

USEFUL CONTACTS

Biotrax, 0161 736 7312, www.biotrax.co.uk – provides information on centres doing psychological as well as medical research

Clinical Neuroscience Research, 7 Twistleton Court, Priory Hill, Dartford, Kent DA1 2EN, 01322 286862

School of Psychiatry and Behavioural Sciences, Room G907, Stopford Building, Oxford Road, Manchester M13 9PT

Being an escort

Not ideal for women, whatever the escort agency's level of honesty, but could be good for men if you go with a legitimate agency.

HOW TO DO IT

Join an agency if you want to be safe and sure of actually getting paid. Lots of escort agencies advertise on the Net and in local papers and men's magazines. If you simply want to be a 'companion' to rich women for the evening it is best to go with agencies that are recommended by friends or that make a point of their ethics.

One journalist went undercover with Platinum Select, had three dates and got £600 cash, two dinners and a night on vintage champagne. 'For £49.99 they would host my details for a year,' he says. 'Subscribers would call me direct and the dates are arranged strictly between myself and the client. Two weeks later, I got my first client. Amy wanted to book for the following evening. "We'll be going out for dinner so wear a suit and tie," she said. She named a time and a restaurant: "I'll need you for four hours," she added. "And, just so you know, there'll be no sex involved." Well, that cleared that up.'

Apparently there is a new generation of career girls who have the money, motives and confidence to use an escort. They can't find a decent man so they turn to escort services. Also, escort adverts have spread from adult magazines to mainstream media, so the stigma is disappearing. The Net also allows women to browse and contact escorts at a safe distance.

Agencies look for attractive, personable, friendly and cultured men who love women and would be an interesting and, ideally, sexy companion for a woman for an evening. You will need to be well dressed, well groomed and great company. Intelligence and a good education would certainly set you apart.

HOW MUCH CAN YOU MAKE?

It depends on how popular you are and how many nights a week you do. Average pay is about £200 a night, and you get your dinner and nightclub entrance paid for too.

COSTS

The only costs involved are travel expenses and money spent on your looks, your clothes and possibly a nice gift for your 'companion'.

TRAINING AND QUALIFICATIONS

You don't need any training or qualifications.

PROS

If you like women and are a bit of a looker this can be a very easy and pleasant way to make good money.

CONS

You may feel used or be bored or annoyed by the women you go out with. You may also find yourself in a difficult or dangerous situation if the woman is part of an outfit that has ulterior motives.

USEFUL CONTACTS

Platinum Select, Platinum House, Chester CH2 3ZZ, 08000 155588, www.platinumselect.co.uk

Police line-ups

It used to be that you could make about £15 quite regularly taking part in police line-ups. Now, though, thanks to technology, you just get a one-off fee for taking part in a video 'line-up'.

HOW TO DO IT

Go to your local police station and ask them about being videoed for identity parades. If they think they may need someone who looks like you they will video you (front, sides, etc) and add it to their library. That's pretty much it! Not hard for a tenner.

HOW MUCH CAN YOU MAKE?

A one-off fee of about £10.

COSTS

None other than travel to the police station.

TRAINING AND QUALIFICATIONS

You don't need training or qualifications.

PROS

This is an easy way of making £10. You don't need to be able to do anything other than stand in a line and, occasionally, read out a phrase or sentence.

CONS

There's less work for women. It could be worrying if witnesses keep picking you out!

Modelling

Every other teenage girl seems to have a desperate need to become either a model or a pop star. Only a few can ever make it to supermodel status, but others can make a bit of a living.

HOW TO DO IT

If you think you have the makings of a model, have some good, professional photos done of yourself and take them round to local model agencies. Most proper modelling work – including catalogues, adverts, magazine spreads and demonstrations but excluding so-called 'glamour' – comes through agencies, so to get anywhere you will need to be on the books of one of them.

If you think you have an 'interesting' face – unusual, characterful, intriguingly ugly even – contact the model agency Ugly. Yes, there really is such an organisation (contact details below). They specialise in interesting-looking people and have regular work for photo-shoots, adverts and even appearances on TV and film. Kasia Hac from the agency says, 'A lot of our character models approached us because they have usually been told they have a "strange", "quirky" or "unusual" look. Obviously with our name we cover all types of characters from the extremes of tattooing and piercing to different body shapes. However, on our books most of our models are very much "everyday" faces. As long as our models are confident and comfortable in front of a camera, age, ethnicity or shape is totally irrelevant.'

Ugly hold auditions once every 18 months where people come in and have a short interview explaining why they want to join the agency and what they can offer. Again, if you think you could work through them, get a set of good and interesting photos professionally taken and send them with your CV and contact details.

Modelling, however glamorous it may look on the outside, is not for the gentle or the faint-hearted, though. When I asked the London agency Models One for a comment they refused, saying: 'Modelling is not really relevant to the title of the book. It's hardly a bit on the side. To make a proper career of it takes such commitment, tough skin, and total driven ambition for it to pay off financially.' True, but if you're young and looking to make money for college or while you're going for acting or singing auditions, it is possible to make some cash this way, at least for a few years.

Modelling is certainly something you can combine with other activities, such as being a student, acting or other work in the entertainment professions. If you have the looks and a strong personality, the pay can be extremely rewarding and, whatever those in the business might say, it's hardly as arduous as, for example, working down a mine, is it?

HOW MUCH CAN YOU MAKE?

Anything from £50 for a small local photo-shoot to millions if you get to supermodel status.

COSTS

You will need to spend money on your appearance – hair, skin, make-up, nails, gym sessions, attractive clothes – and on photography and other elements of marketing.

TRAINING AND QUALIFICATIONS

Although you don't really need any formal training it's good to get expert advice on marketing yourself and even how to carry yourself in interviews and photo-shoots.

PROS

If you've got it, this gives you a chance to flaunt it – and make money at the same time.

CONS

There might be times when you have to have nerves of steel to take the criticism you'll get about your looks. You've got to be confident enough to take a few dents to the ego without losing faith in yourself.

USEFUL CONTACTS

Ugly Model Agency, Suite 1, 256 Edgware Road, London W2 1DS, 020 7402 5564, www.ugly.co.uk

The Association of Model Agents, 122 Brompton Rd, London SW3 1JD, 020 7564 6466

Case study

Theatre director Emma Lucia worked her way through university as a model in the 1980s. 'I did it full-time for a year before I went to university then part-time for three years,' she explains. 'A woman I knew who provided props for magazine shoots suggested that I get on the books of a model agency and she gave me a list of places to go to. One of them sent me off to do test shots which I didn't have to pay for. They didn't take me but gave me the shots and I took them to other agencies and got on the books of one in central London.'

She says that the money was good – £500–£600 a day in those days – but it involved a lot of traipsing round town with her portfolio, sometimes going to ten castings in a day. 'It's ➤

not really a part-time job, although I managed to do it when I was a student,' she adds. 'You do have to be available for castings during the day and you never know when you will get the work. I got paid a lot for the jobs I did but I might not get work for three months or so, so it wasn't that well paid if you even it out. Still, it was a great way to see the world!'

Life modelling

How would you like to make money from just sitting around doing nothing? If that made your eyes light up, try some life modelling for painters and sculptors.

HOW TO DO IT

Contact local art schools and adult education colleges for information on how you can offer your services and an application form. You can also put ads up in local art schools or newsagents offering your services. Once you have worked for a few artists or art schools, word should get about that you are available for life modelling, which will bring in more work.

Life modelling sessions usually last about three hours each, with breaks for rest. They may be for a school or institute class, an art society group or privately for a professional artist or sculptor. Most artists will need a few sessions to get the likeness they are after. For some artists their model is central to the work, involving endless sittings; for others it may be just two hours and a quick reference.

'It's very difficult to get good models,' says sculptor William Fawke. 'Some are hopeless. They might look great, but they're uninterested, can't keep still or can't hold a pose. Actors and drama and dance students are the best in my opinion, but I am pleased to have anyone who is good at holding a pose.'

Zoe Simon, a university graduate, playwright, actor and part-time model in London, says: 'The best school experience was with the Royal College of Art and the Art Academy. Both approached the figure intelligently and challengingly and it was very rewarding. The Heatherley were reliable and good, but two or three other art schools are slow payers – be warned!'

HOW MUCH CAN YOU MAKE?

In London, life models make between £7 and £8 per hour clothed and £10 and £11 unclothed. Outside London the pay is about 10 per cent less.

COSTS

There are no costs other than your travel.

TRAINING AND QUALIFICATIONS

You don't need any training or qualifications.

PROS

This is a very easy way of making money out of your body, so long as you are able to stay relatively still for a long time. You don't have to be beautiful or have a fabulous body. Anyone can do it so long as they have the stamina and willingness to assist the artist.

CONS

It can be cold, uncomfortable and embarrassing. It can also be depressing to see what the artists have made of your body!

USEFUL CONTACTS

The Art Academy, Waterloo, 020 7409 6531

The Royal Academy, Piccadilly, London W1, 020 7300 8000, www.royalacademy.org.uk

Royal British Society of Sculptors, 020 7373 8615, www.rbs.org.uk – contact them for a list of figure sculptors in your area

The Sketch Club, 020 7352 8209, www.londonsketchclub. com – contact them to offer your services to members

Hand modelling

If you have lovely hands that you have kept nicely moisturised and manicured – whether you're male or female – you can make money out of them. It doesn't matter what the rest of you looks like – that won't show!

HOW TO DO IT

The only effective way you can make regular money out of being a hand model is to sign up with an agency. There are various specialist hand model agencies (see below for two of the best) but some general model agencies such as Models One also have hand models. Most of the work is in London, although some major cities such as Birmingham or Manchester will also have jobs available. Outside those places it's best to go to regular model agencies and ask whether they do hands.

Visit the model agencies with your hands at their best, or have some very good photos done of your hands, ideally holding something or in some other sort of action shot, and send them to the agencies. Don't expect too much, though! 'We take very few new people on,' says Steve Barker of Hired Hands model agency. 'We have a few regular models and, mostly, that's all we need.'

If you are taken on you will be asked to go to castings at photography studios or TV production companies for adverts. If you take it seriously you should have a 'hand book' to take with you, full of photographs of your hands in various different poses. Not everyone does this, however.

You will need to keep your hands in very good shape, well moisturised and manicured at all times. Make sure you wear gloves to do the washing-up or gardening, or anything messy.

Hand modelling jobs come up sporadically, as with anything to do with advertising and modelling, and it is not the sort of work you could do if you already have a 9–5 job. If you are able to be flexible with your time during the day, and you can set up appointments at one or two days' notice, this could be a pleasant way of earning money from your body.

HOW MUCH CAN YOU MAKE?

Anything from about £100 to thousands a week if you get adverts that take a long time to film.

COSTS

You will need to buy hand creams and gloves to protect your hands. You may have to pay for regular manicures – unless you do them yourself – but other than that the only cost is your travel expenses.

TRAINING AND QUALIFICATIONS

You don't need training or qualifications, just lovely hands.

PROS

This can be a pleasant and undemanding way of making rather good money if you are lucky enough to be taken on by an agency.

CONS

There are far fewer hand modelling jobs than regular modelling work so very few people get to be on the books of agents. You need to be available during the day and the work is not at all regular. In economic down times advertising is often the first casualty, so you could go for weeks without this extra work.

USEFUL CONTACTS

Derek's Hands, 020 7924 2484, www.derekshands.com

Hired Hands, 020 7267 9212

Case study

Suki Webster is an actress and comedian but supplements her income as a hand model. 'I just fell into it, really,' she says. 'An actress friend of mine is also a nail technician and one day, doing my nails, she said I should be a hand model. Later I went to an agency called Hired Hands who were looking for actresses to work in adverts and they said they'd take me on as a hand model.'

Since then, Suki has had regular work as a hand model. 'I've never taken it too seriously,' she says, 'but I've always had enough work from it.' In London the agencies offer £100 an hour for a photographic shoot and £400 a day for an advertising shoot, with triple pay for overtime. 'The agency's fees are 25 per cent, which is quite high, but I don't begrudge it to them at all,' says Suki, 'because I wouldn't get the jobs myself. I come away with a basic of £67 an hour, after their fee and VAT, which is still good for standing around holding something!'

Suki says that the main attribute you need, apart from good hands, of course, is a degree of confidence that allows you not to shake and to pick things up and put them down in *exactly* the same place. 'Really, when you've got close-up shots, millimetres make a difference. It's not always easy when you've got the ad agency crowding round you and the director barking orders. You need to be confident enough not to let it put you off.'

Film/TV extra

Anyone can be a film extra or walk-on. You don't need any acting ability or particular looks.

HOW TO DO IT

Simply contact some extras agencies and get yourself on their books. You can find a comprehensive list of agencies in *Contacts* (£10.99, Spotlight Publications) although you should be careful who you sign up with. There are some rogue agencies that will charge you money to register with them and then do nothing for you. An agency can reasonably charge you for taking your photograph and including it in their book but it should be a low fee.

Another useful book to look at is *You Can be a Movie Extra* by Rob Martin (£6.99, Titan Books), which goes through all the stages of becoming an extra, how to make the most of it and who to contact. Rob runs the London agency Casting Collective which is well established and has an excellent website at www.castingcollective.co.uk. 'Check with the union BECTU if you want to know if an agency is approved,' he says. 'There are some sharks out there who will charge a fee then do nothing for you, so check them out.'

There are strict rules, set out by the union Equity, as to how much extras should be paid per day and per hour. 'The basic pay is £64.50 a day,' says Rob Martin, 'but you can earn up to £200 if you have to do an hour or two overtime, using your own uniform or special props, doing a night shoot, or all sorts of other things.'

Really experienced extras have all sorts of props and uniforms at home – nurse's uniforms, wigs, police uniforms, chef's hats, and so on. They are also regularly available during the week – most filming work is on weekdays. It really helps if you have a car so that you can get to the more rural shoots. If you have other skills such as being able to ride a motorbike, juggling, rollerblading or playing a musical instrument, that can help you get more work too, but it's not essential.

The most important factor in getting regular work is being available most of the time – including night-times occasionally – and living relatively close to where films are made. If you live deep in the Shropshire countryside it is unlikely that you will get much work, but if your home is in or around London, Leeds, Glasgow, Bristol or another city where films and TV dramas are regularly made, it could be very much worth your while signing up with an agency.

HOW MUCH CAN YOU MAKE?

The basic is £64.50 per day, but you can get up to £200 with 'add-ons'.

COSTS

There are no major costs other than travel and, if you're serious, the cost of replica uniforms, wigs and other props.

TRAINING AND QUALIFICATIONS

You don't need any training or qualifications.

PROS

This is a great way to make money without really trying. Also, if you have books you really want to read – or write – you can get on with them and get paid at the same time!

CONS

You can get very bored if you don't have anything specific to do in the long waits between periods of actual filming. You can only do it if you live in the right area, and you will be away from home for entire days, or nights.

USEFUL CONTACTS

BECTU, 373–Clapham Road, London SW9 9BT, 020 7346 0900, www.bectu.org.uk

The Casting Collective, 317–21 Latimer Road, London W10 5BN, 020 8962 0099, www.castingcollective.co.uk

Ray Knight, 12a Lambolle Place, London NW3 4PG, 020 7722 4111, www.rayknightcasting.co.uk

Case study

John Random is a writer in south-east London and he supplements his income by being an extra. He has an Equity card, but you don't have to have one to do it. 'It's really useful for me because I can write or do some reading when I'm waiting to go on set,' he says. 'I've written several sketches while waiting on set and an entire novel!' John is signed up with three extras agencies which cost him around £60–£70 to join. 'I've been with others but they didn't get me the work so I dropped them. I've been with Ray Knight since I started in 1987, though, because they're so good.'

John often has to turn jobs down because he looks after his son and some days he teaches English as a foreign language, but on average he works as an extra for about a day a week. 'The money can vary depending on what you do,' he says. 'You can get extra money for all kinds of things – using your car, having your hair cut, having your lunch broken into, travelling outside a certain radius from London, having a line or even just a "reaction". All those things can add money on.' You can also get more money for working at night or having your own uniform and props. 'I know someone who specialises in being vicars,' adds John. 'In fact he's got so many costumes he asks them, "What denomination?" He can do Protestant or Catholic. He just looks like a vicar.'

Be a lookalike!

Do complete strangers say, 'Wow, you really look like Jude Law!' or 'Has anyone told you that you look just like Madonna?' You could make money out of this, just by turning up at events and looking like a star!

HOW TO DO IT

If you really think you look like Elton John, Nicole Kidman or

Danny DeVito, contact a lookalike agency (several advertise on the back page of *The Stage* newspaper) and either go to see them – dressed as the celeb you resemble – or send them photographs of yourself (colour is best) looking as much like them as you can manage!

You will need to look like someone who is popular and, ideally, still alive, although some personalities, such as Marilyn Monroe or Humphrey Bogart, are still wanted for all sorts of events and photo-shoots. Looking like King George IV or Robin Day is not going to get you very far. You may find that there are already a few people who also look like the celeb you are wanting to mimic, but that is not necessarily a problem. Some agencies have two or three different people who look like the same celeb, so even if they do have someone already, you could still try.

'Always phone the agency first to get the lowdown on what they want from you and find who to send the photo to and what the address is,' says actress Caroline Bernstein, who occasionally works as a lookalike for Cherie Blair and Mystic Meg. 'Also find out if there is a demand for that particular celeb so that you don't waste your time sending in the photo. Phone and then send is the drill!'

You will not get regular work from this unless you are absolutely the spitting image of someone very much in demand (such as the lookalikes who do the Queen, Prince William and David Beckham), but you could get quite a lot of bookings in a year. It helps to have clothes, wigs and make-up that make you look as much like the person you are imitating as possible. It would also help to study pictures and video footage to see how they walk and hold themselves.

If you are taken on to an agency's books you could be asked to appear at corporate events to 'meet and greet' – that's where you wander around smiling at guests, shaking hands, posing for photographs, etc. – or you could be used for commercials, as stand-ins for the real people, or for PR events. Unless you are very much in demand, most of your work will be in the evenings, although you may get whole days here and there, so it helps to be available during the day as well.

HOW MUCH CAN YOU MAKE?

On the whole, sessions pay around £300-£350 a time, although those who are much in demand can earn a lot more than that just to appear at an event.

COSTS

You may have to buy special clothes, wigs and make-up to make yourself look more like the celeb.

TRAINING AND QUALIFICATIONS

You don't need any training or qualifications, but it helps to have an entertainment background.

PROS

This is quite an easy and often pleasant way of making money. You may be asked to turn up at conferences, parties and photo-shoots, which can be fun and quite glamorous.

CONS

You may not get any lookalike work for the entire year if there is no call for your character. You may find it weird to be liked and fêted for looking like someone else rather than for yourself.

USEFUL CONTACTS

Equity, Guild House, Upper St Martin's Lane, London WC2H 9EG, 020 7379 6000, www.equity.org.uk

Susan Scott Lookalikes, 020 7387 9245, www.lookalikes-susanscott.co.uk

Splitting Images, 020 8809 2327, www.splitting-images.com

www.lookalikes-unite.com – an information site for lookalikes and anyone who would like to become one.

CHAPTER TWO

Time to Spare?

THE OLD SAYING 'Time is money' is true if you can sell services to people who have little of it. If you are unemployed, retired, a student or a homemaker you could sell your time to people who have jobs and money but not enough time to do things they need to do.

Market research

You might be irritated by smiling people with clipboards stopping you in the shopping centre and asking your opinions on mayonnaise, but if you were paid to talk about it, in a pleasant room with food and drink laid on, that would be a different matter, wouldn't it?

HOW TO DO IT

There are a few companies – not many – in Britain that have a pool of people they call on regularly to join a focus group. Most marketing companies like to go out and 'find' their victims on the streets or by cold-calling over the phone. Companies such as Saros Research, however (contact details below), maintain a database that you can get your name on, entering your details such as age, sex, earning level, etc., so that when they are putting together a focus group and want someone like you, they will email you an invitation.

Just log on to their website at www.sarosresearch.com, put in your details and wait for those invitations. You will only be allowed to do two sessions per year with them, but you could also apply to other companies and get extra work that way. The 'work' is very easy. You will go to a local office and sit around a table giving your opinions on a product or an advert or similar. It could be anything from electric blankets to ice cream or BMWs.

You can also make money by recruiting other people for the focus groups. Again, all the details are on the Saros Research website. You earn money each time one of your recruits takes part in some research. When a questionnaire is received and confirmed you earn a bonus of 25p. When a participant takes part in a group you receive a bonus of 10 per cent of their payment.

You can also make about £8 an hour by being on the other side of the fence – interviewing people on the street. Contact Flow Interactive (details overleaf) about this kind of work.

HOW MUCH CAN YOU MAKE?

You can make between £30 and £100 a session depending on what you are talking about in the focus group, plus free food! You can then make a few pounds per person each year if you work as a recruiter.

COSTS

There are no costs other those involved in travelling to and from the focus group.

TRAINING AND QUALIFICATIONS

You don't need any training or qualifications.

PROS

This is a fun and easy way of making some extra cash. It's also a good way to meet other people.

CONS

The work is very sporadic. You can't rely on it for a regular income. Also, you may be asked to fill out a survey each time, which is time-consuming, without actually being asked to attend a focus group, because they use these forms for screening the best candidates.

USEFUL CONTACTS

Criteria, 020 7431 4366, www.criteria.co.uk

Flow Interactive, 020 7482 2424, www.flow-interactive.com

Saros Research, www.sarosresearch.com – fill in the application form online

Case study

Dudu Suleiman is a civil servant who has taken part in three focus groups so far, all of them with Saros Research. 'You have to fill out a questionnaire beforehand, so they can check your eligibility and suitability,' she says. 'Then, you just had to show up at the allotted time and sit around a table with five to six others sharing your opinions on different videos, or products, or taglines they ran by you. Someone from Saros would facilitate the discussion with certain questions, and he/she would go around the tables asking for everyone's opinion.'

So far, Dudu has earned £120 from taking part in these events – you're paid at the end of each session – and she would be happy to do more. 'The good things about it are the fact that it's easy to access the focus groups and gives me the chance to meet people I wouldn't normally get to know. It was also interesting to hear different people's opinions on consumer products and to share my own views on these products. They gave us free food and drink as well which was nice!

'To me, the downsides are that you sometimes wonder how

much they really listen. Also, sometimes you have to fill out numerous surveys/questionnaires in advance, and they only pick you for about one in every five – this made you feel like you were giving them useful marketing feedback without them paying for it.

'Mind you, sometimes you get to do fun things like wine tasting and if you show up late, they still pay you, so I would recommend it.'

Mystery shopping

You may see excitable adverts on the Net about making money and getting freebies just for shopping. This is true, and there are lots of opportunities to make some money in your own time through mystery shopping, but it's not necessarily the big shop-fest they like to make out!

HOW TO DO IT

Thousands of ordinary people in the UK get paid to go shopping, eat out in a restaurant or just pop out for a drink. Fees per visit vary between companies, but are usually between about £6 and £20. And of course expenses are reimbursed so your food and drink are paid for as well.

To get this work you will need to register with mystery shopping companies (see the selection below). You won't have to accept all jobs they offer you, but you will be more likely to get regular work (if that's what you want) and the cushier jobs too if you show that you are willing and flexible early on.

When you go into shops, pubs, ticket offices or wherever you are sent, you will usually be asked to note and report on things such as the decor and tidiness of the place, the number of counters, customers or staff members, staff members' names, what they look like and their job descriptions. You may also be asked to find specific products or seek specific information or work out whether employees are giving out scripted answers to the questions you ask. 'Sometimes you have to ask really stupid questions which can make you feel like a bit of an idiot,' says one mystery shopper, 'but it's never anything really bad.'

The companies will want this information and your till receipts as soon as possible, so you'll need to allow time to fill in the forms, usually within 24 hours. Some companies allow you to do this online; others send you the forms to fill out by hand and post or fax back. The companies will get a copy of your report and will know when you visited: so if they have CCTV you can be sure they'll be watching the tape after they've read your report!

Many mystery shopping agencies specialise in a particular area. Cinecheck, for example, will pay you £8 to survey cinema trailers. They will also reimburse you for your cinema ticket. Field Facts Worldwide audit petrol stations. They'll pay £7 plus £3 for travel expenses. The Mystery Shopping Agency specialises in shopping centres, and you could get up to £100 for a day's work with them.

HOW MUCH CAN YOU MAKE?

It depends how many jobs you do and what kind. Anything from £10 to £500 a week plus a few freebies.

COSTS

There should be no costs as your travel expenses are usually paid for.

TRAINING AND QUALIFICATIONS

You don't need any training or qualifications.

PROS

If you like shopping, eating or drinking out this can be a nice way of at least getting things for free, if not making a bit of extra cash too. You might even be able to tie in a free overnight stay in a hotel if you need to be in a particular town that night.

CONS

The money is getting less, and quite often you are asked to go to shops and eateries that you wouldn't normally touch with a bargepole. 'Nightclubs are the worst,' says one former mystery shopper. 'They're always the sort you wouldn't dream of walking into!' There is a lot of competition, and you may have to do quite a few boring or low-paid jobs before you get the really good ones.

USEFUL CONTACTS

Cinecheck, 0800 5870520, www.cinecheck.com

Field Facts Worldwide, 020 7908 6600, www.fieldfacts.com

High Street Central, www.highstreetcentral

IMS, www.ukims.co.uk

Mystery Shopping Agency, 020 8325 8974, www.mysteryshopagency.com

NOP, www.cybershoppers.nopworld.com

Retaileyes, www.retaileyes.co.uk

Case study

Barry Grossman is a playwright in north London and has supplemented his income for seven years by being a mystery shopper. 'You can get asked to do anything,' he says. 'I've probably done more pubs and restaurants than anything else but you can get odd requests like going to a train station with the timetable and standing on the platform all day timing the trains to see how many are late. It's not always just shopping.

'The pay varies from nothing more than a free meal or drink or free night in a hotel – none of which I do now because I think it's derisory – to earning £250 to £300 for a job that lasts over

➤

a few days. I suppose the average is about £10, and sometimes you get to keep things you buy. I've had a few trips to Tesco where I've been able to keep the things I've bought but you don't get much.

'It's good work if you want to be able to pick and choose the times you work and if you want to be able to say no. There's no contract or anything that you have to sign to say you'll definitely do certain jobs. Mind you, you often have to work your way up so it's a good idea to do some crappy jobs early on so that the agencies get to trust you and give you better jobs later. The downside is that you're sometimes expected to do things for pin money or just a free drink or something.

'I think it's harder to make so much money now than when I first started because like many things it's getting quite crowded. More and more people are coming into it so it's easier for companies to pay people less.'

Babysitting

Anyone can babysit, although if you want to do it through an agency you will need a proven background in some sort of child-care or teaching.

HOW TO DO IT

Babysitting is best suited to women of any age as, although many men make excellent babysitters, most parents prefer the idea of a woman caring for their children rather than a man. If you are already friends with a family with children and they know you well, you might get babysitting work with them, although many people prefer not to charge friends for this kind of service.

Whether you are male or female, however, if you want to work as a babysitter you can advertise your service by word of mouth through friends and neighbours, put adverts in local newsagents and papers, or you could join a babysitting agency such as Sitters, which places babysitters in families all over the country.

If you want to do it properly (and I hope you would) you must first go to your local police station and pay £10 for a police check. You will also arm yourself with a CV, highlighting any job you have had that has been to do with caring for children, and get written references from people for whom you have already worked as a babysitter or other type of carer. If you don't have such references you could get a couple of character references from a former teacher, a doctor, your bank manager or some other professional who knows you well. These are the kinds of things a babysitting agency will want to see, and it would be helpful to you and to your prospective family to have them in a neat folder so that you can readily show your credentials.

If you have had your own children, babysitting should be very easy for you, but if you do not have experience or training in caring for babies it is not advisable to babysit for children under two years of age as you may not be able to cope if they have a medical emergency.

Make sure the parents leave a contact number while they are out, in case of problems, together with a number for their doctor, for the same reason. Before you go to the job, check to see whether they are going to leave you some food. If not, take your own or eat before you go. Wash up any cups or dishes you use while you are there.

If the parents come back after 11 p.m. they should pay for a taxi for you or take you home themselves, unless you have come by car. Your travel expenses should also be paid by the parents, although this is something you can negotiate.

HOW MUCH CAN YOU MAKE?

It depends where you live and how you get the job. On the whole, babysitters are paid a minimum of £5 per hour, rising to £10 an hour in central London on bank holidays or other special times such as New Year's Eve, although the higher rates tend to be negotiated through agencies.

COSTS

There are no costs involved as you should have your travel expenses paid by the family.

TRAINING AND QUALIFICATIONS

You don't have to have training or qualifications but if you work through an agency they will be more likely to take you on if you have a medical qualification or experience, or training and experience as a teacher or nanny.

PROS

This is a pleasant way to spend an evening, particularly if you love children. Quite often you will spend the time simply watching TV or doing whatever you would normally be doing at home.

CONS

The money isn't amazing and you could be stuck with a spoilt or fractious child or baby who never goes to sleep. You also need to be confident in case of emergencies, particularly with babies, who are very vulnerable.

USEFUL CONTACTS

Brilliant Babysitters, 49 Harrington Gardens, London SW7 4JU, 020 7244 6053, www.topnnotchnannies.com (covers homes within the area bounded by the M25)

Sitters, 0800 3890038, www.sitters.co.uk (franchises around the country)

The school run

More and more working parents need someone to pick up and care for their children between the end of school and the time they get back from work. You don't have to be a qualified nanny to do this. Even a retired person with a car and free afternoons could do it.

HOW TO DO IT

Many nanny agencies look for people with proven childcare experience and, ideally, a clean driving licence to do the 'school run'. If you have a background in childcare, teaching, social services, healthcare or medicine, or if you have simply been a full-time parent, contact your local nanny agencies and see whether you can register with them. Look in your local Yellow Pages or contact REC (details below) to find some in your area.

You can also do the school run privately. Look in *The Lady* magazine for private ads from families who need a part-time nanny in the afternoons to pick up the children, feed them, supervise homework and make sure they are happy until the parents come home. In London you can also look through *TNT* magazine or check out www.thegumtree.com or www.greatcare.co.uk for private ads. You could also advertise your services in local newsagents' windows, libraries, and on supermarket and children's clothes shop noticeboards.

Whether you go to an agency or work privately you will need to have an up-to-date CV with no gaps in it that are not explained, a copy of a police check (which you can get through your local police station), copies of any relevant certificates and written references from former employers or professionals who can vouch for your character. You should also have an up-to-date first-aid certificate.

Some parents only need someone to help for two or three afternoons a week, but usually it is five afternoons, generally from about 3.30 p.m till 7 p.m. You won't necessarily need to drive, although you will be more likely to get a good job, and sooner, if you can.

HOW MUCH CAN YOU MAKE?

You should make a minimum of £5 an hour, although in London and the Home Counties it will be more like £8–£10 per hour. If you have three or more children to care for it could be more.

COSTS

There are no costs other than those connected with keeping your first-aid certificate up to date and getting a police check.

TRAINING AND QUALIFICATIONS

You don't have to be trained or qualified in childcare to do this although experience is essential. Having a nanny qualification such as an NNEB or being a nurse or a teacher will help a lot. If you are simply an experienced parent or grandparent that may be enough.

PROS

If you love children – particularly if you have been a parent and are missing your own brood – this is a lovely job to have.

CONS

The money for childcare is not the best and it is easy to have problems with demanding and unreliable parents or with spoilt and difficult children. It is also an enormous responsibility to look after little ones.

USEFUL CONTACTS

The Recruitment and Employment Confederation (REC), 020 7462 3260, www.rec.uk.com – the official body for recruitment agencies including nanny and babysitting agencies. They can send you a list of approved agencies in your area.

Tinies, 020 7384 0322, www.tinies.co.uk – franchises around the country

Top Notch Nannies, 49 Harrington Gardens, London SW7 4JU, 020 7259 2626, www.topnotchnannies.com

Be a doula

If you are a mother you are pretty much qualified to be a doula. Doulas are birth partners and post-birth partners – like surrogate mothers to new mothers – and any woman who has had a baby and wants to help other women get through it happily could become a doula.

HOW TO DO IT

You will need to take a doula course with British Doulas (contact details below), who run four-day courses for women who want to become birth partners and post-birth partners. You do not need academic qualifications to go on the course but it leads to a City & Guilds Doula Profile of Achievement.

The agency will place you in jobs around the country or you can get jobs on your own. If you do it yourself you will have to devote money and effort to advertising yourself, possibly getting a website designed and continuously marketing your service.

You can work part-time or full-time as a post-birth doula, helping around the house, making sure the fridge is full, preparing food for the mother and helping her care for the baby. You can also work as a birth doula – either instead of or as well as post-birth work – in which case you will be with a mother when she goes into labour and throughout the birth, supporting her, making her feel confident and being her champion if she needs someone to speak up for her in the birthing room. Doulas also support fathers and the wider family during and after birth.

HOW MUCH CAN YOU MAKE?

Doulas in Britain make, on average, about £10 per hour for post-birth work and between £200 and £400 for a birth.

COSTS

You will need to pay for the course. In addition you will need insurance and you will also probably want to read books on birth and babies. Apart from that the only real cost will be travelling to and from your jobs and maybe some household equipment.

TRAINING AND QUALIFICATIONS

You need to take the British Doulas course, and it helps to have the City & Guilds Profile of Achievement.

PROS

This is a great way of making use of your experience as a mother. Women of any age can do this job so long as they are strong enough. Some doulas are over 70 and still going strong.

CONS

Only women can do this job and it is certainly not for everyone. If you are at all squeamish or you don't like doing housework, it is not for you.

USEFUL CONTACTS

British Doulas, 49 Harrington Gardens, London SW7 4JU, 020 7244 6053, www.britishdoulas.co.uk

Case study

Pru Guthrie is a full-time mother in east London with two teenage children. She has been a doula for two years, working exclusively through British Doulas. 'If you want to stay at home and be with the children there are very few jobs that allow that,' she says, 'but being a doula means I have the flexibility to work around the children. The hours fit in beautifully.'

Pru works as a post-birth doula, although she would like to do some birth doula work when the children are older – her youngest child is 13 and still needs her around. She works through half-term holidays but takes time off when the children are around at Easter and in the summer. 'I love the work,' she says. 'I love the variety and meeting different mothers and I'm addicted to babies now! I like going to different places and having different experiences with families. As the jobs don't usually last more than a few months each I feel I can go to each job fresh. Also, I enjoy family life myself so I like other people's family lives. It's a very fulfilling and satisfying thing to do.'

Dog-walking and pet-minding

If you hate the gym but want to get out and about then this is an excellent idea. Full-time jobs and busy lives mean that many people don't have all the time they need to look after their pets.

HOW TO DO IT

The best way to start is to ask anyone you know who has a pet if you can be of use to them. Once you have gained a couple of contacts, you may find that your services will be recommended by word of mouth. Also, go to your local vet's surgery and ask whether they would be prepared to put an advert on their noticeboard or in their window.

Pet-minding involves regularly feeding a pet (usually a cat) and clearing the litter tray at someone's house, or looking after smaller animals such as rabbits, guinea pigs or budgies. It's advisable to arrange a police check (see 'Babysitting', p. 36) if you are prepared to go into people's homes.

If you want to dog-walk you should be able to cope with three or four dogs at a time. Always keep them on a lead. Don't forget to check out the rules of your local park. It is also useful to have the details of local rescue centres, and to get to know your nearest dog warden – contact your local council for details.

HOW MUCH CAN YOU MAKE?

Charges depend on your area and what you think people can reasonably afford. Dog-walkers in London can charge up to £15 per dog, but if you are helping an elderly person there is little point in demanding an unreasonable amount. If people like you then they will recommend you to others. Charge dog-walking by the hour and pet-minding by the day.

COSTS

Very little. It helps to have a car to reach people, so petrol could be a factor. Some people may want their dogs exercised in a park rather than around the streets, so you may have to travel around. If you are pet-minding the owners must provide the food and any other necessities such as cat litter. If you want to board small pets in your own home, make sure the owners bring cages (if required) and food with them!

TRAINING AND QUALIFICATIONS

Although you don't need training or qualifications, you could consider a canine first-aid course. Your local vet will be able to give you details.

PROS

Debbie Perrin, who runs Principal Petcare in the Surbiton area (www.principalpetcare.co.uk), says that the exercise and fresh air she gets means that she can eat as much chocolate as she likes without worrying about her weight. Walking really is one of the best forms of exercise, and you will find yourself generally much healthier. These jobs mean you can enjoy the company of animals without the full-time responsibility of keeping one yourself.

CONS

Debora Maria Vila, who runs Cat Care at Home throughout north London (www.catcareathome.com), warns that running these services is a much more popular idea than it used to be. It may be lovely in the summer to be out and about, but don't forget the winter, when it is cold and dark. And be prepared to scoop the poop. Local authorities will fine people who don't clean up after their dog. Also, it is difficult to get away on holiday. You will be most in demand at holiday times, and particularly Christmas, when you might need a break yourself.

See also 'House-sitting and house-minding', p. 55.

USEFUL CONTACTS

UK Pet Sitter. www.ukpetsitter.co.uk. *Also see details above and p. 44.*

Gift fund-raising

Be a face-to-face fund-raiser. Raise money for charity and get paid for it. Just don't expect to be loved by the public.

HOW TO DO IT

Chuggers, charity muggers, direct dialoguers: call them what you will. It sometimes seems impossible to move in Britain's high streets without being accosted by one of these clipboard-wielding fund-raisers.

If you don't mind putting up with the British weather and the sometimes hostile attitude of the Great British Public, then face-to-face fund-raising could be a good way of earning money and helping a good cause.

All you have to do is get a certain number of people to sign up for a regular direct debit donation to the charity you represent. You get paid. They get to feel warm and fuzzy. And the charity fills up its coffers. That's the theory, anyway.

The full-time fund-raisers are recruited and trained by specialist agencies that are paid by the charities. The best known of these are Face 2 Face Fundraising and Dialogue Direct, both run by the Dialogue Group Ltd, Push Ltd, Gift Fundraising Ltd, and Fruitful Fundraising UK Ltd.

The 'chuggers' they take on need to be outgoing and resilient. Most tend to be in their twenties. Unemployed actors do well. No formal qualifications are required but personality and communication skills are important. The agency provides two or three days' training in the mysteries of getting complete strangers to part with their money, then you are sent out in teams of four to eight people to do your stuff in high streets and shopping centres around the UK. So you get to travel a bit too.

The agencies charge charities a fixed rate for each donor signed up to a direct debit monthly donation. And it is apparently profitable for all. Nearly 700,000 people signed up with the agencies in 2002, donating cash to the tune of £34.5 million.

HOW MUCH CAN YOU MAKE?

Between £8 and £10 an hour with the added incentive of a possible raise if you sign up more than the required daily quota of donors, usually two or three a day.

COSTS

None.

TRAINING AND QUALIFICATIONS

No formal qualifications. Just the gift of the gab and a thick skin.

PROS

You get paid to raise money for a good cause, will meet a lot of people, are out in the fresh air and may see some of the country.

CONS

Much of the money raised doesn't go to the charities. They only benefit after the agencies have taken their cut. A lot of people you meet won't want to meet you. Prepare yourself for verbal abuse and the occasional punch if you're really unlucky.

You'll get cold and wet and will suffer sore feet. The parts of the country you see will mostly be concrete.

USEFUL CONTACTS

www.dialoguedirect.co.uk, 01865 297500

www.fruitfulfund.co.uk, 020 7841 0270

Gift Fundraising, 020 7281 6995 – this is an automated recruitment line; you need to leave a message to convince them to interview you.

www.pushconsultancy.co.uk, 020 7749 7850

Delivering

There are all sorts of leaflets and forms that need to be delivered to homes in your area – local papers, leaflets, forms for compiling the electoral roll and so on all have to be delivered by someone.

HOW TO DO IT

Many of these jobs are temporary and are often advertised in your local jobcentre. In London you can be paid simply to stand at Tube and overground stations handing out copies of *Ms London*, *GAT* and *Nine to Five* for a couple of hours one morning a week.

Get hold of some free local newspapers and contact them directly. If you have local takeaways and/or taxi firms, ask them whether they need any help. Hunt out small businesses such as domestic agencies, builders and gardeners which may simply not have the time they need to promote themselves. Also, look in the jobs pages of local newspapers which sometimes have ads looking for people to deliver leaflets and so on. Your local jobcentre may also have this kind of work on offer.

HOW MUCH CAN YOU MAKE?

About £5 an hour on average.

COSTS

None, apart from those involved in travelling to your collection point.

TRAINING AND QUALIFICATIONS

You don't need any training or qualifications.

PROS

Fresh air and exercise. If you are of an outgoing nature you can get chatting to people. If you aren't then just watch the world go by.

CONS

It is not terribly well paid and can be boring if you don't enjoy your own company, so use the time productively. Watch the passers-by and weave the plot of your first novel around some of them. Remember that it's cold work in the winter.

USEFUL CONTACTS

In the London area email distribution@indmags.co.uk to distribute *Nine to Five*, *GAT* and *Ms London* at Tube stations

Jobcentres, www.jobcentreplus.gov.uk

Invigilating exams

Your local education authority often needs invigilators for GCSE and A-level exams, and local colleges, universities and adult education authorities need outside invigilators for their exams too.

HOW TO DO IT

The easiest way to do this at a university or college is to be recommended by a person who already invigilates. The requirement tends to be for someone with a knowledge of, or connection with, the education system. You can contact the various exam boards requesting work or go direct to your local schools and colleges. The other main requirement is that you should have no connection with any person taking the examination. Look in your local paper to see what courses are running near you.

You should receive a short briefing beforehand, but a university or college will give you a written set of instructions and the exam regulations telling you what to do in the event of hearing a fire alarm or if a student is taken ill. One invigilator said that one of her students was so nervous he vomited all over her and she couldn't leave the room to clean up! At the start of a university exam you may find the staff will organise the set-up of the exam. In other cases you will hand out the papers and check that the students have a matching proof of identity.

Depending on the size of the room you will either have to sit the entire time or walk up and down between the desks. If you see any cheating you will have to contact a higher authority. At the end, you will collect the papers.

HOW MUCH CAN YOU MAKE?

A half-day (i.e. a three-hour exam) will pay about £45. You will have to be there for half an hour before the start and after the finish. A two-week stretch of two exams a day will pay between £8 and £18 an hour.

COSTS

None other than travel expenses, although universities will either pay these or give you a small flat fee.

TRAINING AND QUALIFICATIONS

Nothing specific, but a postgraduate student, a retired teacher or a school secretary would be well suited. Otherwise you must be sensible and responsible.

PROS

This is good money for not doing very much if you don't get bored easily.

CONS

You cannot read or write because you have to be alert all the time. It also tends to be seasonal work, mostly in January and in early summer.

USEFUL CONTACTS

The British Council has a list of exam boards, www.british council.org/education/exams/exam_boards.htm

Floodlight is the official guide to courses in London; you can buy a copy in bookshops or newsagents or visit the website, www.floodlight.co.uk

Bar and restaurant work

This is one of the easiest kinds of evening or day work you can get. Pretty much anyone can do bar work, and most can work in restaurants and cafés so long as their English is good enough and they can do basic maths.

HOW TO DO IT

You can often get employment in bars by going into pubs in your area and asking whether they have any work going. Restaurants and cafés often advertise in their front windows for staff, or you can simply go in and ask the manager whether they need extra help.

With restaurants, and often with bars and pubs, you will need to quote your national insurance number and show your CV and references, ideally with evidence of having worked in this sector in the past. If you have experience of catering or working as a chef you can make much more money than you can as a waiter. Try to go for a job that involves specialist cooking if you have experience in that.

There are also several agencies that provide workers for the catering industry. The big agencies such as Reed Employment and Manpower have hospitality and catering sections, as do local jobcentres. They will certainly need to see your CV, your references and your work visa if you are not an EU national.

You can also pick up lots of jobs like these in local papers and magazines and on websites such as www.fish4jobs.co.uk and www.thegumtree.com.

Many pubs and restaurants won't even require a CV or references, or even a work visa (if you are not an EU national), although the better ones will ask to see them.

HOW MUCH CAN YOU MAKE?

Anything from the minimum wage for bar or restaurant work (or lower if you go for one of the nasty burger chains, apparently) up to thousands a month if you are a qualified chef and work every night.

COSTS

There are no costs other than those involved with travel and, possibly, extra laundry for your clothes.

TRAINING AND QUALIFICATIONS

You don't need training or qualifications unless you are going for a job as a chef or something specialised such as a sommelier.

PROS

If you like people, working in this sector can be a great way of meeting people. It also stops you spending money on entertaining yourself by going out in the evenings. If you're good, you could make lots of money in tips.

CONS

It's often hard, demoralising work that is not well paid. You will be working anti-social hours and you will probably have to travel home very late at night.

USEFUL CONTACTS

Jobcentres, www.jobcentreplus.gov.uk

Manpower, www.manpower.co.uk

Reed Employment, www.reed.co.uk

Saturday shop work

This can also be easy work to get if you live near a town with lots of shops or an out-of-town retail park. If the weekends are your only time off, this can be a good solution.

HOW TO DO IT

As with restaurant and bar work, you can often get weekend shop work simply by going into the shops and asking. Smaller ones may also advertise positions in their front window. There are also employment agencies that provide shop assistants, particularly in large cities such as London, Leeds or Manchester. Again, your local jobcentre will also have shop assistant jobs – full-time and part-time – on their books, so look there as well.

Some smaller shops may not ask to see a work visa, but the agencies, jobcentres and larger shop chains certainly will. Having a well-written CV and references will help you. Alternatively, search the websites of larger stores.

HOW MUCH CAN YOU MAKE?

Around the minimum wage, though if you have experience in a similar area of retail you may be able to earn more.

COSTS

None, except your travel expenses.

TRAINING AND QUALIFICATIONS

Experience is useful but no qualifications will be required. A good shop will train you up if necessary.

PROS

Working in a shop where you know about, and are interested in, the things you are selling can be very satisfying. If the shop is small and you like the other staff it can also be great fun. And you will get discounts on goods.

CONS

It is generally low-paid work and is often unrewarding. The larger the shop does not necessarily mean the higher the wage. If you *really* like the goods sold in your shop, the staff discounts could mean you end up spending rather too much of your earnings.

USEFUL CONTACTS

See contacts for bar and restaurant work above.

Also consider ...

- Selling tickets at local theatres, cinemas, concert halls and other events. Just walk in and ask whether there is any work going. Even if there isn't right now, there could be later, so make sure you leave your CV and contact details with them. Also, there are many other ad hoc entertainment-related jobs, such as selling programmes at events, taking tickets, ushering, helping with security and looking after performers.

Debt-collecting

Sadly debt has become a more and more serious problem in recent years, and things don't look as if they are going to get any better. This may not be a job to suit everyone but it is worth considering.

HOW TO DO IT

You need to do this through a debt recovery company. Trawl the Internet and you will soon see that there are a lot of them about – perhaps not as many as companies offering loans, but their websites in turn should have links to debt recovery companies. Alternatively look for job adverts in the local paper or on good job websites.

There are various types of debt-collecting. Debt recovery companies obtain money owed by failed businesses and from business customers who don't settle their invoices. The sort of debt-collecting someone with some spare time can do, though, is collecting reasonably small amounts of money at regular intervals (usually weekly or monthly) from people at their home addresses.

You will collect within an accessible radius, possibly about 5 miles or so, and you have to knock on the door and ask for the payment. This is a job that requires confidence and patience. You will need to be comfortable dealing with people who may not be too pleased to see you.

HOW MUCH CAN YOU MAKE?

Payment will be commission or fee based. Neil Tanner of VBS Debt Recovery (www.vbsdebtrecovery.co.uk) says collectors are paid a commission of £4 on each collection. It is possible to make £40–£70 a week.

COSTS

Your own car and telephone will be necessary.

TRAINING AND QUALIFICATIONS

A debt recovery company should give you training, but it is advisable not to work for anyone who lets you go out on your own straight away. Make sure that you have an experienced collector with you or that you begin by shadowing another collector's rounds. No agent should be obliged to go to a client's house if they have any safety concerns.

PROS

Surprisingly, despite the reasons for their calls, the regularity of visits can mean that debt collectors almost become friends with their clients. Also, you will be helping to hold people accountable for work undertaken on their behalf.

CONS

Personal safety is obviously important. Make sure you undergo a good training programme. You may experience unfriendliness or hostility, but this may not last as clients become used to your visits. This is a job that men probably feel safer doing than women.

USEFUL CONTACTS

www.fish4jobs.co.uk – a good place to find this kind of work

www.thegumtree.com – another good place for this work, but only in the Greater London area

VBS Debt Recovery, www.vbsdebtrecovery.co.uk

House-sitting and house-minding

Many people now own two properties or spend time away on business as well as just having their summer holiday. Looking after a house or flat while the owner is away is a good way of getting a break from your own home and routine.

HOW TO DO IT

House-sitting involves living in someone's home while they are away. You will therefore get free accommodation in return for taking care of their home. You are also making the property safer by being there and so deterring potential burglars. You will have to keep things clean and tidy, and possibly do some gardening or look after a pet. You will be expected to treat the house with respect.

House-minding means keeping an eye on an empty home with a regular, often daily, visit. You may have to water plants or feed a pet cat. For security reasons you will probably have to tidy up the post from the front door (and sometimes forward it), put rubbish in the outside bins and switch lights on and off in the evenings so that the premises don't appear to be unused.

You can start house-sitting and -minding for your friends, family and neighbours, but it is easiest to house-sit regularly by registering with an agency. Andy Pauline of Safehands Sitters, who cover central southern England (www.safehandssitters.co.uk), explains that house-sitting is ideal for someone who needs extra money but has no other responsibilities. His staff are not allowed to leave the premises for more than three consecutive hours. It is a very popular job with retired people, and sometimes freelancers and research students who just need peace and quiet to work.

It is best to present an agency with a police check (see 'Babysitting', p. 36), and you will have to provide a number of references from professional people. The agency will then interview you in your own home. If you are doing this independently the owners will provide a written contract. This should contain all instructions and also guidelines for dealing with any problems that may occur. The contract can then be placed with an independent third party.

HOW MUCH CAN YOU MAKE?

Between £120 and £150 a week.

COSTS

If you work through an agency your costs will be minimal – possibly just to cover personal phone calls. The owners will provide everything necessary plus a float to cover anything you need as you go along (cat food etc.).

If you are doing this independently, an owner could initially request a deposit from you. This would be something like the equivalent of a month's rental of the property which would be lodged with an independent third party and be refunded to you at the end of your stay. You may also have to pay for the utilities you use.

TRAINING AND QUALIFICATIONS

A good house-sitting agency will give you health and safety training, personal safety training, animal welfare guidance and details of their own rules and regulations.

PROS

This is easy, enjoyable work offering relaxing time away from your normal life. Some people enjoy the opportunity to have the company of a pet for a while without the permanent responsibilities.

CONS

You may not be able to leave the premises for more than a few hours at a time. Things can go wrong: if you break anything, for instance, be honest. An agency will have insurance. House-sitting and house-minding are very enjoyable, but remember that they are a serious responsibility.

See also 'Dog-walking and pet-minding', p. 43

USEFUL CONTACTS

Sitters – www.sitters.com

Safe Hand Sitters – www.safehandsitters.co.uk

Cleaning

If you know how to dust, wash up, vacuum and polish there is a huge demand for cleaners all over the country, particularly in big cities.

HOW TO DO IT

You can either go the private route or through an agency. It is per-haps easiest on your own. Start by advertising with a card in the window of your local newsagent, or an advert in the local paper. Otherwise look out for adverts from people wanting cleaners.

If you go through an agency you will need to have a valid

work visa if you are not an EU national, as well as references; it helps to have a CV to show your experience of cleaning for others, or at least of working for others. The agency will interview you, possibly by phone as well as in person. Domestic agencies regularly have private and corporate clients who want everything from a cleaner for three hours once a fortnight to office cleaners who will work every weekday night. It is up to you how much time you want to give.

However you do it, you don't necessarily have to have formal experience in cleaning. If you can show that you have been working somewhere else, that will help to demonstrate that you are trustworthy and a 'worker'. You can be working for people from all walks of life, so it useful to have an easygoing personality as well as a professional attitude to the work. Remember to look clean and presentable yourself when you first arrive, especially for work in private homes. People need to feel they can trust you. Make sure that you understand how much tidying up your employer wants. One person's tidying can be another person's interfering. Discuss beforehand the matter of breakage, because no matter how careful you are, accidents do happen. If you do damage something, always be honest. Agencies will have insurance to cover it.

You don't have to just go the private route, though. You could go into business cleaning. For example, offer a 'total cleaning' service – the kind of service people need when they move home and want to leave the place spotless for the next people, or when they want to rent out their property and a really clean place will help. This is the kind of work you can do as part of another company or, if you have good contacts – i.e. friends who also clean a lot – you could offer the service yourself. Advertise your services in the local and regional press and also contact local estate and letting agents.

There are also several agencies that specialise in cleaning offices. If you are looking for evening and night work, this is the best place to go for it. It is often better paid than private cleaning, more regular and often involves less hassle!

You could also go in for a more specialised form of cleaning, such as carpet cleaning. For this you will need some form of transportation – ideally a van – as you will have to use a special, heavy-duty machine and carpet cleaning fluids. You can advertise your services through local papers, leaflet drops and in local supermarkets and stores. Quite a lot of work will also come through word of mouth. You will need to be strong and possibly have a working partner with you to help move furniture.

HOW MUCH CAN YOU MAKE?

£5–£10 an hour, depending where you are in the country. Office cleaning is similar. For total cleaning you can charge £100–£200, depending on the size and complexity of the job. One typical quote for a team of four people taking half a day is £140 + VAT. Carpet cleaning is similar – £120 for a two-bedroom house taking half a day.

COSTS

You should be provided with all the cleaning products that you will need, so you won't have to do any extra shopping. If you do, however, keep all your receipts so that you can be reimbursed. You will need to be able to travel easily, so if you haven't got a car or access to good public transport, concentrate on finding local work. Agencies should provide training and a uniform for corporate client work. If you do carpet cleaning you will need to buy (or lease) a special machine and buy the cleaning fluids. This could cost you about £1,500.

TRAINING AND QUALIFICATIONS

Agencies may give you some basic instructions and guidelines.

PROS

Jivka Pishtikova, who used to clean privately but now works for Selclene, who cover north London (tel. 0808 155 480), says she loved the freedom of not being tied to a desk, and the time to herself travelling between jobs. She generally got on very well with her employers, some of whom even gave her birthday and Christmas presents.

CONS

People are taking you into their homes on trust and some may try to test your honesty by leaving money lying around in obvious places. Some employers may just treat you like a servant, so try to be flexible and move on to another job if you are unhappy.

In times of recession, services such as carpet cleaning are seen as a luxury, so you could find it hard to get this kind of work in economic down times. You will also have to invest a lot of money at the start which you may not get back.

USEFUL CONTACTS

www.fish4jobs.co.uk – jobs of all kinds here

www.jobcentreplus.gov.uk – many office cleaning jobs are advertised at your local jobcentre

Recruitment and Employment Confederation, www.rec.uk.com – many cleaning agencies are members

Also consider . . .

● Emergency cleaning – armed with a mobile phone and cleaning equipment in your car, you could offer an emergency cleaning service whereby you rush over to a house that has had a plumbing disaster or similar and the owner needs the place to be spotless in a hurry. This is something you could charge a premium for.

● Cleaning up after builders – get friendly with some local building companies or painters and decorators and offer a cleaning service for tidying up when they've finished. Suggest an hourly rate or a total price per job.

● Curtain and upholstery cleaning – you can offer general cleaning once a year or so for houses with a lot of soft furnishings and also specific cleaning of stains. You will need steam cleaners, special fluids and, possibly, a good relationship with a local dry cleaner to do this. Advertise in areas with large, expensive houses that are likely to have a lot of curtains and sofas that will need attention.

Ironing/laundry

There is a demand for people who can iron and do laundry as it is a particular pet hate of many professional men and women. Working and having a family means some people simply don't have the time, while others prefer to be doing something they find more relaxing.

HOW TO DO IT

As with cleaning, you can wash and iron clothes privately or through an agency. If you are doing this on your own, it is probably simplest to stick to ironing. Agencies offer washing and dry cleaning on their premises and so their customers know their laundry is done to a high standard. Your own washing machine may not be as good and may not take the strain of continuous use. Ironing is something that can be part of a cleaning job for an extra hour's pay.

Look out for adverts locally in newspapers and shop windows, or promote yourself in a similar way. Some people have their laundry done regularly, while others may just need it done if they haven't the usual time to do it themselves. Agencies collect the laundry, so you won't have to travel around.

HOW MUCH CAN YOU MAKE?

£5–£8 a load/session, though try to find a deal offering payment for ironing by the hour.

COSTS

If you are doing this privately you will have to collect and return laundry, so a car is very useful. Your employer should either supply you with, or reimburse you for, cleaning supplies.

TRAINING AND QUALIFICATIONS

An agency may give you basic instructions, and of course they will want proof that you can iron. Past experience is helpful.

PROS

You can work in your own home or in someone else's home and be paid for something you don't mind doing. There is also a big demand, so you could get as much work as you want, if you are good.

CONS

Laundry and ironing are physically hard jobs, and in the summer it may be hot work. You may have to work quickly, and you cannot afford to let that black sock get caught up with the white T-shirts . . .

See also 'Cleaning', p. 57

Poll clerk

This is an important job which many people don't think about. Election day polling stations have to be staffed in order for a government to be elected!

HOW TO DO IT

First of all apply to your local authority expressing your interest, and they will put your name on a list. It is better to do this sooner rather than later, so don't leave it until a week before an election as the list will probably be too long by then. If you are successful, you will be sworn in the day before the election. As a poll clerk you will have to issue the ballot papers and register and tick off each person as they come to vote. You will also have to show quite a lot of people actually how to vote. There will be a Presiding Officer in charge of the whole station who does the rest of the paperwork. You can also apply to help count the ballot papers in the evening, but be aware that this is pretty frantic work.

HOW MUCH CAN YOU MAKE?

About £230 a day.

COSTS

You will have to cover travel to the polling station and home again.

TRAINING AND QUALIFICATIONS

There are no special requirements for this job. You will be shown what to do on the day.

PROS

This is a good job if you like meeting and helping people. If you are given a station near your own home, you will be able to chat to all your neighbours. There is plenty to do and the day passes quickly.

CONS

Elections are few and far between so this work really occupies no more than one day a year. You may have quite a distance to travel between your home and the polling station.

USEFUL CONTACTS

For a list of local government websites, www.tagish.co.uk/links/localgov.htm

Plant care and hire

If you have green fingers and some time on your hands, you could help others in your area have healthy, happy plants all year round.

HOW TO DO IT

There are two levels of plant care you can undertake. The simplest is to offer your services as a plant minder for local people when they go away. Put the word around that you are available to do this with a leaflet drop in the area you feel you could comfortably cover and put adverts in local newsagents and newspapers to let people know of your service. For people who don't know you you will need to show that you are trustworthy, so it would probably help to get yourself a police check (pop into your local police station and ask about this) together with some letters of reference from people of note in the area who know you (a doctor, judge or bank manager) or, ideally, people who have used your services already.

You could charge a weekly rate based on where you live, the number of plants that will need caring for and how complicated the care is (orchids, for example, need special knowledge).

Going up a level, you could offer a regular plant hire service as well as plant care. This is quite a big business already, particularly in cities where there are a lot of businesses that like to have plants in or outside their offices but don't want to look after them themselves. But there is no reason why you couldn't set up your own small, local operation if you have a good greenhouse, love plants and have the time to travel around to local offices and homes once or twice a week.

You will probably get more work from businesses than private homes, but why not offer your services to both? Offices and hotels tend to need window boxes and planters filled and watered on a seasonal basis. Become friendly with a local wholesaler of pots and window boxes so that you can get them at a good price. Then it is up to you to grow the plants in your greenhouse and fill the window boxes on-site every few months.

Private homes may also want window boxes and planters, but they may also ask for plants for inside the home and possibly displays for special occasions such as parties or Christmas. If you do not have a flair for flower-arranging, get together with someone who does and then you can offer this special service as well.

Send letters to likely businesses in your area that you think would benefit from your plant hire and care service, addressed to the office services or administrative manager, or the general manager in the case of a hotel. Also, place ads in the local press and in the small ads sections of the business trade press to bring in customers from the public and businesses.

You will need to offer a good personal service to beat off competition from larger firms which may not even be based in your area. Make yourself accommodating at all times – if a business or domestic client has a crisis, try to see them as soon as possible. At least, being local, you can get around quicker than others could.

If you are offering plant hire as well as care you will need a sturdy van that you don't mind getting dirty and a well-stocked greenhouse. Your raw material is plants so, in between jobs, you have to keep tending to your stock and renewing it. You will need a good selection of plants to choose from, particularly big, impressive-looking ones which don't need too much watering for office reception areas.

HOW MUCH CAN YOU MAKE?

Anything from £20 a week for looking after the plants in a neighbour's home to thousands a month if you have a good plant hire and care business.

COSTS

The van, the plants, all the plant growing and care materials and advertising will be your main costs.

TRAINING AND QUALIFICATIONS

Although it is not essential it would really help to have some training and, ideally, qualifications in horticulture and even garden design.

PROS

If you love plants and you have the space in your garden and greenhouse this can be an enjoyable and creative way to make some money.

CONS

There is a lot of competition in the plant hire and care area and it may be difficult to get business. Also, many families have an arrangement with neighbours to water each other's plants, so they may not want to pay for the service.

USEFUL CONTACTS

The Royal Horticultural Society, 80 Vincent Square, London SW1P 2PE, 020 7834 4333, www.rhs.org.uk – they run all kinds of horticultural courses and members can get special deals on plants.

CHAPTER THREE

Space to Spare?

IF YOU HAVE space at home – even if you don't own your own home – you could make money out of it. Think living space. Think storage. Think parking! You'd be surprised what you could possibly sell or rent out. And don't forget the garden. That's a potential money-earner, wherever you live and whatever its size.

Renting out a room

If you have a spare room, renting it out on a temporary or full-time basis is the first obvious way of making money from it. It's a particularly good idea as you can make up to £4,250 a year from renting a room before you have to pay tax on the income.

HOW TO DO IT

There are lots of ways of finding people to rent a room in your home – many of them don't cost a thing. Probably the best, and safest, way is to put the word about among your friends that you have a room to rent, how much it will be, what kind of person you do or don't want, etc., and see who has a friend who needs one. You could even send a 'round robin' email to friends with all the specifications so that they have the details to hand.

There are also websites that you can post on for free. In

London and the Home Counties www.thegumtree.com is a great place to advertise your room. Other websites that cover the rest of Britain include: www.roomsforlet.co.uk, www.property locator.co.uk, www.torent.co.uk, www.letsdirect.co.uk and www.rentomatic.co.uk.

Your local newspapers and advertising freesheets are another good advertising resource, although you will have to pay, or you could simply put a postcard in your local newsagent's window for a small fee. Otherwise you could try a local managing agent, although they will charge a fee. Find them in your local papers or Yellow Pages.

Whoever you decide to take in, even if it is through a lettings agency, make sure you take *and check* references before they haul their bags through the front door. Ideally you should have at least two references, including one from their current employer. A reference from their bank is also helpful. Do telephone the referees yourself, though, as it's very easy to forge a written reference.

It's a good idea to have a written contract between you from the start which sets out the amount of rent per week or month, when it is to be paid and how, and how much notice either side should give to terminate the arrangement. It is reasonable to ask for the rent a month in advance and to give each other around a month's notice, but that is something you can agree between you at the start. Also put in writing what your tenant should do about replacing damaged goods.

HOW MUCH CAN YOU MAKE?

That very much depends on what sort of room you have in what sort of home and, most importantly, *where* you live. It could be anything from about £40 a week to £250 a week if you have a really fabulous place in the heart of London.

COSTS

Once you have taken into account any payments incurred in actually finding someone to rent a room, the only likely costs will be extra electricity and gas usage and any breakages or damage your tenant causes. Make sure you have up-to-date contents insurance (see p. xxx to find out how to get the best deal on this) and always take a deposit – say two weeks' rent – to cover damages when the tenant first moves in.

It is also important to get your gas boiler and any other gas appliances checked by a Corgi-registered plumber once a year (make sure you get the certificate) and to have a smoke alarm fitted.

TRAINING AND QUALIFICATIONS

You don't need any training or qualifications.

PROS

This is an easy way of making money without actually doing any work. If you get someone nice to live with you they can be excellent company and open up a whole new social life and circle of friends for you. One friend of mine met her husband when he came round to look at a room she had to rent, so you never know!

CONS

If you like your privacy this can be unbearable. As the film *Single White Female* demonstrated, you could get the tenant from hell who makes your life a misery. Even if they're not too bad, their habits could simply drive you up the wall and down again. Make sure you phone those referees!

USEFUL CONTACTS

www.inlandrevenue.gov.uk – look here for information on the Government's rent-a-room scheme.

Case study

Barbara McLaughlin is a single mother of one child and lives in Cambridge. She works full-time and studies accountancy part-time. 'I have tried every imaginable way of making extra cash just to keep my head above water and cover my study and child-care costs,' she says. 'I've worked overtime, taken on extra book-keeping work from home, night shifts in pubs and even door-to-door sales of cleaning products with a baby in tow ... Overworked, exhausted, owing money on high-interest credit cards and in desperate need of a new car, I turned to personal finance guides for some ideas. The one I liked best was the rent-a-room scheme as I can earn £4,250 a year "tax free" and this scheme has an added bonus of not needing a babysitter.

'After taking advice from the tax office, friends who rent a room and meeting staff a local language school, I signed a contract and agreed to rent a room to them for their foreign students and opted to host young learners aged between fourteen and eighteen. In the summer season they pay me £98 a week per student and we have a twin room which two of them share and the fee is £196 a week for which I provide bed, breakfast and evening meal. In winter they pay £80 a week per student and they are generally less busy so it keeps the income below the threshold for tax.

'At first I was nervous and thought I would hate having strangers in my home. It hasn't really been a problem as they are so keen to see England they are out most of the time and at the weekend the school arranges excursions for them to other towns and cities. The downside is extra cooking when you fancy a takeaway, extra cleaning, especially in the bathroom, and extra laundry. The queue for the bathroom is a pain in the morning so I combat this by getting up at 6 a.m. and using it first. Even on the worst of days I just stay focused on the pay cheque at the end. My child really enjoys the company of the older kids and has learned some words in other languages, and we have both learned a great deal about other countries and cultures.

We have received some wonderful gifts from our visitors. They like to cook traditional food from their country for us and some of them have invited us to stay with their families.

'Initially I had only planned to do this for one summer to pay off my credit cards and buy a new car, but have found it enjoyable on a good day and even bearable on a bad day. I am now credit-card-free, have a newer car and am paying off my final debt, which is a professional development loan for my accountancy studies which will settled a whole year early. The extra cash is highly addictive and I am already planning to spend the spare cash on a long-haul holiday for summer 2006.'

Foreign students and visiting lecturers

If you can't bear the idea of having someone permanently renting a room in your home, renting it to foreign students or lecturers visiting a local university or college can be a gentle introduction to the process. Students learning English as a foreign language are usually only here for about six weeks at a time, and lecturers rarely stay for longer than a few months, so at least if you don't like their habits you know that it won't be long before they're off your hands and a new person will come along.

HOW TO DO IT

There are thousands of English schools around the country. It's a booming business, and their students need somewhere to stay while they learn. Look in Yellow Pages or on the Internet (enter 'English language schools + [your town]' in Google and see what comes up) and make a list of the schools in your area. Ring them up and ask to be put on their list of local accommodation providers. Good ones will want to see your place before they recommend you, so make sure your home is looking decent before they come round!

English language students tend to be young, from 18

upwards, but are sometimes more mature businesspeople who are over here because they need better English for work purposes. 'They need a nice room in a house that is close to the school, bed and breakfast and perhaps an evening meal, together with a chance to speak the language,' explains Yumus Raiss of the Sels College in Covent Garden, London.

If you would prefer more mature and intellectual guests, and you live near a university, you may be able to rent your room to visiting lecturers. These kind of rentals can last from a week to six months depending on how long the lecturer needs to be in the area. You could find yourself playing host to either British academics or foreign ones. Some may only need to stay part-time, but others will want to be there for weekends too.

Ring up universities and colleges in your area to see whether they have such a scheme. They will want to see your accommodation before recommending it to their people, and they will give you an idea of how much you can charge for it. It is likely that this kind of guest will want somewhere relatively quiet with enough room to study. Internet access would also be helpful, as would a separate phone line for their use only.

HOW MUCH CAN YOU MAKE?

Again, it depends on where you live and what your home is like. In London, for bed and breakfast, you can make £100 a week. With dinner it's usually about £150. If you offer a posh house with a bathroom en suite you can charge around £200 a week.

Outside London, the going rate can vary from about £35 to £80 per week, with central locations in bigger cities getting the top prices.

COSTS

You will need to offer students a continental breakfast which will entail some food expenses. You will also use extra electricity and gas. As with renting a room long-term, it's a good idea to have your home contents insured and to make sure that your insurance company knows you have paying guests some of the time.

If you offer Internet facilities or other office amenities you can include these costs in the rental price.

TRAINING AND QUALIFICATIONS

You don't need any.

PROS

Renting to foreign students or visiting professors can be a great way of meeting new people and learning about foreign cultures. You could find yourself getting on very well with one or more and being invited back to their country for a holiday. It is also useful to bear in mind that whoever is staying with you won't be there for ever, as this takes pressure off the relationship.

CONS

Culture clashes do happen. Anecdotally I have heard that most foreign students are easy to have in the house, particularly Japanese, who are extremely polite and quiet, but some can be difficult, with the most complaints being made about male students from the Middle East.

If you badly need a guaranteed income every week, having students or lecturers may be too uncertain a proposition for you. You may have the odd week or two where no one is renting from you.

USEFUL CONTACTS

The Association of Recognised English Language Services (ARELS), 56 Buckingham Gate, London SW1E 6AG, 020 7802 9200, fax 020 7802 9201, www.arels.org.uk, email enquiries@arels.org.uk

Case study

Journalist April Tod has been renting a room to visiting lecturers and mature students from a local university for several years and finds it an easy way of making money. 'I do it on a part-time basis and it suits my life very well,' she says. 'I am very picky about who I have so I don't have people staying all the time. I can go for months without the right person turning up. The one I have at the moment is a mature student who is doing a three-month course. He is married with children so he's only here from Sunday night to Wednesday afternoon. As I am away a lot we can go for weeks without meeting each other!'

April has a strict rule that she only rents out the bedroom with access to the kitchen and bathroom. 'I don't want to have to share the sitting room as well as it's quite small and I need privacy. I do clean their room every now and then – just put a Hoover around – and they use my sheets and towels, but otherwise they keep themselves to themselves.

'I think that mature students and visiting lecturers or doctors are the best kind of guests to have. They are responsible and they're usually here to work hard so most of the time they're buried in their work in the evening and I hardly notice them. I like the fact that they're attached to the university too because I know their details are on record there and you can feel safe with them.'

April charges £90 a week for her room. 'I used to be on the books of Imperial College in Kensington,' she says, 'but they charged me ten per cent of every booking, which got expensive. Now I just take people from Roehampton University, which is much closer. I'm on a list of accommodation providers that the accommodation officer hands out to people needing somewhere to stay and they contact me direct. Much better.'

Running a B&B

If you have a few extra rooms in your house you could run it as a bed-and-breakfast hotel either full- or part-time, depending on how much free time you have and how much money you want to make. There is more work involved than in just renting a room, and you will have to comply with more legal requirements, but it can be a good way of making your home work for you.

HOW TO DO IT

First, decide whether there is a demand for accommodation of your sort in your area. Do you live in a place that attracts a lot of tourists? Is there a local theatre that has actors needing a place to stay for a few weeks at a time? Is it somewhere where businesspeople often need short-term accommodation? If you live in a dull town, nowhere near transport, where nothing really happens, it will be harder to make money out of a B&B and it may not be worth bothering.

Register your business with local tourist authorities to attract custom. Aim to get into guidebooks, but remember that competition is tough and you will need to offer something special to make a living. You should also keep advertising in as many places as possible to increase the possibility of drawing the punters in. Contact your local theatre and make sure you're on their list. Contact local universities and colleges and large local businesses to get on their lists of recommended places to stay.

Also, have a look at the competition. What are other B&Bs offering in your area? What are they charging? If you think you will need to modify your premises – for example, adding a conservatory restaurant or building extra rooms in the loft – make enquiries about local planning constraints and find out whether you will be able to finance your plans.

HOW MUCH CAN YOU MAKE?

It very much depends where you are, what you are offering, how many bedrooms you have and how often they are occupied. You could make anything from a few hundred a month to a few thousand a month.

COSTS

You will have increased cleaning costs given the extra people coming through your home, as well as extra electricity and gas charges with all the laundry and hot water. You will also, of course, have the cost of providing breakfasts. It is worth doing a very good, high-quality breakfast, by the way, as B&Bs often build their reputation on the standard of their food as much as on the place itself. You will probably also have advertising costs and the expense of starting and maintaining a website if you decide to go for that. Ideally, the longer you last, the more word-of-mouth advertising you will get, if you are good, which is the best and the cheapest sort of promotion you can obtain.

TRAINING AND QUALIFICATIONS

You don't need any training or qualifications.

PROS

You get to meet lots of new people and make money without having to leave your front door.

CONS

People can be difficult, and you have to like them to be able to put up with their funny and often offensive ways. Many also have unpleasant personal habits, and you may find that some cause you far too much work. You are forced to stay in the house – or hire someone to look after things for you, which will cost you – for weeks on end. You won't be able to have many lie-ins as someone has to cook breakfast!

USEFUL CONTACTS

The British Tourist Authority has a booklet on setting yourself up as a B&B. Call them on 020 8846 9000 for the Pink Booklet, which costs £7.99 + p&p. Or look at their website at www.visitbritain.com.

Renting out your home

It may seem drastic, but if you're serious about making some extra money, moving out of your home and renting it out totally can bring in large amounts of cash without too much hassle for you.

HOW TO DO IT

You can either let your place through a lettings agent (you will probably find several on your local high street) or do it yourself. If you do it yourself, find out how much you could reasonably charge for your place and advertise it in local freesheets or on the Internet. If you have the ability, you could even set up your own website to advertise it. Alternatively, put an ad in the local newsagent's window or simply let all your friends know your place is up for rent. You could also contact local large businesses or, if you're in London, embassies to see whether one of their employees would be interested.

If you use a lettings agent they will advertise the place themselves and they will (or should – they don't always) take up references from your prospective tenant for you. Nevertheless, it is a good idea for you to check the references yourself as ultimately it is your property and the buck stops with you.

If you are letting the place yourself, it goes without saying that you should ask for, and check, at least two character references from your prospective tenant, one of which should be from their employer. You should also get a reference from their bank manager. Taking references – and checking them by telephone – is terribly important as you need to be very sure that the person who is going to be living in your home is decent and honest. Once they are in, it is not always easy to get them out.

Once you have found a tenant, draw up a contract with them, including an itinerary of all the furniture and utensils in the property. You can get a sample contract and itinerary in a lettings pack from W H Smith or you can draw up your own. Take a deposit that will cover at least six weeks' rent. This should be given back to the tenant when they leave, minus anything you have to spend on damaged, broken or lost items. Also, make sure they set up a standing order each month, or week. Cash in hand may seem like a good way to get out of paying tax (many people see it in this light) but it can leave you very vulnerable if things go wrong down the line, and it takes time to collect.

One major fear that potential landlords face is how to get bad tenants out if they need to. 'Many problems can be avoided if you do it right from the start,' says Malcolm Harrison of the Association of Residential Letting Agents (ARLA). 'If all your paperwork is correct from the start then if it goes pear-shaped you can apply for an "accelerated court procedure". That means that the paperwork goes to your local county court judge, who is able to issue a "possession order" just from the paperwork without you having to go to court.' This can still take time, depending on where you live and how fast the courts work in your area, so it is very important to do all the checks necessary at the start to make sure you have a trustworthy tenant.

'You need a "good covenant tenant" who will pay when they should and won't cause you problems,' says Malcolm Harrison, 'and it's worth dropping the rent to get someone like that.'

HOW MUCH CAN YOU MAKE?

Depending on where your property is and what it is like you can make anything from £100 to thousands a week (in posh places in central London).

COSTS

If you use a lettings agent to rent your home out they will probably charge you a monthly fee, unless you can negotiate a one-off payment at the start. It's worth haggling because there is quite a lot of competition in the market. Expect to pay no more than 10 per cent of the rental income each month in agent's commission.

One big cost in renting out your home is the occasional need to undertake repairs. You may be lucky and find that nothing goes wrong with the house, but that is unlikely. You may have to have a washing machine mended or replaced, or experience expensive problems with the boiler, roof or drains. You could be faced with all these problems in one year. If you are handy yourself and you have the time, you can save a lot of money by doing repairs yourself, but it's unlikely that you will get away with not having to pay anything for the whole year.

TRAINING AND QUALIFICATIONS

You don't need any training or qualifications to rent out your home, but you might like to read up a bit on it before plunging in. *Renting Out Your Property for Dummies* by Melanie Bien (£14.99, Wiley) is an excellent source book for anyone hoping to become a landlord.

PROS

You should make a significant amount of money without really trying, assuming no expensive problems crop up.

CONS

Unless you can live with your parents or friends for free, you will have to pay rent to live somewhere else. Also, even if you live rent free, you may find that, emotionally and socially, you really can't stand living with others for any longer than a weekend.

You may be very unlucky and get a bad tenant, even after all the checks. They may cost you money by damaging your property and withholding rent for months on end. You can take them to court over this but it is a long-drawn-out process and usually costly.

USEFUL CONTACTS

The Association of Residential Letting Agents, 0845 345 5752, www.arla.co.uk – they will put you in touch with one of their members in your area.

Storage space

If you have a large loft, cellar or a garage that you don't use, you could rent it out as storage for people who are spatially challenged!

HOW TO DO IT

First, work out whether you really have enough clean, dry, accessible space in your home. Empty out areas that you would like to rent out for storage and work out how much space you have in square metres. Ring up local storage companies and find out what they charge and what they offer (e.g. 24-hour access; special locks; extra-large areas, etc.). Work out a rate that will compete with this and advertise in your local papers.

If you have a cellar or garage that has direct access you will be able to charge more because you can offer clients their own key and 24-hour access. As with renting out a room or your home, make sure you have a contract that both parties sign which includes rights and duties on both sides, what access the client will have to their stuff (is it 24-hour or will they have to contact you first to get at it?), how much the rental will be and what period of notice should be given by either side if the stuff is to be removed.

Put the word around among friends first that you have storage space to rent. Most people have quite ordinary stuff that they need to store temporarily, but with strangers you cannot be sure. In fact, if you are renting to strangers it is sensible to include a clause in the contract confirming that their boxes do not include stolen goods, drugs or other illegal materials.

HOW MUCH CAN YOU MAKE?

It depends on the amount of storage space you have and where you live. It could be anything from £5 a week for storing a few boxes in your loft to around £50 for filling a garage in central London.

COSTS

Other than advertising costs and perhaps new locks and extra keys, there should be few costs involved in renting out space for storage.

TRAINING AND QUALIFICATIONS

You don't need any training or qualifications.

PROS

This can be a great way of making money with very little effort or nuisance.

CONS

If someone stores flammable, explosive or biodegradable goods in your home it could seriously damage your property. If you can't offer direct access to the storage area you may be bothered by someone regularly coming and going.

Renting out your driveway or garage

Don't ignore the possibility of renting out parking space on your land if you live near a station or in a busy, urban area with little parking but lots of businesses.

HOW TO DO IT

If you have a garage but no car you could potentially rent it out for others to park in. If you live out in the country or somewhere where there is a lot of space already this will not apply. (There are other ways it could be used, however, such as a rehearsal space for bands.) But in busy urban areas garage parking can be at a premium. In central London, for example, renting a garage can be as expensive as renting a small flat.

You can let your garage through a property letting agent – particularly in major cities – or you could simply put an ad in the local paper, local newsagent or on websites that cover your area. Even if you want to rent it out yourself, it would be worth contacting a few local agents to find out what price they would offer it up for. Once you find someone who would like to rent it, get them to sign a contract that covers what they would pay for damage, loss of keys, etc., and setting out the monthly rent and notice period for cancelling the contract.

Renting out your driveway is even simpler. Put ads in local papers or in the local newsagent, or even on your front gate. If you live near a station, see whether they will let you put a notice up there. Find out how much the station car park charges per day and come up with a competitive price for your drive. For Londoners, there are also websites such as www.londongarages.com that deal solely in garage rental if you want to work through an agent.

Some enterprising residents near Heathrow offer a private 'park and ride' service to air passengers. As it is so expensive to park at Heathrow itself, they offer their driveway or even a parking space on their road and then drive the passengers to Heathrow and pick them up when they return, taking them straight to their car. People who live in Wimbledon rent their driveways out to food, drink and souvenir sellers during the tennis tournament. If you live close to a football ground, airport, station or other venue that people need to park at or walk by, there could be all kinds of ways of making money from your driveway or garage.

HOW MUCH CAN YOU MAKE?

Depending on where you live, you can earn from £10 a day for a driveway in a suburb to £17,000 a year for a garage in Knightsbridge, London.

COSTS

Other than advertising costs and perhaps new locks and extra keys, there should be few costs.

TRAINING AND QUALIFICATIONS

You don't need training or qualifications.

PROS

This is another easy and non-intrusive way of making some regular money.

CONS

You could find that having someone else's car in your driveway causes too much noise, dirt and nuisance long-term. For band rehearsals, you would obviously need fairly distant neighbours and be able to put up with the noise yourself.

Your home as a film set

You would be surprised at how much you can make by allowing a film crew into your home for a day or more. If you live in a posh or even just an interesting place you can rent it out as a film set – prices are around £1,000 a day for somewhere really good!

HOW TO DO IT

Not every home is of interest to production companies but it is often surprising what they are looking for. Contact the BBC locations department, your local film commission or one of the national location libraries in London (see below for contact details) and they will send you a form to fill in about your home.

There are quite a few criteria that the ideal home needs to fulfil. Locations manager Helene Lenszner says, 'Ideally we're looking for generous-sized houses with large rooms, a road with good parking facilities, friendly neighbours who won't mind the intrusion and owners who are relaxed about having a crew of about thirty or forty people in their homes with all the cameras and equipment that go with them.'

If you live in a fabulous stately home you can certainly make a lot of money per day (around £1,000–£2,000) by accommodating a film crew. But quite ordinary homes are wanted too, so long as they are not too far from London or other main film-making cities, there is good parking nearby and enough room for a camera crew to swing a tripod. Some programmes, such as *The Bill*, for example, often need grotty bedsits to film in. They also love homes that have original period interiors, so if you are into fifties decor, for example, consider offering your home for *Heartbeat* or a one-off drama.

You can also hire out your home for stills shots. If it is swanky enough you could get between £1,000 and £2,000 a day, but it needs to be a pretty special house.

HOW MUCH CAN YOU MAKE?

Usually around £1,000 a day, although it would be less for a small place and more for a large stately home. In London, documentary-makers pay around £300–£500 a day.

COSTS

Usually film crews will replace broken or damaged items, although you are often left with damage that you only find later on. Also, if they take over your home for more than a day you will have to find other accommodation for you and your family, which could cost you.

TRAINING AND QUALIFICATIONS

You don't need training or qualifications.

PROS

You can make a substantial amount of money without much time or effort. If you hang around while the filming is going on you could meet interesting people – including well-known actors – and even get a walk-on part!

CONS

Film crews can be *very* intrusive and can break things you would never have imagined could be broken! You will have to move out if the crew is there for any length of time, which can be quite a nuisance, particularly if you have family.

USEFUL CONTACTS

Amazing Space, 020 7251 6661

BBC Locations Department, 020 8576 8863

Sarah Eastel Locations, 01225 460022, www.film-locations.co.uk

Film Locations UK, 020 8393 2423, www.locations-uk.com

Lavish Locations, 020 8742 2992, www.lavishlocations.com

The Location Partnership, 020 7734 0456, www.locationpartnership.com

Location Works, 020 7494 0888, www.locationworks.com

Case study

Five years ago, full-time mother of four Anna Rankin and her husband moved back into her parents' home, Micklefield Hall – a wonderful Georgian house with acres of farmland, near Watford in Hertfordshire. The house is large and needs a lot of upkeep, so the couple's first thought was to hire the place out as a film location.

'It's fantastic when film companies use it as a location,' she says. 'The money's really good but it is a bit erratic so you can't bank on getting a certain amount every year.' Last year the house was used as a location for 12 days, but in other years it has been more.

➤

'It's really fun having film crews around,' Anna adds. 'I've met some really interesting people, including some famous actors, and the children love it. But you do have to be relaxed about it. They can turn the place upside down and you have to not worry about what they're doing to your paintwork or your floors. But they make it all right afterwards anyway so it's not too bad.'

Boarding pets in your home

If you love animals – particularly dogs and cats – and you have a large house or a lot of land, you can make a pretty good living offering holiday homes for pets.

HOW TO DO IT

There are two ways you can do this. Either you can offer an ad hoc service to neighbours, offering to look after their dog or cat in your home while they are away, or, if you have a lot of land and, ideally, a barn or similar that you can convert, you can set up a proper boarding home for cats or dogs.

If you just offer an occasional service for local people, you can put an ad in the local newsagent's and put it about by word of mouth that you can take in animals in your own home. If you have a dog already you will probably meet other dog owners while out walking – an easy way to put the word about. You could also put an ad in the local vet's practice, which should attract a lot of interest.

Setting up a proper boarding home for dogs or cats is another matter entirely. To do this you will need land, and plenty of it. It would also be helpful to have a barn or other outhouse that you could convert for the purpose. Before doing anything, though, you will have to obtain planning permission from your local authority, and this is not easy.

You are required to be licensed under the provisions of the Animal Boarding Establishments Act (1953), which has 57 different conditions. Licences are issued by your local authority. Details can be obtained from the Chief Environmental Health Officer of your council. There are other acts you need to be aware of too, including the Dogs (Amendment) Act (1928), the Breeding of Dogs Act (1973), the Protection of Animals Act (1911) and the Guard Dogs Act (1975).

If you do want to set up pet boarding facilities on your land, first contact Ken Oultram at the Animal Boarding Advisory Bureau (details below) and he will send you an information pack for £10. You can also get help and advice from the Kennel Club, for dogs, or the Feline Advisory Bureau, for cats.

Once you have set up your establishment, you will need to advertise in specialist magazines, set up a website and contact local vet's practices and other animal-focused businesses to market your service.

HOW MUCH CAN YOU MAKE?

For pet-sitting at home you can probably negotiate a price of around £50 to £200 per animal, per week, excluding food and litter. Keep costs down by getting the owners to give you enough food, litter and other equipment for their pet for the whole time they are away.

If you run a full boarding home for pets how much you make will depend on where you are and how many animals you house. On the whole you can make about £15 to £35 per animal, per day, depending on what you offer.

COSTS

For pet-sitting at home there are no real costs other than the time you might have to take to walk a dog.

For setting up a boarding home for pets there are all sorts of costs, including the cost of land (if you don't already have it), the construction of the kennels, legal costs in meeting all the government's requirements, employment costs if you need extra help, cleaning, food and equipment costs, as well as the usual business costs of administration and advertising.

TRAINING AND QUALIFICATIONS

You don't need training or qualifications but it would be very helpful to get advice from the Animal Boarding Advisory Bureau and elsewhere before you start doing anything.

PROS

If you love animals, and you have lots of land that you want to turn into money, this can be a great way of earning extra cash.

CONS

There are a lot of rules and regulations involved in boarding pets, which can be a headache. You may face problems with neighbours complaining about barking dogs all the time, and there may be health issues with animals that are difficult to deal with.

If you are just pet-sitting you may have to be at home more than you normally would in order to care for the animal.

USEFUL CONTACTS

The Animal Boarding Advisory Bureau, c/o Blue Grass Animal Hotel, Clatterwick Lane, Little Leigh, nr Northwich, Cheshire, 01606 891303 – Ken Oultram will send you an information pack on setting up kennels or a cattery for £10

The Feline Advisory Bureau, 'Taeselbury', High Street, Tisbury, Wilts. SP3 6LD, 01747 871872, www.fabcats.org – FAB will give you help and advice on setting up a cattery

The Kennel Club, 1 Clarges Street, London W1J 8AB, 0870 606 6750, www.the-kennel-club.org.uk – they will give you help and advice on the best care of dogs

The Royal Society for the Prevention of Cruelty to Animals (RSPCA), Wilberforce Way, Southwater, Horsham, West Sussex RH13 9RS, 0870 0101181, www.rspca.org.uk

Propagating seedlings

If you have green fingers, a greenhouse and some patience, you can make money out of propagating seedlings and selling them to garden centres, local shops and individuals.

HOW TO DO IT

First, you need to be a good gardener who already has experience in propagating seedlings. A greenhouse is important – the bigger the better – together with a knowledge of popular seeds, the right soil and the right equipment to use.

If you have particular favourite flowers or vegetables that you like to grow, it's likely that they will be popular with others. So when you are propagating seedlings for yourself, fill more trays than you need and sell the extra ones.

Go to your local garden centre, tell them about the seedlings you have and see whether they would be interested. They may tell you about other seedlings that sell well in their shop, so you could start growing those too. Put an ad on your front gate if you want to sell to passers-by; you could also advertise in local freesheets or in your local newsagent's window. Plants and seedlings also sell well at car boot sales, so try these at the weekends.

HOW MUCH CAN YOU MAKE?

Anything from £100 or so a month to £2000 if you work at it.

COSTS

You will have to pay for seeds, seedling trays, soil and the heating and lighting of your greenhouse in the winter.

TRAINING AND QUALIFICATIONS

You don't need qualifications but the more knowledge and experience you have the better. You can do courses in propagating seedlings through the Royal Horticultural Society (see below for contact details).

PROS

If you love gardening and you have a big greenhouse this can be a pleasant and easy way of making money.

CONS

You may find that the patience and amount of work involved are not worth the money.

USEFUL CONTACTS

www.bbc.co.uk/gardening – there is loads of information on all aspects of gardening, including propagating seedlings, in the BBC's excellent gardening section

The Royal Horticultural Society, 020 7834 4333, www.rhs.org.uk

Case study

House husband Michael Garner, who lives with his family in Hampshire, turned his hobby into a money-earner when his first child was born. 'I'd always enjoyed gardening and I used to grow things from seed,' he says. 'You usually have more plants than you need when you propagate your own and I started selling the ones I had left over to local shops. I've been doing it for three years now and I've learned a lot through trial and error. I make about £600 profit a month from something that doesn't take more than a few hours a week.'

Michael was given an 8-foot-by-6-foot greenhouse which he uses for his seedlings once they've been propagated in a warm room in his house, and he says that over time he's learned the cheapest ways of doing things. 'You have to choose the right plants,' he says. 'For example, it costs £2.99 for just six red geranium seeds, whereas for the same price you can get 2,500 foxglove seeds. I also get the pots pretty much for free by going to a local nursery and giving them a tenner for piles of pots that they just throw out.'

The work is seasonal, mostly running from February to October, but he says that if he wanted to he could make more money each month. 'I make about £60 a week just selling plants on a sale-or-return basis to local shops and then about £100 a week at the local car boot sale on Sundays.'

Growing vegetables and fruit to sell

If you have green fingers and a nice big garden (with a greenhouse, ideally) you could sell surplus fruit, vegetables and flowers to individuals, shops or at the local farmers' market.

HOW TO DO IT

Grow more fruit, vegetables or flowers than you normally do and when they are ready to sell put a notice on your front gate to attract passers-by. You could also put adverts in local papers or sell the produce at a local farmers' market (see below on how to find out about one in your area).

If you are already a keen gardener with green fingers, this should not be difficult, although you might like to find out what kind of produce sells best before you start planting the seeds.

You could specialise in organic fruit and veg, which are increasingly popular across the country. Get in touch with the Soil Association (see below) to find out the rule and regulations you have to follow to be able to advertise your produce as organic.

HOW MUCH CAN YOU MAKE?

It very much depends on what you sell and how much of it. Anything from a few pounds a week, if you just sell some spuds here and there, to hundreds a week if you have a large garden and you sell from your front gate and from a market stall.

COSTS

Seeds, compost and gardening equipment will have to be paid for, and there will be the cost of a market stall if you decide to go that route.

TRAINING AND QUALIFICATIONS

You don't need any training or qualifications, although the more gardening knowledge you have the better.

PROS

Make money out of your gardening hobby!

CONS

Gardening – particularly growing vegetables – can be back-breaking work. You need to be strong and healthy to do it. Also, it can be seasonal, with much more produce growing in the spring and summer months than in the winter.

USEFUL CONTACTS

The Association of Farmers' Markets PO Box 575, Southampton SO15 7BZ, 0845 230 2150, www.farmersmarkets.net

The Fresh Produce Consortium, 01733 237117, www.freshproduce.org.uk

The Soil Association, Bristol House, 40–56 Victoria Street, Bristol BS1 6BY, 0117 929 0661, www.soilassociation.org – this should be your first point of contact if you want to grow organic fruit and veg

Hiring out your garden as allotments

If you don't have the time or energy to do anything with your garden yourself, why not let others have the benefit of it?

HOW TO DO IT

If you have a large garden with direct access you could offer all or part of it as an allotment. Mark off a part that you are happy to rent out (probably that you can't see from your home) and let it be known around your neighbourhood that it is for rent.

HOW MUCH CAN YOU MAKE?

Not very much! On average, allotments in Britain cost between £10 and £30 *a year*! This is really only worth considering if you have a large garden that you can't maintain yourself and you don't have the energy to do anything with it. Of course, you can allow for gifts of fruit and veg – and even flowers – from whoever uses it as well.

COSTS

None to speak of.

TRAINING AND QUALIFICATIONS

You don't need training or qualifications.

PROS

If you find it difficult to get about or you really don't have the time to bother with a large garden, turning it into allotments will make it useful and help other people who don't have anywhere to grow things. You might also reap the benefit of home-grown fruit and veg.

CONS

There's so little money in it, it might not be worth the nuisance of having other people walking in and out of your garden whenever they want to.

USEFUL CONTACTS

National Society of Allotment and Leisure Gardeners, O'Dell House, Hunters Road, Corby, Northants. NN17 5JE, 01536 266576, www.nsalg.demon.co.uk

Bee-keeping

If you have a large garden in the country with lots of flowers and space, keeping bees can be a delightful and lucrative hobby.

HOW TO DO IT

First, get in touch with your local bee-keeping society. You can find them through the British Bee Keepers Association (BBKA) website (see below). All local associations run a beginners' course which is a very helpful way to start. Courses may be free or they may charge and add in a half-colony of bees at the end. If they do not include a half-colony you will have to buy this separately.

You will also need to buy a hive and all the protective clothing necessary for dealing with bees, much of which you can often acquire second-hand from your local society. The BBKA has training manuals and runs all sorts of workshops and more advanced training courses for bee-keepers, and it is certainly worth going on these if you are serious about it.

You can make and sell honey from your bees, sell the wax, or make your own candles and other wax products and sell those separately, either at farmers' markets (see contact details, p. 91 above) or craft fairs, or just through local advertising or a sign on your front gate.

HOW MUCH CAN YOU MAKE?

It depends how many bees you have and what the weather is like in any particular year. On average you should be able to produce about 20–40 lb of honey a year from each good hive. Home-produced honey sells for between £1–3 per lb depending on its quality and where you are selling it. Then there are the wax products such as candles and polish that can also bring in extra cash. So with several hives and some time on your hands you could make a few thousand a year out of this.

COSTS

Start-up costs are around £200–£300, but you might spend more money on training courses and more hives later on.

TRAINING AND QUALIFICATIONS

You don't have to be trained to keep bees but, unless you have a lot of experience in it already, it would be a good idea to do a course before embarking on it.

PROS

If you love bees, honey or wax products, bee-keeping is a lovely hobby and it is pleasant to make some money out of it too.

CONS

Some people are badly allergic to bee stings, so it would be impossible for them to do this. Keeping bees can be quite hard work and you need a lot of hives to make any serious money from it.

USEFUL CONTACTS

The British Bee Keepers Association, National Agricultural Centre, Stoneleigh Park, Warwickshire CV8 2LG, 02476 696679, www.bbka.org.uk

Horses and dogs

If you like a flutter you could always go to the dogs – or even the Derby – not as a punter but as an owner.

HOW TO DO IT

If you've got some money to invest and enough to pay for the care and training of a greyhound or, more expensively, a race-horse, you could join celebrities such as Alex Ferguson who have won – and lost – a good deal of money doing this.

Both racing dogs and horses are highly risky investments so really you should mentally write off any money you put in right from the off. With a racehorse there is a lot more money to write off, but then the possible winnings are far greater too. 'We always say that you shouldn't buy a racehorse primarily as an investment,' says a spokeswoman for the Racehorse Owners Association (ROA). 'It's only worth it if you have a genuine interest in the sport.'

If you are interested you will have to shell out a lot of money for a horse – even if you do as most do and buy just a share in one. To buy a horse – usually as a foal – you are looking at upwards of £20,000 as an initial investment. If you just want to own a share, the ROA runs its own partnerships whereby you pay £3,000 up front for part-ownership then £175 a month thereafter for all the expenses. According to the ROA's latest figures the average cost per year of running a racehorse is £16,418. The average annual prize money is £4,572.

Of course, some will bring in a nice return through producing offspring. If you have a horse that has won races and then goes on to breed, you can expect to see a regular trickle of income. You could also get lucky and buy a real winner.

Going to the dogs is a much cheaper option, in terms of both buying and maintaining the animal. If you want to buy a racing dog, it is best to go through one of the trainers at the track where you want your greyhound to race. Most trainers have young dogs in training which they have bought themselves with a view to selling them on to current or new owners. The cost of a greyhound can vary enormously. At 16 weeks old an unraced puppy will fetch between £350 and £1,500, depending on its breeding. The price increases as they get older and more experienced.

The better the greyhound, the greater the price, naturally. A top-class greyhound at one of the bigger tracks will fetch up to £5,000, while the best in the country, those capable of winning races, are worth between £5,000 and £50,000. Keeping a greyhound in training is relatively inexpensive, usually £5 or £6 per day plus veterinary fees as and when required. Arthur Hammond, a director of the British Greyhound Racing Board, says it costs him about £80 a month to train up a greyhound pup. Greyhounds are not allowed to run until they are at least 15 months old, and on average they will be about 18 months old when they first start racing.

When it comes to winnings, Arthur says it depends on the dog and the kind of race it goes in for. 'The prize money is not at a great level but we're trying to get a deal with the bookmakers to bring it up,' he explains. 'If the dog is good quality it will be able to run in open races and the winnings can be £200 upwards. We had the Greyhound Derby a couple of weeks ago and the top prize there was £75,000.' A famous racing dog, Maxi Rumble, has earned his owner £30,000 a year for the last nine years, and he was offered £100,000 to sell him. Stud fees for a good greyhound can also be very lucrative at £1,000 per 'session'.

HOW MUCH CAN YOU MAKE?

Millions if you have a top racehorse that wins races *and* earns money in stud fees. On the other hand you could lose thousands.

COSTS

From about £350 for a greyhound pup to hundreds of thousands for a top racehorse, plus all the food, care, training, veterinary bills, transport and race fees.

TRAINING AND QUALIFICATIONS

You don't need any training or qualifications.

PROS

If you're into horse or dog racing this can combine your hobby with an investment. If you own, or part-own, a successful animal you could make a lot of money.

CONS

Most racehorses and racing dogs cost their owners more money than they win. There are always more losers than winners, so you are more likely to lose than win with this investment.

USEFUL CONTACTS

The British Horse Racing Board, www.horseracing.com

The National Greyhound Racing Club, Twyman House, 16 Bonny Street, London NW1 9QD, 020 7267 9256, www.ngrc.org.uk

The Racehorse Owners Association, www.racehorseowners.net

CHAPTER FOUR

Got a Car?

THERE ARE LOADS of money-making possibilities if you have a car or you know about cars. Don't ignore it as a source of cash!

Minicab driving

The market for minicabs (or private car hire) is huge, particularly in cities such as Manchester, Birmingham or Edinburgh, where driving and parking are getting more and more expensive and annoying.

HOW TO DO IT

To get started it would be a good idea to get a job with a reputable local firm. It is then easier to obtain work. As a minicab driver you now have to be licensed to work. You will need to be vetted by the Public Carriage Office but this is usually arranged by the firm you join. They will look at your police records and generally check your background. To qualify you will need to be over 21, hold a full DVLA, Northern Ireland or other EEA state driver licence and have held it for at least three years.

You will need to have a good, clean, comfortable car. Not all minicabs are clean, but those that are attract more regular and better-paid jobs. It doesn't need to be brand new but it should be in good condition and have four doors. Saloons are best for this kind of work. Some companies will provide a car for you, but then you have to pay them a weekly rental as well as the 'circuit fee' (a weekly payment in return for which they get you work), so it is better if you can use your own car.

As well as a clean driving licence you will need relevant insurance, which will be *much* higher than normal as you are using your car for work – check out websites such as www.the-aa.com, www.insuresupermarket.com and www.moneyfacts.co.uk for the best car insurance rates.

It can be a risky job, so be prepared for that. Keep your mobile phone with you at all times and feel free to refuse jobs if the client looks dangerous or worryingly drunk. Remember, in big cities you really only make money at night as you can't get around easily during the day, thanks to traffic jams, and unlike black cabs you are on a fixed rate per journey, so the longer you take, the less money you make.

HOW MUCH CAN YOU MAKE?

You can earn between £600 and £800 a week, depending where you are working in the country and how many days/nights you do.

COSTS

You need to have a good-quality, four-door saloon. If you own one already then you will simply need to pay for the petrol and regular cleaning (which you could do yourself). The insurance is nasty – about £40–£50 a week, depending on where you live. You will also need to pay the firm a weekly circuit fee.

TRAINING AND QUALIFICATIONS

You simply need to be a qualified driver with a clean licence and a clean police check.

PROS

This is a good, flexible way of making money out of your car when you happen to be free. You can also meet interesting people.

CONS

You need to be tough and you will have to drive for hours on end, which can be tiring and frustrating. You could also be put in dangerous situations at times.

USEFUL CONTACTS

Public Carriage Office – www.tfl.gov.uk/pco, 0845 602 7000, 15 Penton Street, London N1 9PU

Chauffeur work

Once you have done your time as a minicab driver or as a driver for a company, you could go up a notch and become a chauffeur.

HOW TO DO IT

It would help to work for a while for an established chauffeur company to gain experience before going it alone. Once you have decided to do your own thing, buy a good, posh car if you have the money, or arrange finance to buy one. *Auto Trader* magazine is a particularly good place to look for second-hand luxury cars. At the outset you could even lease a quality car – it would mean you would not have to find so much money up front and the whole amount could be set against tax. Also, this arrangement is much more flexible, and if things didn't work out you could simply give it back.

You'll stand a better chance of getting a good, well-paid job if you have been through the one- or two-day course run by the British Chauffeurs Guild. If you attend the two-day course you get membership with no yearly renewal, access to temporary and permanent jobs, a silver cap and lapel badge, a chauffeur's manual, a set of rules and codes of conduct and a diploma of merit, all of which could help you get a good job.

It helps already to have contacts that you know will either use you on a regular basis or will put you in touch with other sources of work. You can also get work by setting up a website advertising your services – just a basic one with a few pages would do. Include photographs of yourself in uniform and your car together with contact details and then promote it on Google and other local search engines.

You could advertise in bridal magazines, in local and national papers and in the business press. In some cases you can offer extra services, such as tours of the area if you live in a touristy part of the country, or special 'minder' services if you have an army or police background or some sort of boxing or other 'tough guy' training.

HOW MUCH CAN YOU MAKE?

According to the British Chauffeurs Guild, rates for temporary or part-time chauffeurs are £8 per hour for a minimum of five hours per day plus £5 travel expenses. For full-time chauffeurs the salaries range from £20,000 to around £35,000.

COSTS

If you decide to go it alone you will need a top-of-the-range posh car such as a Jaguar, BMW or Mercedes. Even second-hand these could set you back £16,000 plus. Insurance will be expensive as you are using the car for work, and these are already pricey cars to insure. Check out the insurance websites above (p. 385) for the best rates. You will also need to pay for petrol, but you should charge this to your employers or clients.

TRAINING AND QUALIFICATIONS

It's not essential but it would help to have one of the qualifications issued by the British Chauffeurs Guild (contact details below).

PROS

You can mingle with the rich and famous, swan around in a posh car in a posh uniform and make some serious money at the same time.

CONS

You may not get enough work to cover the high costs of setting it all up. If you have one full-time client and they drop you your costs will suddenly rocket.

USEFUL CONTACTS

Avis, 020 8326 7310, www.avis.co.uk – offer long-term rentals on luxury cars

British Chauffeurs Guild, 020 8544 9777, www.britishchauffeursguild.co.uk

Hertz – www.hertz.co.uk, 020 8538 5252 – offers long-term rentals on luxury cars

Driving instruction

There are various schools of driving such as the British School of Motoring (BSM) which allow instructors to use their name as a franchise, but you could run your own part-time business training people in your own car instead.

HOW TO DO IT

If you are a good, safe and confident driver you could become an instructor in your spare time, although you will have to devote some effort and money to it at the start. To qualify as a Department of Transport Approved Driving Instructor you need to pass three exams and meet certain requirements including:

- holding a full British driving licence for a minimum of four years;

- having no criminal convictions unless they are spent; and

- being able to read a car number plate at a distance of 27.5 metres when the letter and numbers are 79.4 mm high.

The three exams involve one written test with 100 multiple-choice questions on general driving knowledge and the Highway Code; a second one that tests your driving ability on various kinds of roads; and an instructional ability test which assesses your ability to teach.

If you become really keen and you are a member of the Driving Instructors' Association you could also study for the DIA's Diploma in Driving Instruction.

Once you have your qualification you then have to decide whether you want to work for yourself or become a BSM franchisee. If you join BSM you will have to pay a certain amount each week to the company, depending on what kind of franchise option you have gone for (they have four different ones to choose from). With BSM, you're self-employed and you will get a brand-new dual-control car from them every nine months. One of the options, the cheapest, means you are an associate, and all you get is the car and the name – you have to find your own students. Other options involve you paying BSM more each week, in return for which the company supplies your clients, meaning that you don't have to spend time and money finding your own. Check out their website (details below) for more information.

If you run your own operation you will need to buy a car in good condition (if it is not you could be struck off if Driving Standards Agency officials make an inspection and find your car faulty) and have dual controls fitted. The market leaders for dual controls are HE-MAN in Southampton (023 8022 6952, www. he-manequipment.ltd.uk) and Bestway Dual Controls (020 8581 6677, www.dualcontrols.com). You will also have to do a lot more advertising and promotion of your service in your area. All the money you make you would keep, however!

HOW MUCH CAN YOU MAKE?

Normal rates of pay are around £15–£26 an hour, depending on where you are in the country.

COSTS

You will need to pay for your training and the exams which are likely to come to over £2,000 – BSM trains its own instructors for £2,495 – then you will need to buy a car, if you don't have one already, and have dual controls fitted (which costs between £250–300) and pay for the petrol used each day. Also, you may want to join the Driving Instructors' Association, which costs about £50 a year.

TRAINING AND QUALIFICATIONS

Three exams set by the Driving Standards Agency.

PROS

Once you are qualified and have the right car you can make extra money out of this for years. Even with a full-time job you can have clients who are happy to be taught evenings and weekends. The money is quite good too.

CONS

You really need to be confident that you could make money out of this as the up-front time and money are pretty hefty. Also, you need to have low stress levels given the way some students drive!

USEFUL CONTACTS

The British School of Motoring (BSM), 0845 7276276, www.bsm.co.uk

The Driving Instructors' Association, Safety House, Beddington Farm Road, Croydon CRO 4XZ, 020 8665 5151, www.driving.org

The Driving Standards Agency, Stanley House, Talbot Street, Nottingham NG1 5GU, 01602 474222, www.dsa.gov.uk

The Motor Schools Association, 101 Wellington Road North, Stockport, Cheshire SK4 2LP, 0161 429 9669, www.msagb.co.uk

Food home delivery

Lots of takeaway restaurants need people with vans and cars to transport dinners around town. It's not just suicide scooters that deliver!

HOW TO DO IT

It's simply a question of offering your services to fast-food outlets in your area. Visit the shop or write a letter to the manager. If you are free when they need help – evenings and weekends are the busiest times, of course – they will take you on.

If there are a lot of takeaways in your town it might be worthwhile equipping your van or estate car with something to keep food warm, as you may get a contract from more than one of them. You will also need a mobile phone so that the outlets can get in touch with you immediately to give you more orders.

Some restaurants will prefer to pay you a flat fee for the evening rather than per delivery. It is up to you to decide whether this is worth it. If they offer a vehicle for you to use then it probably would be better to take this option.

HOW MUCH CAN YOU MAKE?

It all depends on where you live, who you work for and how much they are prepared to pay. You will need to set a charge per delivery for specific distances from the shop. It could be anything from £2 to £5 per delivery.

COSTS

The major cost is the delivery vehicle but I'm assuming you have a van or a large car already or you wouldn't be considering this as an option. After that your main costs are petrol and keeping the vehicle clean inside and out.

TRAINING AND QUALIFICATIONS

Just a clean driving licence.

PROS

If you have a car or van already and you are free in the evenings this can be a good way of making a reasonable amount of money if you live in an area with lots of takeaways and lots of lazy residents!

CONS

You have to work unsocial hours and there's no guarantee that you will get enough trips each night to make it worthwhile.

USEFUL CONTACTS

Domino's Pizza – www.dominos.co.uk, 01908 580000

www.pizzajoe.co.uk – a general site listing various pizza delivery shops and chains in the UK

www.roomservice.co.uk – a food delivery company that delivers for various restaurants, mostly in the Greater London area

Nappy delivery

Both disposable and reusable nappies can be delivered and taken away for busy parents. This could also be the start of a larger delivery service.

HOW TO DO IT

If you have space at home – perhaps a large garage or extra room – you could use it as storage for disposable nappies. If you have a baby you will know how many they go through in a week and how much space they take up. Register yourself (or your business) with a wholesaler so that you can bulk-buy nappies cheaply. Then offer nappies, delivered to the door, to parents in your area at a rate that enables you to make a profit.

People will pay extra for the convenience of having these

delivered to the door anyway, but you should make a profit on each pack as you have bought them at a discount already (if you haven't, change your wholesaler!). You can advertise your service through a leaflet drop, ads in local papers and newsagents and even on the Web. If you have a baby yourself you can benefit from the cheaper nappies too.

As we gradually become more environmentally conscious more and more parents are realising that the disposables are harming our environment. Each baby uses over 5,000 single-use nappies, and every one thrown away that reaches a landfill site is probably still there. Eight million disposable nappies, requiring millions of trees, are used and 'thrown away' in the UK every day – nearly 3 billion every year. But they don't disappear – they could take hundreds of years to decompose in a landfill site.

As parents become aware of this terrible legacy that they could be leaving for their children, grandchildren and great-grandchildren, they are going back to the reusable terry nappies. These are quite unpleasant and time-consuming to wash, however, so a number of reusable nappy services have grown up. If you can turn an outhouse or garage into a wash house with several washers and dryers going all day and possibly all night, this might be another service you could offer, delivering clean terry nappies and taking away the dirty ones to be washed.

For this service you would need to include the price of electricity, washing powder and the depreciation of the machines when you work out how much you charge for deliveries. Again, offer your service through a leaflet drop, local ads and also by promoting it in health food shops and maternity shops.

If you didn't want to start all this by yourself you could become a franchisee for a company like Cotton Bottoms. Get in touch with them (contact details below) to find out what package they offer. They are a recognised brand and could enable you to get more clients than you would if you started your own operation.

HOW MUCH CAN YOU MAKE?

It depends what kind of service you offer and how many clients you have. On the whole, a nappy washing and delivery service charges around £50 a month including weekly visits to take away the 'dirties'.

COSTS

You will have to bear the cost of a car and petrol, the cost of buying the nappies in the first place and, if you are servicing the reusable ones, all the costs of washing and drying.

TRAINING AND QUALIFICATIONS

You don't need any training or qualifications for this.

PROS

If you already have a baby yourself this could be a cheap way of getting nappies for your own offspring. It would also be possible to take your baby with you when you deliver – other parents would accept this and even welcome it.

CONS

This is a lot of work for not too much reward. You will have to keep readvertising too as parents will stop needing your services after a year or so.

USEFUL CONTACTS

Cotton Bottoms, 7–9 Water Lane Industrial Estate, Water Lane, Storrington, West Sussex RH20 3XX, 08707 77 88 99, www.cottonbottoms.co.uk

Ads on your car

Taxis and buses do it, so why not your car? If you don't mind driving around with 'Vimto' or 'Heineken' splashed across your bonnet, you could make money without effort this way.

HOW TO DO IT

Look at the adsoncars website (details below), fill in the online form and wait for them to contact you.

The company has a method of putting adverts all over cars that doesn't spoil the bodywork and allows them to be taken off easily in their workshop. Ideally, companies that like car advertising prefer drivers who have a nice, newish car in good condition, live and drive in upmarket areas and do quite a lot of mileage each year.

If you are offered an advert you are not obliged to take it. You may not like the product being advertised or the look of the proposed advertisement, so it's up to you simply to say no.

HOW MUCH CAN YOU MAKE?

Between £70 and £220 a month depending on the car, your average mileage and the size of the advert.

COSTS

None to you.

TRAINING AND QUALIFICATIONS

You don't need training or qualifications.

PROS

This is a very easy way of making a significant amount of money each month without lifting a finger.

CONS

If you care about appearances – or you drive a company car – this is not for you!

USEFUL CONTACTS

www.adsoncars.com – fill in the form online and wait for them to contact you

Car valeting

Car cleaning and valeting can be one of the most profitable sole-trader jobs to be in if you live in or near a wealthy area full of people with more cars than they can be bothered to care for.

HOW TO DO IT

There are two main ways of operating a car valeting service. Either you offer a mobile cleaning operation where you turn up at someone's house and clean their cars there, or you run your business from your garage, or similar, and people bring their cars to you.

If you are looking at this as a part-time, cash-on-the-side kind of operation then the mobile service would be best. You can take it out when you like – perhaps only working at weekends – and then put it away during the week. You will need a clean-looking small van, a good vacuum cleaner and generator, a good water tank and hose, and all the usual cleaning and waxing materials. You should also have proper overalls and look the part. It might help to project a professional look if you have the name of your 'business' painted professionally on the side of your van too.

The useful thing about being out and about cleaning people's cars in their streets is that while you are doing it you and your van are advertising your service and you will probably pick up more work from passers-by or neighbours. You can also get regular work from local businesses. Just offer to come round and clean the cars of any employees who would like the service in the car park. You can charge them individually.

If you wanted to do it from home or nearby then you would need a workshop (perhaps your garage) with plenty of space, as well as all the necessary cleaning equipment. There are franchises for this sort of operation, but this would cost you thousands and would only be worth going into if you wanted to do it full-time.

Do a leaflet drop in the area you want to work in, if you are offering a mobile service, and advertise in local papers. Word of mouth will work well for you here if you are quick, reasonably priced and efficient. Get yourself in the local Yellow Pages and Thomson's Directory and possibly put a card in local car salesrooms and accessory shops.

If you wanted more work you could target taxi firms, fleet managers, car dealers and car hire firms, or look into one of the cleaning franchises around. Also, contact car leasing companies and offer to clean all their cars before they are sent to auction. You could get hundreds of cars each month, if that is the level of work you can handle.

HOW MUCH CAN YOU MAKE?

For hand-cleaning inside and out you can charge between £35 and £40 a time. For a full service, including waxing, you can get closer to £70–80. If you decide to specialise in luxury cars such as Ferraris, using special cleaning fluids and sprays, the cost is usually closer to £300!

COSTS

Obviously there will be the cost of your equipment and ongoing purchases of cleaning products – some of which can be expensive, particularly for top-of-the-range cars. Other than that your main expenditure will be advertising.

TRAINING AND QUALIFICATIONS

You don't need any training or qualifications for this.

PROS

This is a nice outdoor job offering a great deal of satisfaction to those who love cars and enjoy seeing things clean again. It can also be quite a money-spinner if you work at it.

CONS

You will need to work hard to make any serious money. Also, the initial outlay on equipment is quite high however you do it, so you could end up losing money if you don't get enough work to cover your set-up costs.

USEFUL CONTACTS

Autoglym, www.autoglym.com – the company that makes professional cleaning fluids for high-end cars

www.cleanmycar.com – offers franchise opportunities

www.evalet.co.uk – offers franchise opportunities

Car repair

Obviously this is only for those who have a really good working knowledge of all kinds of car engines, but if you do you could provide a much-needed service at a fraction of garage costs.

HOW TO DO IT

If you already have a few years under your belt working for a car repair firm, or you have always naturally been able to mend cars from the year dot, you could set yourself up as a freelance car repairer. If you are good and you offer a well-priced service, word will get around quickly. Everyone has problems finding good, cheap car repairers and you should get regular work without too much of a problem.

To start with you may need a large garage, shed or outhouse on your property to work on the cars, but if you got really busy and wanted to do it more regularly then you would probably need a special workshop, ideally with a pit to work underneath the cars. If you work from home you must talk to your insurers about what you are planning to do. Many of the paints used on cars are highly flammable and it could void your entire home insurance if your workshop was too close to your house. Also, talk to the local council, because there may be planning issues you have to overcome too.

There is also a big demand for mobile car repairers who are willing to do home visits. This is something that a freelance repairer could do easily and well, particularly if you have a good, sturdy van in which to carry your equipment.

As modern cars are increasingly complicated under the

bonnet, repairers working on their own may have to concentrate on mending bodywork and doing simpler jobs that do not need specialist machines. But you could easily make deals with local, larger garages that can do complicated work through which you get a commission for referring jobs that are too big for you to take on.

Advertise your service in local car accessories shops and in newsagents' windows. Your main client base, though, should come through word of mouth. Many car repairers specialise in certain makes of cars or vans but this may not be an immediate option.

Make sure you give estimates for jobs, not quotes, as you don't want to be tied to an amount and then find it takes much more time and more parts to complete the job.

HOW MUCH CAN YOU MAKE?

You should be able to earn at least £40–£50 an hour if you go to people's homes and around £35–£45 if they bring their cars to you.

COSTS

You will need a number of good tools – many of which you may have already – which will set you back at least £5,000–£10,000. If you are mobile you will need a good van, and if you work from home you will need to equip a workshop, including buying in ramps or even building a pit for working underneath cars.

TRAINING AND QUALIFICATIONS

Ideally it's a good idea to be qualified in car mechanics, but it's not essential if you are running your own business. Look into NVQ, BTEC and City & Guilds courses at your local college. You can even do evening classes in basic car maintenance.

PROS

If you love tinkering about with cars it will make you very happy to have a proper business excuse for doing so!

CONS

You won't be guaranteed regular work and you could have a problem if you specialise in cars that very few people own. It is also dirty, smelly and often frustrating work!

USEFUL CONTACTS

www.automend.com – claim they can find parts for any make and model of car

City & Guilds, 1 Giltspur Street, London EC1A 9DD, 020 7294 2800, www.cityandguilds.co.uk

www.haynes.co.uk – all the Haynes manuals available here

Car buying and selling

If you love cars and you've spent years poring over car magazines and hanging around car auctions, you could make money as a dealer.

HOW TO DO IT

First and foremost in this business you need to know a good car from a knackered one. You need to be able to go to car auctions and pick up bargains that you can sell for a profit later on. You should study car magazines and have a subscription to *Exchange and Mart*, *Parker's Guide* and *Auto Trader*. You should also check prices and vehicles available on websites such as www.honestjohn.co.uk, which features reviews of cars, www.parkers.co.uk, which features reviews and prices, and www.autotrader.co.uk, the website of the magazine.

You will also need to be a bit of a salesperson. You don't have to be an Arthur Daley or a dodgy dealer, but you do need to be able to engage with customers and get them to buy rather than just look.

You could offer your services to individuals and local garages, acting as an agent for them at car auctions, working out first of all what they want, then buying the kind of car they need and taking a commission. If you get a reputation as someone who is honest and knowledgeable then this could be the quickest and cheapest way of dealing, as you have a guaranteed sale each time you buy and you don't have to put up your own money.

You could also buy cars at one auction, tart them up and then sell them for a profit at another auction. Or, if you see bargains you know would sell locally, buy them at an auction then sell for a profit through newspapers and free ads papers. 'Small cars do well,' says PR agent Xavier Adam, who has occasionally bought and sold cars for profit. 'There's a big market for them with new drivers, retired drivers, learners and people in cities who want to be able to park easily.'

The main UK auctions are Manheim and British Car Auctions. There are various local ones but they tend to be of a lesser quality. If you are not an account holder with the auction companies they will insist on a 10 per cent deposit on anything you buy. 'Be aware of false bids from car owners and the auctioneer bidding the price up,' says Xavier Adam. 'Sometimes if you ask in the office they will tell you a reserve price which will allow you to know what the owner is looking for.'

HOW MUCH CAN YOU MAKE?

You can make thousands a year if you know what you are doing and you shift a lot of cars. If you just do one or two a month, though, you will probably just pick up the odd few hundred here and there.

COSTS

You will need to buy the cars in the first place, unless you act as an agent for others at auctions. You will also need to advertise your service in local papers and probably on the Net.

TRAINING AND QUALIFICATIONS

You don't need any training or qualifications – just an in-depth knowledge of cars.

PROS

If you love cars and you're a good salesperson, this could be a great money-earner.

CONS

More and more people are getting clued up about cars, thanks to the Net, so it may be harder to make money from them. Also, customers have become extremely suspicious of the second-hand car market and will expect to see a full service history etc., even with very cheap cars, which is largely unrealistic.

USEFUL CONTACTS

www.honestjohn.co.uk – a really good car review site

www.parkers.co.uk – the website of the monthly publication

Furniture removals

If you are strong and you have a good-sized van, you could make some useful cash moving furniture and boxes of stuff for private individuals.

HOW TO DO IT

You will need a good, sturdy, capacious van, strong arms and, sometimes, another strong friend as a helper. You should advertise your service in local newsagents, the Yellow Pages and through leaflet drops, but once you get known as a good, reliable and reasonable mover you should get most of your work through word of mouth. It is very hard to find people who will deliver for a reasonable fee, so keep your charges fair and you will be in constant work.

If you would like regular work, get in with relocations companies, estate agents, estate management companies, storage places and even concierges in posh blocks of flats. They are all people who are asked occasionally to recommend small removals people or 'a man with a van'.

HOW MUCH CAN YOU MAKE?

It depends where you are and how many jobs you get. On average you will probably get between £20 and £70 per job.

COSTS

You will need to pay for the van, the petrol and, on busy days with heavy items, for a helper.

TRAINING AND QUALIFICATIONS

You don't need training or qualifications.

PROS

There is a big demand for this service, which will suit you if you are strong and enjoy heavy work. You should get jobs through word of mouth.

CONS

It can be back-breaking work and it is particularly bad when you get heavy, bulky objects to take up several flights of stairs.

Case study

Andrew Gray, a former minicab driver, says he has not had to advertise his furniture removal service in London for at least 18 months. 'I got into it through a friend that I used to minicab with,' he says. 'I started off helping him then started out on my own. I advertised for the first two years in the gay press and local magazines like *Time Out*, but then stopped and I haven't needed to advertise since. All my work comes by word of mouth. I get other kinds of work through it too. For some of my clients I also do furniture assembly, furniture restoration and some painting and decorating – but only if I like them!'

Andrew says he spends about £2,000 on a second-hand van which lasts him about two years. 'You don't want anything too good because they get bashed about, particularly in London.' He also has two or three men he can call on if he needs extra help. 'I pay them £10 an hour with a minimum of £40,' he explains. 'I tend to charge £40 per job if it takes less than an hour and then £30 an hour after that, or £15 per half-hour. If it's a really easy, small job I'll just do it for £20.'

Dispatch and courier services

You don't have to be a driver to be a courier. If you are a motor-cyclist or a cyclist you can make money carting packages around town.

HOW TO DO IT

Most large courier companies are constantly looking for drivers, motorcyclists and cyclists to work for them. It is a tough job – even life threatening to the motorcyclists and cyclists – and there is quite a high turnover of staff.

As a motorcyclist or cyclist you will be expected to provide your own transport. Car and van drivers either use their own vehicles or drive the company's. Some dispatch companies specialise in bicycle couriers and they supply their own bicycles and outfits. If you are a keen cyclist and take pride in your work, this is the sort of company to go for.

Given that most of the work comes from local businesses, the hours will generally be office hours, so it would be no good for someone who already works during the day. Also, according to Derek Olrog of Hays Couriers, one of the biggest courier companies in the country, most couriers work full-time as the outlay in insurance and other payments is too high to make it worthwhile taking on part-time staff.

'We need drivers and motorcyclists who are responsible and know their way around town,' he adds, 'but cyclists need to know their way even better because if they go the wrong way they don't have the speed to catch up with themselves quickly enough.'

HOW MUCH CAN YOU MAKE?

Couriers tend to get paid by the job and you can't know in advance how many jobs you will get in a week. Cyclists are paid the least per job and van drivers the most. The amount you make will depend on where you work and how many jobs you get.

COSTS

The only costs will be repairs to your vehicle and fuel, if you have a car, van or motorbike.

TRAINING AND QUALIFICATIONS

Just a driving and/or motorbiking licence and a knowledge of the area you work in.

PROS

If you love driving, motorbiking or cycling and you like being out in the traffic all day, this is a great job.

CONS

It can be dangerous (bikers and cyclists regularly lose their lives in London and other big cities), frustrating and dirty. It is also only really a day job and, primarily, a full-time job. There are few part-time opportunities available.

USEFUL CONTACTS

The National Courier Association, 7 Canons Road, Old Wolverton, Milton Keynes MK12 5TL, 01908 317892, www.nca.couk.com

CHAPTER FIVE

Home alone?

E VEN IF YOU have children or an elderly parent, or you are not mobile enough to work outside the home, there are all kinds of ways you can make money without leaving your front door. Remember, if you have a computer there are now even more ways. Check out Chapters 10 and 13 for more ideas.

Childminding

If you want to stay at home to look after your children but would like to make money too, this is a particularly good way of doing it.

HOW TO DO IT

As a childminder you can look after other people's children while you're tending your own, although you're only allowed up to six in total: that's up to three under-fives and up to three more between five and eight years old. The first step is either to contact the Children's Information Service for a recruitment pack or preferably to attend an instructional session in your local area.

You can find a lot of information about childminding and how to get into it on the website of the National Childminding

Association, or just ring them direct (your local council will have the number for your nearest branch). You will need to go through some training first and you, your family and your home will need to be approved by your local council before you can even be put on their list.

Once you are approved, you will be included on a list that the council sends to families who enquire, and you may be contacted by one that is close to you. If you are taken on, the parents will drop their children off at an agreed time in the morning and then pick them up in the afternoon. You will be their 'mum' or 'dad' for the day, playing with them, feeding them and looking after all their needs.

HOW MUCH CAN YOU MAKE?

'There's no fixed fee per hour, per child,' says Kay Lyons from the National Childminding Association, 'and it varies all over the country, but the average pay per child is about £2.30 per hour for full-time care and £2.44 for part-time.'

COSTS

A £14 Ofsted registration fee once your checks are complete – and then a fridgeful of healthy drinks as well as toys, videos and games.

TRAINING AND QUALIFICATIONS

Anyone looking after kids younger than eight has to be registered with Ofsted and undertake a childcare and first-aid training programme (although this can be completed within the first three months). You and any adult in the household will also have their police records checked to ensure that you are suitable for the job.

PROS

You can do this from home during hours normally devoted to your own kids anyway.

CONS

Huge responsibility for below-minimum-wage return.

USEFUL CONTACTS

Children's Information Service, www.childcarelink.gov.uk

National Childminding Association, www.ncma.org.uk

Case study

Jan Holt from Essex, gave up her marketing job when she had her first child. Having been a full-time mum she did not want to go back to the grind of working in an office again so she took up childminding. After contacting the local council and being accepted by them she was put on the area's childminding list.

'I love it,' she says. 'I have a pair of twelve-month-old twin babies to look after and my children, who are three and four, really love them and miss them when they're not there. They love coming home from school to play with the babies.' Jan has the babies for about 40 hours a week, and earns £80 per child. 'I can't think of any other job that could fulfil caring for my kids and making money at the same time,' she says. 'It's perfect!'

Fostering

Imagine 24/7 childminding with a whole wealth of responsibilities and expenses on top – that's fostering! Unlike adoption, which is permanent, fostering can involve caring for one or more children (from babies to 18-year-olds) for days, weeks or months at a time. The only thing the kids have in common is the need to be separated from their original domestic surroundings and placed in the care of someone responsible. So is it you?

HOW TO DO IT

Contact your local social services department or an independent fostering agency (links to both can be found below). Fortunately, there is plenty of support and advice available to help you with these choices.

In general, foster carers can be anyone – young or old (from 21 to retirement age), rich, not so rich or even unemployed, male or female – and some agencies will even consider applications from gay or disabled carers, although this is a grey area, subject to interpretation of the child's immediate circumstances. The determining factor is usually whether you have the time, space and temperament suitable for doing the job – and the evaluation of whether you are up to it is a lot more stringent than any 'real' parent has to go through. Here too, though, there is help available – for instance, if your home is not immediately suitable but *you* are, there are grants available to bring it up to standard.

Naturally, *your* needs are important too, especially when it comes to deciding which type of foster care you are best suited to. Roughly speaking there are five types.

1. Emergency care – when a child needs to be moved from their immediate situation as quickly as possible while their full needs are being determined. This can last from a single night to a few weeks.

2. Respite care – just for a few hours at a fixed time every day or week, perhaps to relieve an over-stretched parent or carer.

3. Medium-term care – often when a tricky family situation is being resolved; the kids will stay with you but will have increasing access to their parents, for instance.

4. Remand care – kids (usually teenagers) who are protected by a court order. (NB: this can be the trickiest of all and requires carers with great patience and particular skills.)

5. Long-term care – kids who cannot return to their original families and need more permanent care.

HOW MUCH CAN YOU MAKE?

Between £50 and £220 per child per week depending on local council rates (although the Fostering Network recommends a minimum of £120 per child per week). You can also receive further allowances and grants for childcare, educational, domestic or even holiday expenses. These can exceed £200 per child per week, depending on circumstances and region.

With fostering more than almost any other 'job', however, it's really important that you do it for the love of children rather than the need for money. Most of these children have already been through difficult or even hellish times, and the last thing they need is foster parents who don't care and are only in it for the cash.

COSTS

The average cost of raising, feeding and clothing a child is well over £6,000 per annum, which makes it the second-most expensive commitment in your life apart from your home. Don't underestimate it.

TRAINING AND QUALIFICATIONS

Foster carers need the same skills as parents and must also work alongside the local authority or birth parents. Naturally, there are rigorous security and safety checks to ensure you're up to it. Fostering agencies will require you to go through their own training procedure.

PROS

For the right people, fostering can be immensely rewarding on every level, particularly if you love children and are very patient, kind and generous.

CONS

It is hugely challenging as you often get children who have been abused in various ways and can be difficult, hurtful and even dangerous. This is not the 'try before you buy' alternative to adoption many people assume it to be.

USEFUL CONTACTS

www.adoption-net.co.uk – advice about fostering and adoption (which is exclusively long-term and governed by different rules)

British Association for Adoption and Fostering, www.baaf.co.uk

---

Case study

Jane and Martin Morgan have been short-term foster carers for seven years, looking after over a dozen charges in that time. 'Short-term can be the hardest of all, because the kids think they're getting an instant family – and it's rarely as simple or permanent as that. Once you're known as reliable carers, the money's not bad – but there're always easier ways to make money.'

Teleworking

Although the name sounds strangely old-fashioned, as telecoms become cheaper and modems get faster, teleworking will become more attractive to workers and employers alike. Currently, less than 5 per cent of European employees work from home, but this is expected to rise to nearly 15 per cent by 2015.

HOW TO DO IT

Teleworking can cover almost any job that doesn't physically require you to be at a set location: virtual assistant, call handling, bookkeeping, telesales, database management – you name it. And the key to finding work in any of these areas boils down to a combination of your abilities and your powers of persuasion – both of which you will need to the full. One obvious first step, for instance, is to talk to your current employer about which parts of your job (or indeed your entire department's output) could be done just as efficiently and more cheaply from outside the office.

'Oh, look, a flying pig!' you may be thinking, but recently the TUC (www.tuc.org.uk/economy/tuc-7666-f0.cfm) successfully secured the minimum wage for teleworking – demonstrating that it is being taken seriously and dispelling fears that tele-workers will end up as cheap labour to be exploited by unscrupulous companies. So if you enjoy a close, trusting relationship with your boss and can back up your argument with facts and figures, it's well worth a shot.

Not convinced? Then try the second and much more common path to teleworking; set yourself up as a freelancer and start flogging your services by phone, advertisement or website. It won't be easy, especially at first – but there's more advice on building websites and setting up your virtual stall in the sections below.

Martin Keel works two days a week from home as a systems analyst for a mobile telecoms company. 'Teleworking is something a lot more office workers should be aware of. If you have a job that could equally well be done from home, why shouldn't you just walk up to your boss and say, "What about it, then?" Any reasonable employer would at least consider it. Don't laugh, one day we'll all be doing it!'

HOW MUCH CAN YOU MAKE?

This depends on your skills. The beauty of teleworking is that you don't have to worry too much about pricing – any competitive charge for the job will usually be cheaper to the employer than paying for desk space, insurance, heating, lighting and a full-time staffer to do the same task. Despite the best efforts of the TUC, however, teleworkers rarely settle for less than £10 per hour, regardless of the job. Don't be greedy, though – remember you're starting a business here, and early clients are like oxygen; nothing will grow without them!

COSTS

Obviously, you need to be switched on. We're talking G3 mobile, ADSL connection to a ninja-fast laptop and a car ready to take you anywhere at a moment's notice. Only by proving you can handle any eventuality from home will you ever persuade an employer to risk letting you watch Wimbledon on company time!

TRAINING AND QUALIFICATIONS

Because out of sight is out of mind, qualifications, or at least long-term on-the-job experience, are especially important in teleworking.

PROS

In 50 years the idea of 'going to work' may well be a novelty. Teleworking is one way silver surfers are already enjoying the last laugh over the rest of us.

CONS

You'll need a very understanding employer and all your powers of persuasion.

USEFUL CONTACTS

www.learnthenet.com – an excellent introduction to IT, telling you all you need to know about the basics of using computers, software or websites

The Telework Association, 0800 616008, www.tca.org.uk – a useful source of tips, courses and teleworking opportunities

Virtual assistant/secretarial

A prime example of teleworking in action, virtual assistants (VAs) are there to help small businesses who can't afford full-time secretarial support or need to delegate occasional typing or admin work.

HOW TO DO IT

There is no set way a VA business operates; sometimes you'll get an orderly trickle of calls or emails to send, next it might be a David Brent-style stream of emails to be sent, consignments to be traced, reports to be written up and meetings to be rescheduled ... oh, and can you do it all by three? If you can you definitely have the aptitude to make a VA – but if you do, you're somewhat missing the point.

Because now you're self-employed, other people's inefficiencies are only your concern if you want them to be. Teleworking is about persuading clients to do things better, cheaper and faster, and indeed choosing only those clients who make your life easier in the process.

Of course, this assumes you have systems (and clients, for that matter!), but these will develop as you grow in confidence and experience. In the first instance, you'll need a spare room (or at least a clear desk, away from the kids, TV or any distraction), a phone, a modem and a PC – packed with all the usual software applications (see below) – and the ability to correct unintelligible emails while talking to suppliers you've never heard of about products you don't understand. Think you can do all that?

Good. Now break out the Yellow Pages, call all your friends or log on and start looking for clients. Sadly, the endless trawl for business is one thing the Web has not changed; you still have to generate leads one by one, persuade them to take you on, and chase them till they pay. There are no magic websites where clients gather together in the hope of finding their dream virtual slave (well, there are, but you really *don't want to be hanging out there!*).

That said ... try a Google search (www.google.co.uk) for the term 'virtual assistant' and see whether any of the larger VA agencies are recruiting. In fact, email them anyway and see whether they can be persuaded!

'My first bit of advice is not to give up your day job, if you have one,' explains a spokeswoman from VA bureau www.avirtualsolution.com. 'Just because you have a computer and can operate a few software programs does not mean you can become a virtual assistant ... I understand my limitations. I am not the greatest graphics designer in the world. I use another VA for all my graphics design work. I do the websites and she does the graphics.'

HOW MUCH CAN YOU MAKE?

Clients are charged a fixed hourly or daily fee (not including phone calls, postage costs, etc.), but what you earn depends on the level of service you offer. Agencies charge up to £150 per client per day, but typically you would charge between £10 and £20 per hour for routine secretarial work done by phone or email.

COSTS

Telephone calls, stationery and ideally a permanent Internet connection such as ADSL.

TRAINING AND QUALIFICATIONS

None specifically. You will need to be familiar, however, with Windows, word-processing (i.e. Microsoft Word), email (i.e. Outlook Express) and contact management software (i.e. Outlook), as well as having an excellent telephone manner. Typically, all calls must be answered within three rings, all emails and letters answered the same day – and yes, clients are notorious for calling up and testing your efficiency.

PROS

An excellent use of home-alone time that will rise in popularity as teleworking, instant messaging and video conferencing become more commonplace.

CONS

To make real money you have to be essential to your clients, not just helpful. Specialise in using a particular software package so you become known as a specialist rather than just becoming a virtual dogsbody.

USEFUL CONTACTS

The Alliance of UK Virtual Assistants, www.allianceofukvirtualassistants.org.uk – hints, tips and a localised bulletin board to promote your services www.avirtualsolution.com – one of the online agencies

Tutoring and therapies

Everyone has a skill they could teach to (or practice on!) others – see Chapter 6 for more on this subject. Tutoring is an excellent use of home-alone time, however, and one that will increasingly become Web-based. If you are not completely tied to the house, check out Chapter 8 for more information.

HOW TO DO IT

In financial terms, it's common sense that teaching one to one (music lessons, say) tends to be less profitable than classes (yoga, say). All this is changing, however, with the advent of webcams, instant messaging and video conferencing. With a little research and a small investment, you could be teaching a dozen pupils in six different countries how to do the lotus position, all at the same time and all paying £35 an hour for the privilege.

Naturally, it'll take a bit of tweaking and a few computer crashes along the way, but there are plenty of online guides to help you, including the excellent http://computer. howstuffworks.com. And if you can't stand all this jargon stick to piano lessons, because there's no avoiding it.

HOW MUCH CAN YOU MAKE?

When it comes to teaching from home, you're restricted to the standard local rates. Piano teachers make between £10 and £25 per hour session, whereas yoga teachers with classes of five can earn hundreds a day – so see what your rivals are charging and price yourself somewhere in the middle. Obviously, you'll need to advertise locally, and this is one area where a Web presence won't help you at all, unless the skill can be taught online – in which case your income is restricted only by your ingenuity and the speed of your PC and Web connection.

COSTS

Don't think people will pay good money to squat in your cellar. You'll need a spare room, appropriately decked out for the class or therapy you provide. For online tuition you'll need a webcam (£30–£100), an ADSL connection (around £20 per month) and a sound grasp of video conferencing and instant messaging.

TRAINING AND QUALIFICATIONS

Again, depends on the skill. Nobody's going to pay good money to learn from a gifted novice, however, so paper credentials count for a lot here, whatever you're teaching.

PROS

Correctly handled, this can be part social and part professional – subsidised leisure, really.

CONS

When the class begins, you realise that teaching takes a lot more preparation and organisation than you thought.

USEFUL CONTACTS

www.useyourheadteach.gov.uk – the government's guide to becoming or returning to teaching, some of which is useful in terms of home tuition too

www.ability.org.uk – primarily a help portal for disabled Web users, but also a gold mine of links to sites on holistic medicine, alternative therapies and self-improvement

> ### Case study
>
> Mark and Sharon Jagger teach pottery classes from their converted cottage outhouse in Llangollen. They promote mainly through word of mouth and cards in windows, but are considering a website – 'I doubt anyone will be rushing up from London to be taught by us,' explains Sharon, 'but arty things look good online – and we were thinking of selling our ceramics that way. So yes, we're dot-com wannabes, I suppose . . .'

Proof-reading

A perfect job for home workers with an eye for detail. Publishers still tend to work from printed manuscripts, however, so it's not as email friendly as you might think.

HOW TO DO IT

Do a Web search for book publishers in the subject area you prefer. Don't be indiscriminate or think you can bluff your way through; a medical proof-reader who doesn't know what 'endoginous' means is wasting everyone's time and will never get any work! Proof-reading tends to suit people with a real eye for detail; and not necessarily the ones you might think. Teachers tend to be excellent whereas journalists, now so spoiled by syntax- and spell-checking software, are probably less so.

Supposing you do have the skills, however, where do you find the work or convince it to come to you? Alas, it's down to our staple combination of flagrant self-promotion and patience. You could try checking out some of the better-known freelance writing portals such as www.freelancewriting.com, but work posted in such places tends to be very poorly paid. In short, don't expect to be proof-reading the next Harry Potter any time soon.

Having specialist knowledge, however, greatly improves your chances. Remember that medical gobbledegook we mentioned above? Well, if you did know that 'endogenous' means 'of internal origin' (and spotted my deliberate spelling error) then there are all kinds of pharmaceutical companies, publishers and researchers who may be very pleased to hear from you.

Alas, there's no magic formula for finding such potential clients, but trawling for them using the search engines doesn't take long and emailing them by the dozen is virtually free. Just keep your messages short, persuasive and witty.

HOW MUCH CAN YOU MAKE?

The Society for Editors and Proofreaders (www.sfep.org.uk) recommends a minimum hourly rate of £16.50 for proof-reading and £18 for copy-editing – although curiously they suggest a higher rate of £19 for the easier job of online editing. These rates can vary when proofing long or highly technical copy.

COSTS

Occasional postage and telephone costs.

TRAINING AND QUALIFICATIONS

Obviously journalistic, writing, sub-editing or previous proof-reading experience is handy, as is neat handwriting and good word-processing skills. You should also have a rock-solid command of English and any subjects you claim to specialise in.

PROS

Regular work that can be immensely satisfying for book lovers.

CONS

Usually laborious and painstaking. No room for error.

USEFUL CONTACTS

www.pgdp.net/c/default.php – for those who want to practise their proof-reading skills, this is a charitable venture
designed to make e-books freely available to everyone; sign on
and brush up at the same time

www.sfep.org.uk – The Society for Editors and Proofreaders

Writer's research

There are all sorts of organisations and individuals that need
research done for them. Novelists and other types of book
writers are obvious candidates, but also TV programmes, film-
makers and writers need someone to research topics, and the
work can often be done from home.

HOW TO DO IT

If you have a good education, and are perhaps a writer or academic, you will already have many of the necessary skills for
researching, although it helps to have worked as a researcher
either in an academic or a media environment.

Finding work is mostly a question of putting up and answering ads. The Society of Authors has a quarterly journal called the
Author in which researchers can advertise their services to
writers. A classified ad costs 45p per word with a minimum fee
of £5. Contact the society on 020 7373 6642 to place an ad.

You could also look at writers' forums such as
www.writersservices.com or www.writernetwork.com. Needless
to say, struggling authors are rarely big tippers and usually looking for 'collaborators' rather than paid researchers, but don't forget that this is a business to you, not a work of fiction!

Many writers and academics will put ads up on noticeboards,
or on the intranets, of universities or colleges for researchers, so
look there if you are able to. You can also look in *The Times Educational Supplement* and general trade magazines for jobs advertised. Once you have started, however, if you are good, efficient
and reasonably priced you should get work through word of

mouth. Authors, journalists and producers often ask each other for recommendations for researchers or assistants.

Researching complicated subjects in painstaking detail isn't for everyone, so if you find this is for you, there are plenty of commercial opportunities in any number of fields. The *Guardian*'s jobs section often has research vacancies, some of them freelance or part-time, so head for http://-jobs.guardian.co.uk, enter the word 'research' and see what you can dig up for yourself.

HOW MUCH CAN YOU MAKE?

'It depends what you can get away with!' says Jo Hodder of the Society of Authors. 'It also depends on the project or the type of book.' Researchers can generally expect to be paid between £8 and £20 an hour depending on their expertise and knowledge base. TV researchers are paid £120 a day – at least, that is the NUJ rate, although not all TV companies will honour that.

COSTS

Phone calls and travel if you need to do it. Nothing else unless you have an Internet package that is not an all-in package.

TRAINING AND QUALIFICATIONS

Ideally you need to be educated at least to degree level or something similar in your research subject.

PROS

If you have an academic or enquiring mind this can be a fascinating occupation. Also, the vast majority of research can now be undertaken on the Internet or over the phone, so most of your work can be done at your desk.

CONS

If you are really house-bound you may not be able to do too many research jobs as there is a limit (though quite a wide one) to what you can find out on the Web and by phone. To do it properly you will probably need to visit libraries or even museums once in a while – possibly some abroad – to research an obscure subject.

USEFUL CONTACTS

www.bris.ac.uk – Bristol University's Careers Advisory Service has lots of information for researchers and would-be researchers looking for work

The Society of Authors, 020 7373 6642, www.societyofauthors.co.uk

Answering service

So many people work for themselves now that the demand for office services such as people to answer calls when they're out is pretty strong.

HOW TO DO IT

Advertise your services in local business magazines and newspapers, local chambers of commerce and on the Web. You will need to guarantee that you can answer calls for them – if they redirect them to you when they go out of the office – during office hours or whatever hours they need.

Many such services charge per call, which you could do too, or you could charge a flat fee by the day or by the week. You will need a good phone manner and a quiet room in which you keep your phone (no screaming kids or barking dogs in the background) and a computer with which you can send the messages by email to your clients.

HOW MUCH CAN YOU MAKE?

It depends how many clients you have and how much you charge. On its own it may not bring you a great deal of money, but combined with a general virtual office service it could be a useful money-earner (see Chapter 13 for information on setting up a virtual office).

COSTS

No costs as people phone you and emails are free if you have an all-in package or broadband.

TRAINING AND QUALIFICATIONS

You don't need any training or qualifications.

PROS

This is an easy way of making some money without leaving your home, assuming you have a good telephone manner and a clear mind.

CONS

It is hard to get this kind of work and it may not bring you enough money on its own.

USEFUL CONTACTS

Executive Business Services – www.ebs-secretarial.co.uk – a virtual secretarial business that often contracts out telephone answering services

www.virtual-secretarial.co.uk – a site that offers all kinds of virtual secretarial services

Need More Time Ltd – www.needmoretime.co.uk, 0845 458 5888 – offers call handling and virtual PA services

Accepting deliveries

This is a tenuous one, but if you live in a built-up area full of people who are out at work all day, you could offer your home as a regular delivery spot for everything from letters to sofas.

HOW TO DO IT

Do a leaflet drop around your area offering your home as a delivery spot. Keep the prices low – say £1 or even less for accepting letters and parcels.

If neighbours take you up on the offer make sure you get all the details of the delivery – the name on the parcel, roughly what time it is due to arrive and any contact numbers or other details for the company delivering. Once you have taken delivery of the item, leave a message for your neighbour and they can come and collect it when they get back.

If you prove to be reliable and in at all times, word should get around and you should find more and more people gradually using your service. For accepting bulkier items you could charge more, assuming you have the room to house the things until your neighbours come to collect them.

HOW MUCH CAN YOU MAKE?

Very small amounts at first, but you never know, it could grow!

COSTS

Just the cost of a leaflet drop and the odd phone call here and there.

TRAINING AND QUALIFICATIONS

You don't need any training or qualifications.

PROS

This is a very easy thing to do if you are stuck indoors all day. It will also introduce you to your neighbours!

CONS

Delivery people are notoriously unreliable and you could find yourself not even able to pop out to the shops as you wait and wait. The recompense for this hanging around will be very small.

Indexing

Have you ever wondered who compiles the indexes at the end of factual books? Well, it's probably a professional indexer!

HOW TO DO IT

If you are interested in doing indexes you are probably already a big reader and are naturally a patient sort who likes attention to detail.

To be a good indexer you have to understand the main themes of the book and organise the index by key words: people, events, subject matter, and so on. You also need to be a vigilant reader and have the ability to work to a publisher's or author's brief. It is an arduous but much required job.

You can get work by making good contacts with publishing houses and getting yourself on the database of the Society of Indexers (see details below). If you are good and work at your contacts with editors within a company you like, you will get regular work from them.

It is possible to get work without any training but you are much more likely to get it if you have done a course. The Society of Indexers runs a distance learning course for trainee indexers, which leads to accreditation status. There are also seminars in various parts of the UK for beginners as well as experienced indexers.

For many people indexing is a second career through which they can use expertise developed in some other field. It may be combined with other publishing-related work such as copy-editing, proof-reading or abstracting.

You will need a computer with specialised software to automate routine processes such as sorting, formatting and printing, and to ensure greater accuracy and consistency. This will allow you to concentrate on the wording and content. Completed indexes are usually sent to publishers in electronic form, usually as email attachments.

HOW MUCH CAN YOU MAKE?

The Society of Indexers recommends rates of £16–£30 per hour or £1.20–£5 per page. You may get rather less than this when you start, though.

COSTS

The Society of Indexers' course costs £400 and you pay £60 to become a member of the society, which seems to be an essential if you want to get work. Other than that there should be no major expenses if you already have a computer to work on.

TRAINING AND QUALIFICATIONS

You need to be trained by the Society of Indexers to have a serious chance of getting work.

PROS

This is an intellectually challenging and potentially interesting way to make money. You can easily do it from home, often in your own time (unless the publishers have a tight deadline), and you will learn things as you go!

CONS

Indexers often have to work during unsocial hours, including evenings and weekends, to meet publishers' tight deadlines. The work can be mentally and physically exhausting.

USEFUL CONTACTS

The Society of Indexers, Blades Enterprise Centre, John Street, Sheffield S2 4SU, 0114 2922350, www.socind.demon.co.uk

Book design and layout

Books used to be designed by hand in publishers' offices until the advent of computers and special book-designing software. Now individuals do it at home or in their own offices.

HOW TO DO IT

Quite a lot of freelancers who lay out books have already done it in-house for at least one publishing house. Even if you haven't, however, and if you have a good eye for design and enjoy reading, you should pick it up quickly – it is not complicated.

You will need a good computer – Apple Mac is the favourite for all types of design work – and the relevant software. You may already be familiar with 'desktop publishing' (DTP) through Microsoft Publisher, but the two packages mostly used by professionals are the long-established QuarkXpress and newcomer from Adobe called InDesign.

In addition to DTP software, you are likely to need a good graphics package such as Adobe Photoshop to enable you to create graphics and work with photographs and illustrations. As a freelance designer, you will need a CD burner so that you can create CDs to send to the publisher, and you will need a decent Internet set-up so you can send and receive large documents and graphics quickly and reliably.

After that it is a question of making contacts and getting the work. Contact as many publishers as you can, showing them examples of your work. It may also help to advertise in the *Author*, the quarterly journal of the Society of Authors, offering your services as someone who could design books for self-publishing authors or small-time publishing houses while you are learning.

HOW MUCH CAN YOU MAKE?

Rates of pay vary according to the type of project and your speed of working. A simple text-only book will earn you a few hundred pounds, whereas a highly illustrated four-colour book will pay more – but you will need to have acquired very good skills to reach this level.

COSTS

Nothing, other than the cost of a book layout software package – between £300 and £1,000 – if the publishers themselves do not provide it for you.

TRAINING AND QUALIFICATIONS

There are a range of courses on book design, from evening classes through to postgraduate level. Check your local evening classes institute or contact the London School of Printing and Publishing.

PROS

If you enjoy designing and you are a quick worker, this is a good way of making extra cash at home. There are no major costs once you have bought the design software.

CONS

It is quite a competitive area and the pay, as in most areas of publishing, is not that great.

USEFUL CONTACTS

London School of Printing and Publishing, Elephant and Castle, London SE1 6SB, 020 7514 6569, www.lcp.linst.ac.uk

The Society of Authors, 020 7373 6642, www.societyofauthors.co.uk

CHAPTER SIX

Got a Hobby?

IF YOU'RE CREATIVE or you enjoy activities that other people
enjoy too, make some money out of them!

Antiques dealing

If you have an eye for acquiring items from auctions,
salesrooms, fairs or even car boot sales and charity shops, why
not mark them up to their real value and sell them on to the
public?

HOW TO DO IT

There are lots of ways to get into antique dealing and you don't
have to be rich to start with. If you're starting out or would just
like to meet more like-minded people and get some advice, then
spend some time going around the smaller fairs where you can
find some of the best bargains.

As with any kind of collecting, it's important to get as much
information and knowledge as you can along the way. Look at
specialist antique magazines such as *BBC Homes and Antiques*
and the *Antiques Magazine* (www.antiquesmagazine.com). Also,
invest in the latest edition of *Miller's Antiques Guide* (£22.99,
Mitchell Beazley) or Judith Miller's *How to Make Money out of*

Antiques (£4.99, Mitchell Beazley) and other helpful books on the subject. The more you know the less you are likely to be ripped off in this most confusing world. It is very easy to buy something that you shouldn't and lose a lot of money if you start in ignorance.

To start off with you could buy items you know about from car boot sales and charity shops and then sell them for more money on eBay or to specialist shops. As you become more knowledgeable and confident, you could open a regular stall, a home-based dealership or even a shop. If you do get to this stage, it's very useful to become a member of the British Antique Dealers Association (BADA) or the Association of Art and Antiques Dealers (LAPADA). The benefits of belonging to one of these include the information and advice you'll receive, along with representation at government level, trade fairs and the guarantee you can give to your customers.

To get into either organisation, though, you do have to work, as the requirements from both are that you're VAT registered, have been trading for at least three years and have references, and have been accepted by the Associated Board of Directors. If you are just dealing in antiques on the side it's unlikely that you will get to this stage.

If, on the other hand, you want to get into the area of conservation and restoration, there is the option of taking the more academic route via a training course at one of the country's leading centres, such as West Dean College in West Sussex or Lincoln University.

You might even fancy yourself as an auctioneer. The best way to get started is as an office junior or porter in the saleroom. You will probably be expected to choose a speciality such as silver, furniture or jewellery. Depending on how they progress, trainees can be running their own auctions within a few years.

HOW MUCH CAN YOU MAKE?

How much you make obviously depends on how much, and what, you have to sell. You will need to know your stuff and pick up the killer bargains. It could be anything from a few quid here and there selling nice bits of china on eBay to hundreds or even thousands if you buy a valuable antique for a fiver at a car boot sale and it gets top price at Sotheby's.

COSTS

You will need to buy the antiques in the first place and you will probably have auctioneer's commissions to pay if you sell them in an auction house. You may also need insurance for what you're selling. If you want to join BADA or LAPADA membership involves an annual fee, and you will also have to bear any marketing and advertising costs.

TRAINING AND QUALIFICATIONS

It's only really in the area of restoration and conservation that you should have a qualification. A passion for antiques and experience within the industry would be sufficient qualification for setting up a business. It is always helpful, though, to have some kind of relevant qualification in, say, art history, and some knowledge of running a business is vital.

PROS

Dealing in antiques is a great way to meet like-minded people, and as you do so you tend to benefit from their expertise and pick up more knowledge yourself.

CONS

It is easy to lose a lot of money by buying the wrong things and then not being able to sell them. Until you have a lot of knowledge in your specialist area you may well make costly mistakes, including buying fakes and forgeries. To do really well in the antiques business you also need quite a lot of money.

USEFUL CONTACTS

www.antiques-uk.co.uk – a great general site with a facility for searching for particular pieces that you might be looking for

Antique Collecting, Antique Collector's Club Ltd, 5 Church Street, Woodbridge, Suffolk IP12 1DS, 01394 38 55 01

Antique Dealer & Collectors Guide, Statuscourt Ltd, PO Box 805, Greenwich, London SE10 8TD, 020 8691 4820

The Association of Art and Antiques Dealers, www.lapada.co.uk

www.bbc.co.uk/antiques/atg – this section of the BBC website has a full list of the year's antique fairs and events throughout the country

The British Antique Dealers Association, www.bada.org

West Dean College, Diploma Course Office, West Dean, Chichester, West Sussex PO18 0QZ, 01243 818219, www.westdean.org.uk

Art dealing

Use your knowledge of art history and the contemporary art scene to pick out valuable works and sell them on.

HOW TO DO IT

This is a bit like antique dealing – it's always a good idea to go round the smaller art fairs and even car boot sales in order to meet people with similar interests and pick up some bargains. It is important to get as much information and knowledge as you can along the way. Being an artist yourself will help, but you can get a lot of information from reading books on the history of art, going to exhibitions and lectures and reading magazines and papers such as the *Burlington Magazine* and *Apollo Magazine*. These publications and lectures will give you access to professional opinions and the latest news in the art world.

One event to watch out for is the annual 'Secret Exhibition' at the Royal College of Art which includes the work of 750 secret participants, including celebrities and graduates of the college itself. Around 1,500 original postcards are sold to the public for £35, and in 2002 one buyer actually bought a Damien Hirst pen drawing which was later valued at £900.

If you are investing in prints, limited edition prints are obviously the best buy, and the fewer there are of them the better – it's not always worth buying from a large edition.

Once you are more established, it's definitely worth joining an organisation such as the Society of London Art Dealers (SLAD). This offers a weekly magazine on the art world, a listing in their member directory, and invaluable help and advice on a range of issues affecting art dealers from VAT legislation to the regulations concerning the import and export of art.

Organisations like this will also help you decide where to hold exhibitions. The SLAD website, for instance, offers a list of galleries and the areas they specialise in.

HOW MUCH CAN YOU MAKE?

This will depend on how successful you are at picking up something worth selling, but if you become good at it then you could well make thousands.

COSTS

You will have to bear the cost of buying prints or paintings first, unless you sell paintings by new artists and simply take a commission. You will also have to meet the cost of advertising and marketing and of hiring somewhere to show the paintings.

TRAINING AND QUALIFICATIONS

You might be able to build up your knowledge through experience, but it's a very good idea to have a degree in art history, or to attain some other kind of qualification in the subject, just to fill in any gaps in your knowledge, if nothing else. This will be invaluable in helping you speak with confidence and authority when liaising with potential customers.

PROS

A chance to use your knowledge of art history to select unrecognised or undervalued works and benefit from their sale at the correct price.

CONS

This isn't an easy way to make money. You need an extensive knowledge of art history together with an appreciation of the changing market.

USEFUL CONTACTS

Apollo Magazine, 1 Castle Lane, London SW1E 6DR, 0207 233 8906

The Burlington Magazine, 14–16 Duke's Road, London WC1H 9AD, 0207 388 1228, www.burlington.org.uk

www.invaluable.com – if the worst comes to the worst and some of your paintings are stolen, this is a site designed to help you get them back; it searches extensively through the world's auction catalogues

Society of London Art Dealers (SLAD), 91 Jermyn Street, London SW1Y 6JB, 020 7930 6137, www.slad.org.uk

Collecting

Collecting is big in this country and it's amazing how much money you can make by buying things in charity shops, at car boot sales and on the Internet and then selling them on for a higher price.

HOW TO DO IT

People usually collect things because they like them and want to own them rather than for their investment or sales potential. Once you become interested and knowledgeable in a particular area, however, you might want to sell some things you don't want any more or that you have two of. There is a whole host of things you could collect, and they don't have to be posh antiques. Quite amazing things are being collected now and are making serious money for their owners. Here are a few to consider:

Chopper bikes

If you are wondering what to collect as an investment it's always a good idea to go for things that young boys covet but probably can't afford. Such is the case with Chopper bikes. The mass-produced Mark 2 version which came out between 1972 and 1980 – most famously in yellow, red or purple – cost around £35, a lot of money for parents in those days. Thousands of youngsters did not get the bike they longed for. Now those disappointed 12-year-olds have jobs and children of their own and suddenly they can buy their own Chopper – and more! Recently one collector who had kept his black-and-chrome Chopper in mint condition – storing it in his bedroom with a blanket over it for over two decades – sold it on eBay for £1,900 plus carriage. Go to www.rcoc.co.uk for more information.

Electric guitars

Guitars belonging to famous rock stars such as Eric Clapton, Pete Townshend and B. B. King change hands for thousands at auction. Even a piece of a guitar smashed on stage by Pete Townshend will fetch a good price. As rock gods become even more godlike the prices are going up – a Jimi Hendrix Flying V is now worth around £1.5 million – so it is worth buying guitars from the best names you can afford and keeping them for a few years before selling at a higher rate. Christie's has regular sales, so keep an eye on their website at www.christies.co.uk.

First edition books

You can pick up a good, collectable first edition very reasonably. 'It's possible to get a nice first edition of a Graham Greene for under £100,' says Ros Godlovitch of London-based Valentine Books. 'There are lots of copies of many of his books available to buy.' To start a collection you could simply contact an antiquarian bookseller, or go to one of the many antiquarian book fairs around the country. Members of the Provincial Booksellers' Fairs Association hold sales regularly, although *the* big antiquarian book event of the year is the Olympia book fair in June. It is possible still to find a gem in charity shops and at car boot sales, but it is getting harder all the time. You can also sell through booksellers or on the Internet if it is not a truly major work. Go to www.aba.org.uk for more information.

Old maps

Antique maps seem to be a very good area in which to start a collection, particularly from a financial point of view. 'Maps have rocketed in value over the last fifteen years,' says Daniel Crouch of the Shapero Gallery in London. 'Maps that sold for about £100 at the end of the 1980s are now about £1,000. However, it's still a relatively inexpensive thing to collect, compared to other types of antiques that people go for.' Clearly it is possible to part with thousands for a map, but it is also possible to buy good-quality, interesting maps for under £100. 'You should buy the best example you can afford, not necessarily the most expensive, if you are serious about collecting,' says Philip Curtis of the Map House in London. 'It is better to buy a lovely example of an inexpensive map than a poor example of an expensive one.' Check out www.map-fair.com for a list of map fairs around the world.

There are many, many other things you can collect and buy and sell to make money in the short- and long-term. Examples include Barbie dolls, silver, stamps, Action Men, Star Wars memorabilia, vinyl records, classic cars, classic motorbikes, wine, antique jewellery, 1950s paste jewellery, fans, jukeboxes, erotica, postcards – the list goes on! Obviously, you will be a better and happier collector if you collect things you are genuinely interested in. That way it will be less of a business and more of a money-making hobby. The only big drawback is that if you *really* love what you are collecting you may not want to sell any of it. If that happens, you will end up spending money instead of making it!

HOW MUCH CAN YOU MAKE?

Anything from a few pounds a month to several thousand if you pick something up cheap that turns out to be very valuable at auction.

COSTS

You will have the cost of buying things in the first place, and possibly the expense of renovation, storage and insurance, as well as travel costs to and from sales.

TRAINING AND QUALIFICATIONS

You don't need any training or qualifications.

PROS

This is an enjoyable way of making money out of a hobby. As more and more people are collecting more and more unusual things, you could find that you can corner the market in a new area and make money before anyone realises that the things you are collecting are becoming valuable.

CONS

You may need to spend a lot of money in order to make some. If you become too attached to your collection you may not make any money at all.

USEFUL CONTACTS

www.bonhams.com – the website for Bonhams the auctioneers

www.christies.co.uk – the website for Christie's the auctioneers

www.ebay.co.uk – this is *the* site for buying and selling collectables

www.sothebys.co.uk – the website for Sotheby's the auctioneers

Case study

Peter French, a marketing manager in Bedfordshire, has been making extra money for the last year selling football collectables on eBay. 'On average, I make about £200 to £250 per month in clear profit, after all eBay fees, postage costs, etc.,' he says. 'The best month I have had was just over £500. The best sale was of a programme for the 1953 FA Cup Final [the 'Matthews Final' – so called after Stanley Matthews]. I bought it for £80 and resold it for £150 a couple of months later. Another good deal was a bulk purchase of thirty copies of the 1979 European Cup Final programme, featuring Nottingham Forest, which cost me £3 each, but which I have gradually been selling off for anything from £6 to £10 each.'

Peter has been collecting football memorabilia for years as it is a particular love of his. He says that before he even started selling items on eBay he did a lot of research. 'I watched the prices for various items for about six months, and actually jotted down the final auction prices of literally hundreds. That showed that online auctions can be very unpredictable, but also taught me some invaluable lessons on how much to bid, and also which items sell like the proverbial hot cakes, and which are like the pink wafer biscuits in the selection pack. I would advise everyone to watch auctions in their chosen field very carefully for a few weeks before jumping in.'

He admits to still making mistakes with some transactions, though, even with his experience. 'There have been several occasions when I have ended up selling an item for less than I paid for it, because of the unpredictable nature of the auctions. An item that sells for £10 one week can go for £30 the next. Probably the worst I have made was through carelessness – I bought a programme on eBay for over £100, and when I received it there was writing on the front cover [which reduces the value considerably]. I hadn't noticed this on the photo with the auction, and the seller refused a refund. Now I'm stuck with it, and I haven't had the courage to try to resell it to see quite how much I overpaid!'

Sewing, dressmaking and altering

People who can sew are becoming few and far between, as are people with the time to learn. If you can make clothes, or alter or mend them, you will be in demand.

HOW TO DO IT

If you have been making clothes or altering them for friends and family to the point where you know you can do it and you enjoy it, offer your services to the public through adverts in the local press and, if you can, through leaflets in local fabric shops.

If you are good, a lot of your work will come through word of mouth. This, however, can also lead to too much work at any given time, and because of this it can be handy to know friends with similar skills who can take some of your work on. Being part of such a network will also drive work your way when business is slow.

If you would like regular work, contact local dry cleaning outlets which often offer an alterations service as well. Some department stores and posh fashion shops also offer this and often need people to do it. Many people simply want a dress or suit for which they have material and a pattern made up for them. A basic advert in a local magazine is often all it takes to bring them in!

HOW MUCH CAN YOU MAKE?

Prices for this kind of service will vary depending on where you're based, so ask around – possibly in fabric shops and dry cleaners – to find out the going rate. Average rates are about £5–£10 per hour with a minimum charge of £10.

COSTS

While you can expect your customers to supply their own items of clothing or fabric you can't really ask them to provide thread, unless they need a special kind for their design. So you need to get a good supply of thread, a range of different needles for your machine (and also some for any hand work you might have to do) – and, of course, a good sewing machine.

TRAINING AND QUALIFICATIONS

There are courses you can go on to refine your skills and learn new techniques, but you may well have learned all you need to know over a lifetime of mending and altering clothes for your family.

PROS

If you're good at what you do, you'll get a lot of business through word of mouth. The expenses are fairly low and it's a job you can do during hours that suit you – as long as you have enough time to get the job done within a reasonable deadline.

CONS

This can be quite back-breaking and eye-straining work for relatively little money. There may be too much or too little work for you at any given time.

USEFUL CONTACTS

Skillfast UK, 80 Richardshaw Lane, Pudsey, Leeds LS28 6BN, 0113 227 3333, www.skillfast-uk.org – the UK's skills council for the textile, apparel and footwear industries, they offer a list of relevant courses and qualifications

Dress designing

More and more professional women (and some men) are looking for a good designer to make tailor-made clothes for them. If you can do it well you could get a lot of work from it.

HOW TO DO IT

The big area in dress designing is of course designing wedding dresses. This is probably the one time in a woman's life when she's most prepared to pay for tailored clothes. While it is an asset to specialise in wedding dresses and ball gowns, doing the more mundane jobs such as suits and alterations keeps the business coming in. In any case, specialising means working at a very high level, and you will have to be experienced and confident. If you are, then your main task is just to get the word out that you exist!

You can, for instance, advertise your services in the local press, and it would definitely be a good idea to put an ad in a local shop that sells fabric. If they don't normally advertise, you could say that you'll steer some business their way by referring your customers for material.

If wedding dresses are your forte then you may find it useful to advertise in one of the many bridal magazines, or have a stand at a wedding show.

In an age when people use the Internet more and more, it would be a big asset to have some kind of online presence in the form of a website that showcases your work in a portfolio, giving details of your experience and qualifications if you have them. It also adds an air of professionalism to your business if you can direct customers to your work online.

If you need to brush up on your skills or just get some more inspiration for new designs, there is an array of courses you could attend, either full-time or part-time alongside your current job. The London College of Fashion is an obvious candidate, although there are a lot of smaller institutions offering training at all kinds of levels. Most adult education centres have at least one dress-designing course, and they usually also offer pattern-cutting courses and other specialist sewing and design classes.

When it comes to selling, make sure you have the right attitude. You may think that when you first start you have to keep your prices low to get the business off the ground – but you can shoot yourself in the foot if you make them too low since this implies that your work is not as good as others'. Do some research into the going rate for dress design in your area and adjust your prices accordingly. Somewhere in the middle would be a good place to start.

Cultural capital is something that will make your prices soar once you're established. If you can get a reputation for your work, people will be willing to pay a lot for it – they may even feel happier with a higher price, with its implication that what you do 'must be good'. Don't be afraid to put your fees up if you sense you can – it's the price of fashion.

With good practical skills you can also extend your services to tailoring clothes to give you a more solid business base.

HOW MUCH CAN YOU MAKE?

Fashion is a notoriously tricky business, so you could make very little if your designs are not attractive to many people. On the other hand you could make a nice living if you come up with the right look. It's important to get an idea of how long it will take you to do a range of different designs as people will often ask you for a quote on the spot and you need to be able to work out an hourly rate for yourself.

As a rough guide, it's been stated that newly qualified designers can earn about £12,000 in their early career, progressing to about £25,000 or more once their experience and reputation increase.

COSTS

The good thing about this is that after you've got your sewing machine you don't normally have to buy materials in until you've got a job to do, and then you should have an idea in advance as to what you will require. This is an easy business to run from home, but once you are more established a workshop could act as a good shopfront.

TRAINING AND QUALIFICATIONS

You don't need training or qualifications but it would help a lot to do some dress-designing and pattern-cutting courses, even if it all comes naturally to you.

PROS

You can work from home quite easily. Because you're working on a commission basis, you will only need to invest time and money when you've definitely got a commission. While the demand for wedding dresses is seasonal, there is a much steadier call for ball gowns and party dresses.

CONS

The demand for tailor-made clothes can vary, so business can fluctuate. Customers for this kind of product are notoriously difficult, so you may often find yourself having to work far longer than you anticipated for the same amount of money simply because you keep having to change the design. People expect you to match shop prices at times, while as an individual it costs you far more to make a dress than it does a factory.

USEFUL CONTACTS

CAPITB Trust, Richardshaw Lane, Pudsey, Leeds LS28 6BN, 0113 239 3355, www.careers-in-clothing.co.uk

Fashion and Design Protection Association, 25 Watsons Road, Wood Green, London N22 7TZ, 0208 888 1213, www.fdpa.co.uk – consultants and advisers on intellectual property and the protection of your designs

The Grafton Academy of Dress Design, 6 Herbert Place, Dublin 2, 01676 3653, www.graftonacademy.com

London College of Fashion, 20 John Princes Street, London W1G OBJ, 020 7514 7566, www.lcf.linst.ac.uk

Millinery

These days, hats can be more of an artwork than something to keep your head warm.

HOW TO DO IT

Like dress designing, hat-making is a skill you probably already have if you're considering going into business with it. If you're a beginner, however, and you have an inkling you could do it, it's certainly something you can train in and maintain as a hobby until you're really good.

If you need training, start with a general-interest course and progress from there on to an intermediate programme and workshop, or into a more specific area such as couture, conceptual headwear or even tiaras. Some professionals have found it useful to go to factories and see how hats are made on a production line.

As with art, fashion is a matter of cultural capital – someone notable showing an interest in your work gives it instant credibility. Your task is therefore to bombard the right people with your portfolio, a concise account of your ideas and a short biography. To appear worthy of their attention, though, you've got to build up a following from the ground, so start small with your first contacts. Find your nearest boutiques and independent retailers and try to persuade them to buy your work or display it in return for a percentage of the profits from any items sold.

HOW MUCH CAN YOU MAKE?

When you start off, you'll need to base your price on the cost of the materials plus the time it takes to make your creation multiplied by a suitable hourly rate. Once you get a name for yourself, though, you can start charging 'designer prices', especially if you get your work into respected outlets.

COSTS

If you do need to brush up on your skills, the fees in a place such as the Wombourne School of Millinery start from £65 for one day, rising to around £300 for more detailed instruction. You'll also need your own millinery equipment, including a traditional wooden block (around £50) and all the materials. It might also be a good idea to invest in a few books on the subject for tips and inspiration.

TRAINING AND QUALIFICATIONS

There are several courses you can go on in the London area, the London College of Fashion and St Martin's College being notable options. Outside of London many adult education centres offer millinery and design courses, as do big design centres like Leeds College of Art and Design and Edinburgh College of Art.

PROS

Having little functional purpose, hats are all about design, so that means you can be as creative as you like – as long as your creations have appeal.

CONS

The main disadvantage of designing hats is that they could be unpopular with everyone. It can also be a seasonal business, with customers mainly buying around the time of Henley, Ascot and the prime wedding months of June to August, but not much at other times.

USEFUL CONTACTS

London College of Fashion, 20 John Princes Street, London W1G OBJ, 020 7514 7566, www.lcf.linst.ac.uk – courses here cover some areas of millinery, including conceptual headwear and trimmings

Wombourne School of Millinery, Mill Lane Farmhouse, Mill Lane, Wombourne, Staffs. WV5 OLE, 01902 893 683, www.hatcourses.co.uk – offers a range of courses with a website full of information on the subject

www.leeds-art.ac.uk

www.sendler.co.uk – Jeanette Sendler teaches millinery in Edinburgh

Handbag-making

You don't have to be Lulu Guinness or Jasper Conran to make handbags. Handbag design has exploded recently, and women are buying more than ever.

HOW TO DO IT

The good thing about handbag-making is that you don't have to conform to any conventional design. As long as you can make something fairly functional that looks good, chances are you'll attract interest, and if your designs fit the market then you're likely to sell.

While it's good to have your own style, it's important too to think of your market – what kinds of fabrics and colours your target audience are looking for. For instance, if you're using leather, which is going to bump the price up, you must come up with a creation that will attract people with more money than the youth market, who would rather pay less for cheap and cheerful PVC.

The best way to sell your work is, of course, to get it into some shops. If the shops you approach are reluctant to buy stock from you, you could ask whether they will just display your items in return for a cut of any profits made. As your reputation grows, more outlets will be prepared to buy the stock from you direct. You can also sell your designs at markets and at the many exhibitions and shows around the country, such as Top Drawer at Earls Court, London (www.eco.co.uk), and the Homes and Gardens show at Olympia in London.

It's also a very good idea to have an online shop in the form of a website if you, a friend or a web designer can create one. Remember that it's very important to ensure that you are noted by search engines when people enter terms such as 'handbags', 'designer', 'unique', etc. If you're not sure how to do this, it's definitely worth enlisting the help of a professional website designer, as this will steer a lot of traffic your way.

HOW MUCH CAN YOU MAKE?

Unless you've got ground-breaking ideas and tremendous enthusiasm, this is something you might want to keep as a hobby to start with, as you'll only make a little at first. A good reputation and a classy website, though, will mean you can put your prices up to whatever trendy people will pay, and you could make thousands each year.

COSTS

Your costs will depend on your materials, so it's a good idea to have certain designs you can replicate at a fixed price with cheaper materials. If you want to make bags to customers' specifications then stress to them that you need to discuss the costs of their design before giving them a price.

In addition to materials, you may need to pay for postage and packaging if you're advertising on the Internet. You will also have advertising and Internet costs.

TRAINING AND QUALIFICATIONS

There are a couple of specific courses in handbag-making but more generally it is included in courses on design and fashion drawing. It would also help you tremendously to do a course in starting up a fashion business.

PROS

Nowadays, with novelty bags being so popular, you can be as creative as you like without having to stick to any rigid conventions. If you love handbags this can be a great hobby out of which to make some money.

CONS

It's a competitive area so you have to come up with something very original to make a mark. Also, customers can be very fickle. You might not find anyone who likes your designs enough to be able to sell them.

USEFUL CONTACTS

There are probably more courses specialising in handbags than you'd imagine, so do check out your local adult education centre.

London College of Fashion, 20 John Princes Street, London W1G OBJ, 020 7514 7566, www.lcf.linst.ac.uk

Hampers

Everyone loves hampers – particularly at Christmas or on special occasions such as birthdays or at seasonal events. The big stores such as Harrods, M&S and Fortnum's do them, of course, but there is nothing to stop you making and selling your own.

HOW TO DO IT

Designing a hamper is an art in itself. You have to know what makes a balanced hamper, what the demand is and how to make it look attractive enough for people to pay for this luxury item. Some hampers are aimed at special occasions such as Christmas, Easter, Valentine's Day or Henley Regatta. Some specialise in sweet things, chocolates, cheese, smoked salmon or champagne and truffles. Some include a teddy or a plant or bath salts. Most hampers use long-lasting foods in tins, packets or bottles, which are the easiest to work with as you don't have the worry of the food going off. Others specialise in fresh fruit and home-made cakes and biscuits, which can work very well but only if you really know what you're doing.

If you are a good cook and, perhaps, already sell your produce (see below, p. 172, on how to make money out of baking and other food production), then creating a hamper that includes some or all of your best-selling items would make sense, particularly in your local area. You could put out special adverts a month or so before Christmas, Easter and Valentine's Day promoting your special hamper gifts. Remember, though, that if you are selling home-made food and drink you need to comply with Department of Environment, Food and Rural Affairs (DEFRA) regulations. Look on their website (details below) and on the Business Link website for information on this. You can also call the Food Standards Agency for information.

There are two main ways you can market hampers. One is to sell locally to delicatessens or direct to local people. Another is to set up a national or even international service.

Obviously the local route is the easiest, particularly if you are just doing this in your spare time, or if you are known locally for your cakes, jams, cheeses or whatever is your speciality. Make sure there's a need for this service by going round to local grocers, delicatessens and gift shops and seeing who would be prepared to buy and sell your hampers, or put one on display with your card attached. Selling through shops means that you would not necessarily need to offer a delivery service too. If the shop delivers anyway you could arrange for them to send out your hampers and pocket the charge for that. Alternatively you could ask local stores of any type to stock a leaflet advertising your hampers – possibly offering them a commission for referral.

If you are interested in offering a national or international service you must look on it as more of a business. Browse the Internet and you will find that there are already several companies that offer mouth-watering hampers of all kinds, delivering all over the UK and in some cases (look at www.hamper.com or www.hampers.uk.com) around the world. You will have to offer a service that sticks out from the competition – maybe it involves your special, home-created foods, or is more competitively priced, or has its own special gimmick.

If you are going to produce a lot of hampers each week it may be worthwhile hooking up with a national delivery service, or speaking to the Post Office or other postal service about prices for sending hampers. Make sure you factor delivery charges and, if necessary, VAT into all your prices. It makes sense to set up an attractive and accessible website, but you can also whip up interest in your service through adverts in national magazines and newspapers and, if you can, through press releases that lead to mentions in these publications.

Businesses are often keen to give staff hampers as 'Christmas bonuses', so this market can be tapped through ads in the business and marketing trade press, as well as direct marketing letters to local and/or national businesses (start with local businesses as they should be easier to sell to). You could also take a stall and sell your hampers at local fairs, agricultural shows and farmers' markets.

Creating the hamper itself will involve buying as much at wholesale prices as possible. Look on the Internet and in trade magazines for the best low-price baskets, ribbons, tissue, coloured plastic and tags that you can find. Many nice non-perishable goods can be bought at wholesale cash and carrys, so join your local one.

HOW MUCH CAN YOU MAKE?

It depends how many you sell each month and what your profit margin is. It could be anything from £100 to thousands a month.

COSTS

You will have to meet the cost of the packaging as well as the foodstuffs themselves. If you are making some of these then you will also have to pay for power, wear and tear on cooking equipment and packaging for the individual items. You will also have to bear the cost of advertising your service – website, leaflets, etc. – and, possibly, some PR.

TRAINING AND QUALIFICATIONS

You don't need any training or qualifications for this, although some training in sales and/or food retailing would help.

PROS

Hampers are lovely gifts to receive and to make. If you are creative and you have a knowledge of and interest in food and drink, this can be a fun and absorbing way of making money – almost a hobby.

CONS

There is a lot of competition in the market, particularly beyond the local level, and the costs are quite high. If you include perishable goods you could lose a lot of money if they don't sell. Delivering goods is also an extra complication and a potential burden.

USEFUL CONTACTS

Business Link, www.businesslink.gov.uk

DEFRA, www.defra.gov.uk

Food Standards Agency, 020 7276 8000

Sweet-making

If you're the type of person who likes to make sweets at Christmas and for personalised gifts, why not make some money from it?

HOW TO DO IT

With the competition you will face from confectioners, you really need to use the 'home-made' aspect of your product as the selling point. Ideally you should be able to come up with recipes that taste nicer than shop-bought sweets. It can also help build a reputation if you specialise in one area, such as chocolate or fudge.

However, to get people's attention in the first place, you're going to have to be good at the packaging as well making the sweets. Maybe you think you could cope with this on your own by having simple bags or wrappings and just putting your label on them using one of those excellent design packages you can get for the computer. If you can afford it, though, it's a good idea to outsource your ideas to a design company.

If you set up a website, some of your produce may have to be shipped abroad, or nationally at least, and you'll need to consider the types of inexpensive packaging you can use for this. A good website for this is www.e-pack.co.uk. For the actual gift boxes themselves try www.kmapackaging.co.uk, which offers plain gift boxes starting from around 35p each.

If you do have a forte for creating aesthetically pleasing parcels, then you might consider moving into the higher end of the market, offering to make gift packages and wedding novelties.

While you can put adverts in shops and the press for special dates such as Valentine's Day and Christmas, a good way to promote yourself is to get your sweets seen and sampled in a market. There are always markets going on at the weekend, so have a look in the local press and find out about the regular events you can take part in. Hiring a stall at the smaller events shouldn't be too expensive but might still put a dent in your profits – so you might consider sharing a stall with someone else. If you get a name for yourself and become confident that your sweets are selling well, you can move up to setting up a stall in some of the bigger markets.

Another very good way to market yourself would be on the Internet. While people may not often be looking for hand-crafted confectionery, by having an Internet presence you're much more likely to get the attention of any who are searching for it. Building a website is one thing, but it's even more important to get it recognised by search engines such as Yahoo and Google. You can find out about search engine optimisation on a number of websites including www.searchenginewatch.com/webmasters, www.searchengines.com and www.howipromotemysite.com.

If you go for the top end of the market and start making some money you can also start showing your goods at trade shows such as Top Drawer (www.topdraweronline.com) where you can get a stand and display your wares to shop owners and press.

HOW MUCH CAN YOU MAKE?

Once you've established a strong reputation you can start charging higher prices, but first you need to get as many people as possible trying your sweets. Therefore, start at a lower price. You won't be able to match the supermarkets if you want to make a profit – but people will generally pay more for the novelty and individuality of handmade sweets.

COSTS

While you'll need to bear in mind the cost of transport, advertising and cooking utensils, your biggest expense will of course be your ingredients and your packaging materials.

TRAINING AND QUALIFICATIONS

As with any business involving food, you can expect to get visits from environmental health officials, so it would definitely be worth going on a course that deals with hygiene as well as health and safety. For some general information on the rules and regulations, go to the Business Link website (www.businesslink.org.uk).

PROS

Sweets might be plentiful in the shops but this also leads to people looking elsewhere when they want a special gift.

CONS

If you don't sell your produce, it will usually have to be thrown out after a certain period of time. Also, sweet-buying can be seasonal.

USEFUL CONTACTS

National Market Traders Federation, www.nmtf.co.uk – this has a list of markets all over the country with contact details for each one

www.timeout.com – if you're in or on the outskirts of London,

Edinburgh or Dublin, this is an invaluable guide to the markets and events at which you could try for a stall

Pottery

It is harder to make money from pottery in these days of mass production, but if you are good and your work is distinctive, you can make money selling it in local tourist shops and galleries.

HOW TO DO IT

Perhaps one of the best ways to get your work out there is simply to take it along to a crafts shop with a summary of your history to leave as a small display. Another good idea is to market your work in major tourist centres, jumping on the souvenir bandwagon.

A very good resource for finding events as well as getting general advice is www.studiopottery.com. This also has a great section where you can advertise your services to other potters and lovers of pottery. Another good site for finding out about events and gatherings is the one run by the Crafts Council (www.craftscouncil.org.uk), which organises a range of events throughout the country.

When you're more established it's likely that shops will buy stock directly from you, but while you're starting out you may have more success in finding platforms for your work if the retailers don't have to make any financial outlay.

To learn more about presenting yourself and your work, you can attend courses at various colleges and universities, including St Martin's. This would be of great benefit because success in this field really does depend on your ability to market yourself and increase your customer base.

HOW MUCH CAN YOU MAKE?

As always, this depends on the items you're selling and how respected your work becomes. A full-time potter starting out could expect to earn about £8,000 per annum, so you could potentially make a few thousand in your first year. On the other hand, if your style is not to other people's taste you could be lucky to make £100!

COSTS

In addition to materials such as clay and paint, you'll need a pottery wheel and some kind of oven or kiln. Because of this it's a good idea to rent a proper studio if you can, or kit out a shed or convert the garage.

TRAINING AND QUALIFICATIONS

The likelihood is that if you're interested in making a living in this specialised area you'll already have some experience. If you're still looking to learn, or simply to improve the skills you have, there is a range of qualifications you can attain. You could start with evening classes, so ask at your local adult education centre.

PROS

This is a great chance to be creative, as people looking for hand-crafted pottery will often be going for the novelty factor or a signature style that stands apart.

CONS

You do need a lot of equipment, which can be expensive, and you may also have to change some of your ideas if you find your work isn't popular.

USEFUL CONTACTS

Association for Ceramic Training and Development, St James House, Webberley, Longton ST3 1RJ, 01782 597016, www.actd.co.uk

www.craft-fair.co.uk – in addition to giving lists of craft fairs in Britain, also offers a wealth of advice ranging from sourcing materials to advertising space

Metier, Glyde House, Glydegate, Bradford BD5 0BQ, 0800 0930444, www.metier.org.uk

National Society for Education in Art and Design, The Gatehouse, Corsham Court, Corsham SN13 0BZ, 01249 714825

www.popularcrafts.com – dedicated to craft projects and suppliers

www.studiopottery.com – useful resource for all new potters

Curtains and soft furnishings

Making your own soft furnishings isn't just a way of saving money – you can turn a profit by making them for others too.

HOW TO DO IT

If you have a sewing machine and you're confident about making curtains and soft furnishings, all you need to do to start yourself off is get the word out. Let friends and family know that you are for hire and that can start the word-of-mouth recommendations, which are always the best. While you can take advantage of any free advertising space in your local press or online, a very good place to advertise would be in a furnishing fabric shop. This way it will be the people who need things made from fabric who will read your ad.

Other good places to advertise would be shops selling things for the home, as these are likely to attract people looking to redecorate. Remember to stress to shops that any customers you get you will direct to them for their home wares or fabric.

HOW MUCH CAN YOU MAKE?

The best way to work out a good wage for yourself is to assess how long a job is going to take and then decide on an hourly rate that you're happy with. This should help you get a reasonable price for the job, and as you get more skilled you'll be able to make these judgements and complete the work quicker. A rough idea of the hourly rate for making a pair of curtains, for instance, is around £10.

COSTS

Customers have to pay for their own material and will normally bring it to you. Your main costs will be a sewing machine, other sewing tools and advertising.

TRAINING AND QUALIFICATIONS

If you've been making soft furnishings like a pro for a while then you need only go on a course if you want to brush up your skills. There are a lot of courses for people who want to take this up, however. If you're already very good on a sewing machine and want to move into other areas, you could go on a beginners' course in general soft furnishings. On the other hand you may prefer to specialise in one area, such as cushions, in which case there are many courses to choose from that are more focused on a single skill.

PROS

You get to put your practical skills to good use and offer a service to people who want something original but can't sew themselves.

CONS

There may be times when you have too little work, and if you're working alone there may also be times when you have too much.

USEFUL CONTACTS

Most local education authorities offer soft furnishings courses, so ask at your local centre.

Catering and cooking

If you're a good cook, but don't want the rigidity of working in a restaurant, your own catering business could be the answer.

HOW TO DO IT

To consider this business you really do need a background in food so that you have a feel for ingredients, costing, and also what you're capable of alone – or with whatever help you have at hand.

One major consideration when starting up a catering business is that you need to get the approval of your local authorities before you begin trading. In fact if the premises you're using haven't been used for commercial food preparation before, you may even need planning permission. The government-sponsored Business Link network for small businesses and start-ups can give you information on this. Go to www.businesslink.gov.uk, follow the links to the health, safety and premises sections, and you will find information on all aspects of adhering to the laws.

Once up and running, you will also be visited by someone from your local environmental health department, who can offer you advice but can also prosecute for serious breaches of health and safety regulations. Another raft of regulations with which you will have to comply is in the area of weights and measures and appropriate labelling and pricing.

After you've established a range of sample menus you could provide, and also have an idea of the kinds of specifications you could handle, you need to advertise in your local press. Once you're more established an ad in the Yellow Pages would be a big help, and if you don't mind cold-calling new businesses this would also be extremely advantageous, as you'll have a lot of competition.

As well as generating your own business, you can check out websites such as www.moca.org.uk which list work available at any given time; www.caterer.com is also very useful in illustrating the variety of work available as well as offering advice on how to get it.

To get bigger jobs such as corporate events and weddings, the best contacts you can have are the event organisers in your area.

The good ones will be easy to find in your local directories and on websites such as www.yell.com, and once you've done a couple of successful jobs you should approach these with sample menus and references.

As you gain experience you will become better at pricing and setting up menus, but if you're at all unsure, some time shadowing an experienced caterer or working in a restaurant would definitely be a good idea.

HOW MUCH CAN YOU MAKE?

Clients are charged by the head according to the type of food they require. A cold buffet might be anything from £6 to £10 a head rising to up to £20 for a more substantial fork buffet. Full meals might be £30 and upwards – depending on what's involved. How much you personally make out of it depends on what you pay for ingredients, utensils, power and staff.

COSTS

If you're cooking on a big scale, then you will have to consider the cost of gas and electricity in addition to the ingredients upon which you'll base the cost of your services. Keeping within the food safety laws is also expensive as you have to keep food stored in special ways and at particular temperatures, so you will need the proper equipment to do this. There will also be the costs of advertising, travel, utensils and possibly staffing.

TRAINING AND QUALIFICATIONS

If you think you've got enough experience in the cooking field, it's still worth making sure you're up on health and safety regulations among other things – www.moca.org.uk offers a list of courses that are helpful in this area. You can also go to cookery and catering courses at your local adult education centre.

PROS

This offers a chance to have more independence than you would working in a restaurant and, best of all, you can do away with the boss. There's a constant demand for caterers, even from private individuals, and while this is likely to increase at certain times of the year, celebratory events throughout the year will bring you a pretty constant supply of work.

CONS

You have to have a method of transporting your produce to and from the premises. This is also an area in which work will frequently come at weekends, holidays and evenings, so you have to be prepared to work these anti-social hours.

USEFUL CONTACTS

Hospitality Training Foundation, 3rd Floor, International House, High Street, Ealing, London W5 5DB, www.htf.org.uk

Mobile and Outside Caterers Association, Centre Court, 1301 Stratford Road, Hall Green, Birmingham B28 9HH, 0121 693 7000, www.moca.org.uk

Springboard, 3 Denmark Street, London WC2H 8LP, 020 7497 8654, www.springboarduk.org.uk

Tourism Training Trust, Suite 6, Caernarvon House, 19 Donegall Pass, Belfast BT7 1DQ, 028 9032 0625, www.tttni.com

Cake-making and decorating, jams

Jam-making and cake-making bring in money at fairs and, if you're good, you can supply local tea shops and upmarket delicatessens.

HOW TO DO IT

It's as simple as making the food, and selling it. The main challenge is to stay abreast of fairs and fêtes in your locality. The best way to get your cakes sold in a shop is simply to go round cafés and delicatessens, identify which sell home-made produce and talk to the manager. If you offer a free sample of your best recipes, you'll soon have some outlets interested.

As with any business involving food, you can expect to receive visits from the environmental health department, so it would definitely be worth going on a course that deals with hygiene as well as health and safety. For some general information on the rules and regulations, go to the Business Link website, www.businesslink.org.uk.

There are all kinds of lines you could go into when it comes to specialist foods: pâtés, preserves, biscuits, pastries, home-made ice cream, ready-made frozen dinners and specialist celebration cakes are just some of the things you could make and sell.

If you get really good you could start selling to delicatessens and large, upmarket food outlets such as Harrods and Selfridges. For this there would need to be something very special about your produce – organic jams, unusual-recipe chutneys in unusual pots, celebration cakes that no one else has thought of, and so on. You will need to spend more time on your 'hobby' to make this work. It involves having a brand, specially printed labels, attractive and unusual packaging, and workable distribution.

You could also check out local farm shops, craft fairs and markets to see whether you can get a stall selling your own beautifully packaged jams, preserves or cakes. You could advertise your cakes in local papers and wedding magazines or contact local pubs to see whether they want someone to offer ready-cooked lunches or nicely prepared sandwiches. Make the most of friends and existing contacts by offering to do the catering when someone holds a party or function.

It can be a complicated business, but for some this has brought in a respectable amount of money each year. If you think you could be on the verge of making it big, or even medium-sized, in the specialist food area, get as much help and advice as you can from your local Business Link and anyone else who is in the same line of work.

HOW MUCH CAN YOU MAKE?

It depends how much you produce and what level of sales you get. It could be anything from a few pounds at a local fête to thousands a year if you sell specialist cakes for weddings or have an upmarket range of jams and chutneys you sell to, say, Selfridges and local delicatessens.

COSTS

In addition to the ingredients you need to buy, you'll also have to pay for transport, power, packaging and advertising, including maintaining a website if you have one.

TRAINING AND QUALIFICATIONS

As with everything, there's bound to be a course that could help, but this being a more traditional activity, learned in the home, the chances are you know all you need to and, as they say, the proof is in the pudding.

PROS

You can usually work from home – a house with a good kitchen is ideal for this kind of work.

CONS

There's more work than making the food involved – you've got to shop for the ingredients and transport your produce to the outlet. As it's perishable food you're dealing with, you could find yourself having to throw a lot away if it doesn't sell quickly enough.

USEFUL CONTACTS

Business Link, www.businesslink.gov.uk – offers advice on the health and safety guidelines with which you will have to comply

http://cleanup.food.gov.uk/ – lots of information on food safety

www.lifestyle.co.uk/business/plans/catering-business-plan.htm – online help with setting up a catering business plan

www.tradingstandards.co.uk – useful information on food labelling

Also consider . . .

- Birthday-cake-making for dogs and horses – yes, really. There is a market for this. If you know about dogs or horses or other pets, you can concoct delicious (to them) 'cakes' for their birthdays. Many pet-owners are highly sentimental about their animals and will pay for a 'cake' made of the kind of foods they like. For inspiration, check out the dog birthday cake recipe on the Blue Peter website at www.bbc.co.uk/cbbc/bluepeter/active/bakes/ bake_dogcake.shtml. Start selling to neighbours and friends who have pets and then you could broaden out with a website that advertises your service.

- Business celebration cakes – if you are particularly good at cake decorating you could offer specially tailored creations to businesses as part of their marketing plan. Cakes with the company's logo or in the shape of, and looking just like, a new product of theirs, can sell for good money. So if you are a good artist as well as an excellent cake-maker, offer this as an idea to local businesses first and see where you get. Prices tend to start at £100 per cake.

Greetings cards

It may be irritating that there seem to be more commercial occasions than ever before – but not if you're making the cards.

HOW TO DO IT

The actual making of the cards isn't hard – it's just like being back at school. You don't, however, want to make something that looks worthy of a classroom wall. With so many cards around, you have to be sure you have a good idea to set your product apart from the others. This may lie in your artistic talent, or, as seems increasingly the case with shop cards, your sense of humour.

You can get the bits and pieces needed for making attractive cards all over the place now. Websites such as those of

Craft Creations and Baker Ross sell all manner of card-making materials. You can also find wiggly eyes, furry pipe cleaners and the like in some supermarkets. Looking around your home for decorative bits can save a lot of money. You can use old wrapping paper as background or download something suitable from Internet sites (www.magicalkingdom.co.uk, for example); old buttons, bits of ribbon and even sweet wrappers may also come in useful.

Invest in *Crafts Beautiful* magazine, which often has inspiring ideas for cards and other crafts. It also has adverts for suppliers of craft materials, which could be useful.

Make up a portfolio of cards and take this round a variety of places such as art and gift shops and stationers. Quite often you can sell them on a 'sale or return' basis through these outlets. Just speak to the manager – they can only say no!

HOW MUCH CAN YOU MAKE?

You could turn about 50p–£1 profit on each card you make, depending on the cost of your materials and whether you sell to shops (which will want them cheaper) or direct to the public.

COSTS

For basic designs, you won't need much more than card and envelopes, but materials can be as elaborate as you can afford, including beads, lace and pressed flowers – as long as you think it'll attract the buyer.

TRAINING AND QUALIFICATIONS

Courses can certainly help you hone your illustration and design skills, but it is perhaps more important to have imagination and simply keep an eye on market activity. Where better to find inspiration than in a card shop or in craft magazines and books?

PROS

You get to be as artistic as you like and if customers like your designs they're likely to come back for something different to give on other occasions. Making cards is also a relaxing and fulfilling way to spend a few hours here and there.

CONS

Business will fluctuate at different times of year, and it may take some flexibility in your ideas to come up with something that proves popular. The card market is also very competitive and crowded, so you may have to push to get your work even into local gift shops and stationers.

USEFUL CONTACTS

www.astitchonline.com – provides accessories for sewing crafts which can be used in making cards

www.bakerross.co.uk – more materials for making cards

www.craftcreations.co.uk – lots of materials for making cards

www.craftworkcards.uktradingco.com – blank cards and decorative bits

www.thepapermillshop.co.uk – a good source for paper and card

Picture framing

You might be surprised at how easy this craft is now with the advent of new technology which does away with the need for brute strength.

HOW TO DO IT

With the right equipment you can set up a studio in your home or garage, and given the high demand for picture frames you're likely to attract a lot of interest from advertising in the local press. You could approach local bookshops that sell prints and offer to work for their customers.

To start off, you need four things: a mitring machine to cut mouldings at the correct angles (around £1,200); an underpin, which holds the two sides together while you attach them (around £600); a mount cutting machine (around £300); and a glass cutter (around £30).

While some of this equipment can be picked up from classified ads, the best source is one of the many picture-framing fairs that take place across the country. Website www.clubframeco.com is an example of one from which you can get all the materials you'll need to start up, whereas sites such as www.craft-fair.co.uk and www.craftscotland.org offer a list of the year's fairs if you'd rather see the items before buying.

HOW MUCH CAN YOU MAKE?

Marking your frames up by four times what they cost you to make, you can make a good living, averaging around £8,000 per annum if you keep it on a part-time basis.

COSTS

As you'd expect, your costs will vary in accordance with the price of your materials. The other major expense will be that of your toolkit. Should you buy all your equipment new, it will set you back around £2,200, but you can always look out for second-hand pieces of equipment in your local press.

TRAINING AND QUALIFICATIONS

The machinery that has recently come into the industry has made the work far less labour intensive and less skilled than it was previously. The real skill nowadays lies in choosing the right mounts and frames to complement your pictures.

PROS

There's a high demand for framing, and if you work from home the fact that you don't have to pay rates means you can undercut the shops while providing the same quality of product.

CONS

It can be difficult to publicise yourself if you don't work from a shop and you already have competition from other framing outlets.

USEFUL CONTACTS

There are quite a few institutions that offer courses in picture framing and also restoration should you want to move into that area as well. Ask at your local adult education centre.

www.clubframeco.com – an online store from which you can buy equipment and materials

www.craft-fair.co.uk and **www.craftscotland.org** – these give detailed lists of the arts and crafts fairs around the country

The Fine Art Trade Guild, 16–18 Empress Place, London SW6 1TT, 020 7381 6616, www.fineart.co.uk

www.pictureframer.com – an American website which offers some general advice to those wanting to enter the market

---

Case study

Kent-based artist Toby Fraser has picture-framing equipment in one room in his house and makes regular money framing pictures and prints for a local second-hand dealer. 'I've known him for a while and we just have an agreement that any prints he gets he sends to me to frame,' he says. 'He can ask a lot more for them if they're framed well and he knows that I have a good eye for colour, which is very important in choosing the mountings, and that I'll do it at a better rate than the commercial picture framers.'

He also frames prints that he picks up at car boot sales and in second-hand and charity shops which he then sells at local auctions at a profit. The prices vary but he has made between £180 and £400 for a set of six prints, once he has allowed for the costs of buying and framing them. Sometimes he will buy an old book that is not valuable in itself but has nice-looking colour plates which he will take out, frame and sell separately or as a set.

'I take private commissions as well as working for a few shops,' he says, 'but it all comes from word of mouth. I've never advertised, it's just evolved naturally. I charge between £15 for a small job for a friend up to £75 for a large job, which is better than you could get on the high street.'

Toy-making

Make toys and sell them at craft fairs, fêtes and on the Internet, or to toy shops.

HOW TO DO IT

The key aspect of toy-making is the initial idea, so the first thing you need to do is think of something that kids would like.

Because safety is such an issue you really need to join a society such as the British Toy and Hobby Association (BTHA). This involves you sending your toys off for testing to prove their compliance with the association's safety standards. Becoming a member, however, means that you receive help in protecting your business interests, representation at all parliamentary and EU levels, toy safety consultancy, PR support for the industry and allied issues, the use of the association's Lion Mark toy safety symbol, and as well as discount on space taken at the toy fairs they hold.

Another very good organisation to look at is the British Association of Toy Retailers. Their website, www.batr.co.uk, offers detailed market research and advice and contacts in areas such as marketing, safety and retailing. You can find lists of other toy fairs across the country on websites such as www.collectorsgazette.com/fairs, and if you want to research the shops in your area, a local directory is available from the BATR website.

Because you can't compete with the brightly coloured, plastic world of mass-produced toys, it's usually better to go for more old-fashioned items such as cars, trucks, trains, teddy bears and dolls, and other soft toys for girls. Skilled professionals have gone into business making rocking horses that sell for a lot of money – often to wealthy, professional women who weren't able to have a horse as a girl!

HOW MUCH CAN YOU MAKE?

It's a good idea to charge about four times what it costs you to make the toy. The prices you can charge range enormously, from £2 or so for very small items such as collectable characters made from pistachio shells to the £1,800 plus you'd pay for a rocking horse or £2,000-plus for a top-quality doll's house.

COSTS

As always this depends on the materials you're using. Aside from this, you really do need to get your toys lab-tested for safety, or you risk facing a lot more in legal fees! Also, you may have to allow for packaging and travel costs and advertising and Internet fees.

TRAINING AND QUALIFICATIONS

For this kind of work you need skills in sewing, woodwork, metalwork or plastics, and just as importantly you need to study the current legislation and safety standards.

PROS

Because kids have wild imaginations, you can be as creative as you like. If you enjoy crafts and have always loved toys, this is a great way to spend your evenings and make money.

CONS

You need to be sure that your products are safe for children. There are many conditions involved in becoming a member of the associations that deal in child safety, including sending your products to testing labs to get their approval. It can also be hard to sell your toys if they don't appeal to children or their parents.

USEFUL CONTACTS

British Toy and Hobby Association, 80 Camberwell Road, London SE5 0EG, 020 7701 7271, www.btha.co.uk/general.html

British Toymakers Guild, 124 Walcot Street, Bath, Avon BA1 5BG, 01225 442440, www.toymakersguild.co.uk

www.dollshouseworld.com – a site on which you can advertise anything you make that relates to doll's houses

Musical instrument-making

This is a specialist field, but if you are already musical and have a skill in making a particular instrument you could make money out of it.

HOW TO DO IT

There's no doubt about it – this is a skill. If you don't yet know whether you can do it then either attend a course to learn about it or don't even go there! If you've been doing this kind of thing for a while, your only real challenge is to find buyers. And of course working in this area, the best place to advertise is in music shops. Music teachers and music schools might also take adverts or hand out leaflets, so contact those in your local area.

While you might be thinking big – like Eric Clapton, who remade his own electric guitar – it's best for a newcomer to start with the simpler items, which may even have a bigger market. Pan pipes and recorders, for instance, are a lot easier to make than a violin, and their popularity among less musical people means you can sell them from a market stall and offer them to shops that perhaps specialise in other things, such as souvenirs or arts and crafts.

To take this up as a profession you must have excellent wood-work and metal skills, good dexterity, patience, and an under-standing of pitch and harmony.

HOW MUCH CAN YOU MAKE?

This being a skill, you can charge a fair amount for the finished instruments. You need to consider the number of hours you devote to each, though. You might get £5 for a penny whistle, while a beautifully hand-crafted violin will fetch something between £250 and £500.

A rough guideline is that part-time instrument makers can earn between £4,000 and £10,000 annually once established and if business is good.

COSTS

This will depend on the materials, so if you're not making an instrument to order materials need to be a big consideration. If you're starting out, it's not a good idea to make very expensive instruments – start with middle-of-the-range products, upgrad-ing later, once you have more of a reputation (and more money to spend).

TRAINING AND QUALIFICATIONS

It's possible to enter this field without academic qualifications but it's advantageous to have good woodwork skills and also some knowledge of running a business. For instance, you can do a foun-dation degree in Musical Instrument Technology at London Met-ropolitan University. This is a two-year course requiring maths at GCSE (A–C)/S grade (1–3) and one A-level or equivalent.

PROS

This is a skill that very few other people have. It can also be a very satisfying and relaxing hobby.

CONS

Most people who buy musical instruments are simply enthusiasts looking to the regular retail outlets. You may not be able to compete with the cut-price, mass-produced versions of your instrument coming from Japan or the United States.

USEFUL CONTACTS

Common Ground, PO Box 26064, Kilmarnock KA2 0YG, www.commongroundscotland.com – offers a range of courses on making instruments including pan pipes and dulcimers

The Institute of Musical Instrument Technology (IMIT), PO Box 118, Southsea, Hampshire PO4 9YP, www.imit.org.uk

www.learndirect-advice.co.uk/helpwithyourcareer/ jobprofiles/profiles/profile958/ – offers advice on the industry along with details of current courses

www.musicalinstrumentsales.co.uk – a site on which you can advertise your instruments and get in touch with others in the industry

Photography

It can be hard to break into the more artistic side of photography, but there are ways you can use it to make some money while you're building up a portfolio.

HOW TO DO IT

You can make a living out of all kinds of photography, but the biggest source of income for most is from weddings. To be effective you need to be skilled, not only at taking the pictures, but also at dealing with groups of people at a particularly emotional and sometimes stressful time. Business can vary; May to September is likely to be your busiest time – accounting for 80–90 per cent of the work – with the rest of the year being relatively quiet.

Another good source of income will be family and baby portraits. This requires particular patience, and with babies you need something to get their attention and make them smile. A little dog, for instance, is usually a winner.

You can prove your worth by getting a portfolio together, featuring pictures from a relative's wedding, perhaps, and a few portraits. A very good way to start out is to approach some of the photographers listed in the Yellow Pages and ask for a Saturday job. Shadowing another photographer and getting occasional jobs to do yourself will mean you'll soon be advertising as an experienced photographer yourself. If you are doing weddings, then remember to dress as though you're a guest – don't just turn up in jeans and trainers!

After you've worked on a freelance basis, there are prospects for finding permanent and full-time employment. Press photographers are employed by provincial/national newspapers; medical photographers by hospitals and medical schools; scientific/industrial photographers by universities, industrial firms and the Civil Service. Other employers of permanent staff include the forces (particularly the RAF) and the police.

HOW MUCH YOU CAN MAKE?

While it's a good idea to gauge the prices charged by other photographers in your area, you could expect something in the region of £100 to £200 for a wedding, which will normally take about three to four hours. A general guideline is that trainee photographers can make around £8,000 per annum, specialist photographers around £12,000, and more established professionals £20,000 upwards.

TRAINING AND QUALIFICATIONS

There is a myriad of courses teaching the fundamentals of photography, right through to advanced techniques. A course on presenting yourself and your work would also be highly beneficial, especially if you want to get into the more artistic side of photography.

COSTS

To go it alone – and even to be taken seriously when approaching other photographers – you'll need your own equipment. You can always pick this up second-hand, but as a rough guide to buying your own new, a camera will cost you about £500, a flashgun around £300, a lens £400–£600 and a light meter and reflector each around £100. So to start up, you're looking at expenses of around £1,500.

If you think that's bad, just remember that anything could break down at any time, so professionals will normally have a spare of everything in case this happens during a job. You could therefore be spending something like £3,000, but if you don't have that kind of money at the moment, working for another photographer is a very good route into the industry.

PROS

It's a great way to use your talent, meet people every day, and potentially make a lot of money for a few hours of work.

CONS

You could experience quiet months outside the wedding season. It's an overcrowded industry and you need to have tenacity to become established.

USEFUL CONTACTS

The Association of Photographers, 81 Leonard Street, London EC2A 4QS, 020 7739 6669, www.the-aop.org

British Institute of Professional Photography (BIPP), Fox Talbot House, 2 Amwell End, Ware, Herts. SG12 9HN, 01920 464011, www.bipp.com

National Council for the Training of Journalists, Latton Bush Centre, Southern Way, Harlow, Essex CM18 7BL, www.nctj.com, 01279 430009

There are lots of other crafts and hobbies that you could make money out of. If you already enjoy a particular craft, consider how it could be turned into a money-making operation on the side. Some crafts you could make money out of are:

- basket-making
- calligraphy
- candle-making and other wax products
- crocheting
- embroidery
- enamelling
- engraving
- gilding
- jewellery-making
- knitting
- lace-making
- leatherwork
- metalwork
- patchwork
- printmaking
- quilting
- rug-making
- silversmithing
- stained-glass-making
- weaving, spinning and dyeing
- wood carving.

CHAPTER SEVEN

Are You Practical?

S O MANY PEOPLE have so few practical skills that if you are at all handy, and willing to take on small jobs, you will never be short of clients.

DIY and odd jobs

If you are good around the house, offer your services locally as an odd-job man (or woman) willing to take on any bits and pieces that neighbours can't do themselves.

HOW TO DO IT

You don't strictly need qualifications – all you need is to think about which areas you can confidently work in. For example, people need help with painting, tiling, decorating, gardening, plumbing and even smaller jobs such as hanging pictures and changing a fuse.

You can advertise in your local supermarket and papers or in the newsagent's window, and if you do a good job word of mouth will soon bring in some business. There are also some websites that act as directories for odd-job people.

Many people are put off by high call-out fees charged by full-time plumbers, electricians, and so on. If you charge little or nothing for the call-out and then charge by the hour you will be more in demand. Sticking to your local area – whatever radius you want – you won't spend much time travelling anyway.

Some companies that offer a similarly general service charge call-out fees while others just charge by the hour. Look in the Yellow Pages and the local press to find out what services are on offer in your locality so that you know which will be the best approach in offering a competitive rate.

It would be helpful to get a police check – these cost £10 from your local police station – as you can show this to new, elderly customers who might be worried by a stranger coming round. You may also find that you could get regular part-time work with a local institution such as a nursing home, or at a school or office block. This kind of work often comes through word of mouth as well as through adverts in the press or in employment agencies.

HOW MUCH CAN YOU MAKE?

As a general guide, you could make around £30–£50 for your first hour of work, and about £20–£40 for every hour after that. Remember that larger jobs, such as painting, will attract lower hourly rates.

COSTS

You probably already have many of the tools you need, although you may need to replace and update these more often when you are working for others. Apart from updating your toolkit your only other expense will be travel and personal liability insurance, which you will need to cover you when in other people's houses.

TRAINING AND QUALIFICATIONS

There are a lot of areas you can work in where the only qualification you need is common sense. But for any plumbing that goes beyond bleeding a radiator or changing tap washers, something like a Corgi qualification will be essential. You might also like to do extra training to improve and build on your existing skills.

Contact the Construction Industry Training Board or the British Plumbing Employers Council for information on their courses.

PROS

A lot of the work requires you only to have common sense and practical ability. People are likely to call on you again in the future if you do a good job, so you shouldn't need to pay for advertising once you've had a few customers.

CONS

You might have to travel quite a bit, and without a company to back you up it's down to you to get your money, settle any disputes that might arise and, in the worst-case scenario, pay for any damage you may cause.

USEFUL CONTACTS

British Plumbing Employers Council (BPEC), 02476 420970, www.bpec.org.uk

Construction Industry Training Board (CITB), 01485 577700, www.citb.org.uk

www.friday-ad.co.uk/ – if you are in the South, your local *Friday Ad* would be a good place to put an ad; a lot of them are free, although other, more prominent ones charge

www.cityneighbours.com – a website you can advertise on.

Carpentry

If you've got a talent for woodwork, you could hire out your services, even think about extending into areas such as fitting kitchens and designing furniture.

HOW TO DO IT

If you're experienced and confident, let it be known that you can put up shelves, make cabinets and fit kitchens for money. Don't underestimate the value of word of mouth. Doing a few small jobs to begin with for friends – or even offering the odd small freebie in your first weeks – will be a platform from which to display your skills and expertise, and then you'll find that you need only retain a few clients to make a decent living.

To get on to the books of the shops that do kitchens, you have to prove your worth. You'll either have been in the trade for a long time and have some very good references, or you'll have a recognised qualification along with some experience.

Once you get established, if you want to do more of this you will really need a studio to work from, since you'll be creating a lot of mess and a lot of noise. Having commercial premises where customers can find you can also be advantageous. You can advertise in the local press at first, upgrading to more expensive ads in publications such as the Yellow Pages as you progress.

If you're better at the general jobs such as shelving and basic cabinets, units and fittings, then it's best to be flexible. It's only really worth specialising if you're very good at the more expensive jobs such as cabinet-making, staircases and furniture design.

HOW MUCH CAN YOU MAKE?

It's generally recognised that, once established, you can make more money from a carpentry business than you could from an average office job. What you earn will depend on the area in which you specialise. For instance, if you were to specialise in the skilled area of making cabinets you could expect to earn about £8,000 a year if you worked on a part-time basis. Working on more basic jobs, however, will bring in more work, even if each job is for less money.

COSTS

Tools are essential, and the cost of these can run into thousands. A lot of carpenters find that they start with the essentials and build up a collection over the years. This kind of work is messy and loud, so after a while you will need to pay for a space in a suitable location that you can use as a studio, and you will probably also need to pay for advertising in the Yellow Pages and local publications.

You might also like to pick up a few handbooks on the subject in case you do hit upon jobs you've never had to tackle before.

TRAINING AND QUALIFICATIONS

While there are a lot of qualifications, short courses and training schemes in this area, the best qualification is still experience. Only from this do you get an understanding of the whole process, from specification, through design and planning to the finished article.

If you do need some training, though, and you're between 16 and 25, you can do a three-year Construction Apprenticeship Scheme (CAS) in England and Wales or a four-year apprenticeship in Scotland registered with the Scottish Building Apprenticeship and Training Council. Working this way means you earn a wage at the same time as following the training programme.

PROS

Word of mouth and satisfied customers are likely to keep business coming in even if you only start with a very small customer base.

CONS

Working with noisy equipment means you will usually have to stick to daytime hours. You can reach a stage where you actually have too much work to do alone, and yet at other times business might be slow.

USEFUL CONTACTS

Construction Industry Training Board, Bircham Newton, King's Lynn, Norfolk PE31 6RH, 01485 577577, www.citb.org.uk

The Furniture, Furnishings and Interiors National Training

Organisation (FFINTO), The Poplars, off Wollaton Road, Beeston, Nottingham NG13 9HH, 0115 922 1200, www.ffinto.org

www.thelocalweb.net – a website that covers local services

Case study

Sean Gannon is a carpenter in Brighton. His interest in carpentry began four years ago while he was working at a wood recycling plant. The plant attracts a lot of this kind of business as customers often need help in crafting the wood into various items such as shelves and furniture. 'This was an excellent way of learning from other skilled carpenters while also saving up enough money to open my own workshop,' he says. 'Also, it paid the bills while I was trying to pay off some other debts.'

Another bonus was the fact that demonstrating his skills in the wood recycling plant allowed him to build up a loyal customer base so that, when he opened his workshop, he found that advertising was almost unnecessary. The amount of work he was offered meant that in the end he literally had to give up his day job to take it on.

'One of the downsides is that sometimes you have more work than you can cope with alone. It can all come in in a rush and you can't always get extra help in just like that. I've had to turn work away sometimes, which hurts! Also, you can't work into the night, even when you need to, as the neighbours will complain.'

He estimates that the value of his toolkit now runs into thousands of pounds, but says that this has been built up over the years and provided you aren't doing anything too specialised you can get by with the basics.

Assembling furniture

If you've mastered the black art of furniture assembly, you're likely to be in demand, as so few seem able to do it!

HOW TO DO IT

As a furniture assembly genius your main task will be to make people aware that you can do it. As with many skills you can get a lot of work through word of mouth, but you can also promote yourself through ads in newspapers, newsagents' windows and local websites. It's also worth contacting companies that provide flat-pack furniture and finding out whether they can put customers in touch with you when they buy the kits. Some who offer this service put posters up near the furniture stores giving their phone numbers so that clients can contact them while the idea is at the forefront of their minds.

Joining an agency is also a great way to open your services out to an established customer base. Agencies that cover various parts of Britain include Flatpackers UK (www.furniture-assembly.co.uk), who are usually on the lookout for self-employed workers to join their team. (They will also give you a handy price guide for different items of furniture.) Also, try Unpact (www.unpact.co.uk) and check the Web for more that might cover your area.

HOW MUCH CAN YOU MAKE?

Most companies that do this kind of work have a fixed fee for different items of furniture. For example, you might charge only £15 for a cot whereas a wardrobe would cost more like £50. Find out what agencies in your area are charging, then offer a more competitive deal.

COSTS

Papers like the *Friday Ad* or *Loot* will often let you advertise for free or will charge just a small amount for a bigger or more prominent ad. With a lot of self-assembly furniture the tools are provided for you, so you're not likely to need much more than the basics in your toolkit, which you probably already have.

TRAINING AND QUALIFICATIONS

You don't need qualifications, and if you're good at assembling furniture then you've probably already had all the experience you need.

PROS

This is a way of making money while meeting people and getting to travel around your area.

CONS

You may get a lot of time-wasters who don't really want to pay for something they know they should be able to do themselves. Many flatpacks are so badly made that you will often need more than basic skills to put them together, using extra tools and your own accessories such as nails and screws.

USEFUL CONTACTS

Flatpackers UK, 01784 477420, www.furnitureassembly.co.uk

Unpact, www.unpackt.co.uk

Painting and decorating

Anyone who is experienced and skilled in painting and decorating can get work this way, as so few other people are!

HOW TO DO IT

There's not a lot to painting, but with the more complicated jobs, such as wallpapering, tiling and putting up borders, you do need enough experience, and ideally on-the-job training, to be confident that you can do it.

Because people often advertise for this kind of help, you have the option of answering adverts as well as putting out your own. It would be worth taking advantage of the free adverts available in local papers such as the *Friday Ad*, as well as putting ads in shop windows; you can even start up your own website to give details of your services, which provides an online presence for those searching on the Internet.

You may want to work on a very ad hoc basis, and just respond to adverts or general demand around your neighbourhood. In this case, it would be fair to use their ladders and simply take your own brushes along. As you get more established you should get your own kit together, including ladders and even a van to take you around. Once you are established you could take an ad out in the Yellow Pages, since this will steer a lot of business your way even if it is more expensive.

HOW MUCH CAN YOU MAKE?

It may surprise you to learn that a painter in London can demand between £100 and £150 per day. The normal rate anywhere else is more like £50 per day. An established painter is likely to assess a job and give a fixed price before starting.

COSTS

If you want to start up properly, you'll need to spend a fair bit on your own ladders (around £500), perhaps a van and also public liability insurance which will cover you should you damage anything or injure yourself (£400). You'll also have to allow for the cost of advertising, of course, unless you get all your work by word of mouth.

TRAINING AND QUALIFICATIONS

While experience is probably the best qualification, there are courses offered by most local education centres, often accredited by City & Guilds. A head for heights is a prerequisite!

PROS

You can get a good rate of pay for your time and pretty regular work.

CONS

You may be faced with cleaning and preparing pretty uneven or unclean surfaces. Business can slow down in the winter months as Christmas approaches and will normally only pick up again in February. You may need to renew equipment such as brushes on a regular basis, which can add to your unforeseen costs.

USEFUL CONTACTS

www.paintingdecoratingassociation.co.uk – representing over 2,000 professionals in the country, this association aims to provide advice on the industry along with a code of conduct

www.yourlocaltradesman.com – interactive business service for finding local work

Gardening

We are more aware of the value of our gardens than ever, thanks to the plethora of gardening programmes on the TV, and yet few of us have the time to do anything with them.

HOW TO DO IT

Unless you've got skills in design, you're more likely to be offering your services in the more mundane areas of mowing, pruning, planting and sowing seeds.

A lot of your work is likely to come through word of mouth, but by all means take advantage of any free adverts you can place in the local press and online. Because gardens are often on show, a good tactic is to drop a leaflet through the doors of houses desperately in need of some green fingers. Target the more upmarket streets in your area as their residents are more likely to have the money to spend on 'staff'.

When advertising in shops, it's always good to target places your market base will frequent. For instance, garden centres will attract gardening enthusiasts who may still require help with certain tasks.

HOW MUCH CAN YOU MAKE?

The ongoing nature of gardening means that once you've got a few satisfied customers you're likely to get regular work from them. While it's worth negotiating a price that both parties are happy with, it's reasonable to ask for around £10 per hour, depending on where you live and what other gardeners are charging.

COSTS

Although most people have their own tools, you will definitely need an array of your own. In addition, it's also very handy to have your own lawnmower and a large car or even a small van to transport these around.

TRAINING AND QUALIFICATIONS

For the routine tasks you need only a bit of experience. You definitely need to be physically fit and strong enough to deal with occasional lifting and pulling up strong roots. If you are interested in learning more, you could get a National Vocational Qualification or a Diploma in Horticultural Studies.

PROS

This is perfect work for people who love nature and the outdoors and have green fingers. In addition to one-off jobs, you're also likely to get some ongoing work with institutions or communal gardens.

CONS

This is seasonal work so you will probably need to find something else to supplement your income in the winter. It can also be pretty demoralising when the weather's bad. It is very physical and demands a strong and fit person.

USEFUL CONTACTS

www.commonwork.org – one of the sites you can check out to learn more about gardening and the natural environment

www.gardeningdata.co.uk – a useful source website for gardening

Horticultural Trades Association, 19 High Street, Theale, Reading, Berks. RG7 5AH, 01734 303132, www.the-hta.org.uk

The Royal Horticultural Society (RHS), www.rhs.org.uk – the national society for all things to do with gardening, which offers training courses and support

Window cleaning

Got a bucket, a cloth and a head for heights? You could be a window cleaner.

HOW TO DO IT

Apart from these, all you need is a ladder. With a van to get around in, you can advertise your services in the local papers, and once you've got a network of clients you will have regular work.

It really can be as easy as this, particularly if you target those parts of your local area where people are cash rich but time poor (or simply can't be bothered) and would be pleased to pay someone to reach up to their top windows.

You can also get work simply by doing a leaflet drop around your area. If you want more regular work get in touch with whoever is in charge of the buildings management of office blocks locally. They often need window cleaners on a monthly or even weekly basis.

HOW MUCH CAN YOU MAKE?

Depending on where you are, the number of windows, and whether you're doing residential or commercial buildings (charge the latter a bit more!) you can ask for anything between £4 and £25 per building. Window cleaners will go back to the same house every three to six weeks.

COSTS

It's advisable to have a van or a large car to transport your equipment around. Other than that, the costs for detergent, clothes, chamois and a scraper or two are fairly minimal.

TRAINING AND QUALIFICATIONS

Although you don't need any qualifications, it might be worth picking up a few tips from the experts ... on safety if nothing else. A good website for this kind of information is www.windowcleaners.uk.com.

PROS

The nature of the work means you can keep going back to the same houses in the future.

CONS

You have to be willing to work in some pretty bad weather conditions or your business could suffer.

USEFUL CONTACTS

Master Window and General Cleaners, www.window cleaners.uk.com – they endeavour to provide information on all aspects of the trade

Wood-stripping

This is another activity that is gaining in popularity as TV programmes encourage us to strip and repaint everything.

HOW TO DO IT

Although you've probably heard that the technique most often used is an 'acid bath', the solution is normally an alkaline one of caustic soda. For this you'll need a workshop in an area where there's a big enough demand for the service. A location in an area of Georgian, Victorian or Edwardian houses with moneyed owners would be ideal, for instance, whereas you'd probably have less luck in a newer area.

You can target the older houses with leaflet drops as well as advertising through cards in shop windows and taking advantage of the free adverts available online and in your local press. If you can, target any DIY shops that have space to advertise in order to attract the attention of people in the process of decorating.

HOW MUCH CAN YOU MAKE?

'A household door costs £25 plus VAT,' says Debbie Neal of Malmesbury Strippers, 'but other, more complicated furniture would be priced individually.' Get a rate card or an idea of pricing from a similar business, as prices are likely to vary a great deal depending on the area in which you're working and the kinds of items that are brought in most.

COSTS

You may already have space in your home to set up a workshop – perhaps you could convert your garage or a shed – but because of the fumes and mess that come with this job it would be advisable to rent a space somewhere else as a workshop. You will also need to pay for the stripping solutions and protective clothing.

TRAINING AND QUALIFICATIONS

You definitely need to know about the different types and ages of wood to gauge how long they need to be dipped for. Several books on wood-stripping and wood care will help.

PROS

There has been more demand for the natural wood look in recent years and there can be some good business in areas of older houses.

CONS

It's a rather unpredictable market. A lot depends on what's in fashion and, as with other interior design, it's a business that's going to suffer in recessionary periods.

USEFUL CONTACTS

www.malmesburystrippers.co.uk – wood- and metal-stripping company in Wiltshire

www.periodproperty.co.uk/article023.htm – a very good guide to the equipment and experience you'll need

www.uktoolshop.com/tool_books/bookspart1.htm – offers guides to wood-stripping and finishing

Hedge-trimming

There is a lot of demand for this in the suburbs, though less in cities or the country.

HOW TO DO IT

Just by walking around your area, you'll be able to gauge whether you think there are enough gardens with hedges to sustain your business. This is one of the best ways to publicise yourself as well – simply by knocking on doors and offering your services or doing a leaflet drop in the wealthier areas. It would probably be best to start working over the weekends and gradually build up from there.

Putting up an advert in a local garden or DIY store will also attract the attention of potential customers, and if you do a good job you're also likely to get a lot of business through word of mouth.

HOW MUCH CAN YOU MAKE?

You can normally charge around £20–£30 per hedge, but this will vary depending on the area in which you're working and of course the size of the hedge.

COSTS

Apart from the hedge-trimmer and saws, it would be handy to have a vehicle to carry them and also to take away the hedge cuttings, which should be part of your service, unless the householder has a compost heap or similar that you can use. You will also need personal liability insurance as you are doing a potentially dangerous job on someone else's land.

TRAINING AND QUALIFICATIONS

You don't need training or qualifications but you do need to be highly competent and experienced.

PROS

The hedges grow back – and if you do a good job, you'll be called back. It is also a satisfying and rewarding job for anyone who enjoys gardening and the outdoors.

CONS

As with all outdoor work, there will be times when you have to withstand some pretty bad weather conditions. It is also a seasonal activity so you could be overworked in the spring and summer and twiddling your thumbs over the winter.

USEFUL CONTACTS

www.commonwork.org – one of the sites you can check out to learn more about gardening and the natural environment

Gutter-clearing

Not exactly glamorous, but you would be surprised how much of a demand there is for people who can do this dirty job.

HOW TO DO IT

If you can stand the heights, this is a service that is needed all year round – you just have to let people know you're available. Because so many people need this kind of help it might be worth taking out an ad in your local paper as well as advertising on noticeboards in shops.

Leaflet drops in homes all around your area would also help you get work. Remember that the busiest time of the year for gutter-clearing is autumn and early winter when the falling leaves clog up gutters everywhere, so it is worth timing your leaflet drop for that season.

HOW MUCH CAN YOU MAKE?

Although it's worth checking what other people are charging for the service in your area, the average price you could charge is somewhere around £75 per job.

COSTS

You'll need a vehicle to carry a tall ladder and cleaning rods. You should be able to pick all this up for around £1,500. You will also need public liability insurance.

TRAINING AND QUALIFICATIONS

This is one of the simpler jobs that people generally can do for themselves but just don't have the time for (or don't want to do). So as long as you've done it before and are confident and stable on a ladder, you should be fine.

PROS

This is money for fairly straightforward work that a lot of people simply don't get round to.

CONS

As with all outdoor work, you'll have to put up with some pretty bad weather at times. It's also messy and you've got to have a head for heights.

USEFUL CONTACTS

UK Guttering Supplies, www.gutteringsupplies.co.uk – useful if you know how to repair and replace guttering, as this can be a good additional service to offer

Drain-unblocking

This is another dirty job that no one wants to do, so you can charge more for it than for other handiwork.

HOW TO DO IT

If you're sure you can do the job, you can start advertising locally, maybe for weekend work at first, and build your business from there.

It's worth advertising in the local press and in supermarkets and shops. Once you're more established you can progress to more expensive ads in the Yellow Pages and so on.

To do it properly you should arm yourself with a high-pressure water jet and a van in which to house the machinery. This will set you back at least £2,000, but for tough jobs it will be worth the money.

HOW MUCH CAN YOU MAKE?

You can normally charge a flat rate of about £70 or a call-out fee of, say, £40 with an extra charge on top for the work.

COSTS

In addition to your travel expenses, you will have to pay for equipment such as rods and suction pads, ideally a high-pressure water jet and a van too. You should also get professional indemnity insurance. All together it will probably cost you £3,000–4,000 to set up.

TRAINING AND QUALIFICATIONS

Experience is a must, but a general handyman can do this kind of work, so you don't need to be a plumber. It could help to take some plumbing training. See your local adult education classes or one of the private training businesses (details below).

PROS

This kind of work normally only requires a handyman with a bit of extra knowledge of drains – so you don't need to be an experienced plumber. It is also quite well paid considering the level of skill needed.

CONS

It's not a fun job, and you will often have to deal with sewage and the other joys that come with drains. You can only do this kind of work if you can handle – let's not mince words – muck. Not really that big a deal, but worth considering, especially if you're also unblocking toilets and sinks.

USEFUL CONTACTS

www.plumbworld.co.uk – all the equipment for all kinds of plumbing jobs you never knew you needed

The PlumbSkill Centre – Highlea Farm, Witchampton, Wimborne Minster, Dorset BH21 5AA – private training in all aspects of plumbing, 01258 841441, www.plumbskill.co.uk

Fast Track – Unit 8, Penraevon Industrial Estate, Meanwood Road, Leeds LS7 2AW – private training in all aspects of plumbing, 07709 186715, www.plumbtraining.co.uk

Fence-erecting and treating

You will get more of this kind of work in the country or suburbs than in cities, but there is always a demand for it all over Britain.

HOW TO DO IT

If you have some experience in the field, your first task is simply to walk around your locality and gauge whether or not there are sufficient gardens to make your business worthwhile. To target customers you can then drop leaflets into the households that may be interested and advertise in your local press and in shops.

You will need to be a good carpenter and handyman and also be able to do basic painting and decorating. It will also help to develop good relationships with local timber merchants so that you can buy pre-cut wood at a discount which you can then make a profit on when you sell it to your customers. If you go in for fence-painting as well you will need compressors and paint guns to do a proper job.

Your customers will be responsible for the legality of the fence but it will help if you can advise them on whether they should contact their local council or not. Planning permission is required if you want to erect a fence higher than 1 metre (3 feet 3 inches) which fronts a public road. Permission is also required for any fencing higher than 2 metres (6 feet).

You will need to know what kind of fences are safe and which are not in different situations. For example, will the fence be exposed to high winds? All fences, particularly those 1.2 metres (4 feet) or higher, require very sturdy posts. An open fence – for example, chain-link – is stronger in high winds as it offers little resistance.

'I get a lot of fence-painting work in what I call barbecue weather,' says Sean Carney of Teesside Fence Care. 'That's between June and August when people are out in their gardens a lot and they want the fence to look nice.'

HOW MUCH CAN YOU MAKE?

'It depends on the work involved,' says Sean Carney. 'Each job is priced individually: it depends on the ground, what needs to be done and the size of the fence. The least I charge is £38 to £50 for one post, but for a whole fence it goes by yardage rather than hours. A 30-foot fence would be about £200, but it depends on the area and the style you want.'

Carney also treats fences and charges between £120 and £200 each time. 'If you look after a fence and treat it once every two years it'll last a lifetime,' he says. 'Untreated fences will disintegrate after about five years.'

COSTS

You will need a van and basic tools, and if you are going to offer a fence-painting service as well you will need to part with at least £1,000 for the compressors and electric guns.

TRAINING AND QUALIFICATIONS

Although there are all sorts of relevant courses, the best qualification for this specialised job is experience of similar work.

PROS

Once you're confident in doing the work it is fairly straight-forward. It's a great job if you like the outdoors, and also a good chance to meet people.

CONS

The work can be very seasonal with less business in winter. You have to be prepared to work in all weathers.

USEFUL CONTACTS

www.gardeningdata.co.uk – information on fence erection

Teesside Fence Care, 01287 635580, www.fencecare.co.uk

Door-to-door security

An unusual earner, but you don't have to be a locksmith to do it.

HOW TO DO IT

In such an age of fear, you'd be surprised how few people have spyholes and door chains in their homes. Advertising in the local press may well bring in some business, but probably the best way to get a good number of jobs per day would be to go round and talk to people about it face to face. For back-up there's usually a recent article in the local press with a scare story about burglaries in the area.

Contact manufacturers to find out bulk prices for spyholes and door chains so that you can buy them cheaply and make money on the package as a whole. With a drill and the basic accessories of spyholes and door chains you can get the job done quickly without entering the house. It does help, though, if you don't look like a criminal!

If you get established you may be asked to work on locks too. Locksmithing requires some training to start with, so contact the Master Locksmiths Association (contact details below) about their courses and services.

HOW MUCH CAN YOU MAKE?

This depends on how good you are at selling your service and doing the job. If you charge £10–£15 per job, you can see that you'd need around ten jobs a day to make £100.

COSTS

Once you've paid for the drill and screwdrivers, these are fairly minimal. The cost of the spyholes and door chains will be passed on to the customer.

TRAINING AND QUALIFICATIONS

Although it would obviously help to have some kind of qualification or know-how in the building field, all you really need is confidence that you can do the job. If you move into locksmithing you will need proper training. A basic week's course run by the Master Locksmiths Association costs around £1,200.

PROS

You can decide your own hours, you get instant money for your labours and, aside from all this, you're providing a useful service to your local community.

CONS

You need to be prepared for a lot of rejection and sometimes even abuse if you are going round door to door. You also need to accept that you will have some very slow days, so it helps if you're not the type of person who'll be affected by this.

USEFUL CONTACTS

Banham, www.banham.com

The Lockshop Warehouse, www.lockshop-warehouse.co.uk

Master Locksmiths Association, www.locksmiths.co.uk

Yale, www.yale.co.uk

Property manager

It's really hard to find a good managing agent who will look after residential property. If you're organised, efficient, honest and rather handy yourself, you could be in demand.

HOW TO DO IT

It helps to have contacts with estate agents, lettings agents and people who live in blocks of flats or houses that have been turned into flats, because most of the work you will get in this area will be through personal recommendations.

As a property manager you will be responsible for setting and collecting the quarterly or annual service charge from residents. You will also be responsible for the general maintenance of the block – organising plumbers, decorators, electricians, builders, roofers, etc., where needed, and paying them out of the service charge.

Of course, if you can do these jobs yourself – and the residents are in agreement – you can undertake the work and charge the full amount to the house, rather than paying outside workers. On the other hand, if there are too many demands on your time this can become very annoying. 'I've spent the last two years fixing boilers and washing machines,' says an ex-property manager who just got fed up with the job and handed it over to a friend.

HOW MUCH CAN YOU MAKE?

Property managers tend to charge 10–15 per cent of the total annual service charge, so how much you make each year depends on the number of residents, the size of the property and the service charge.

COSTS

You will probably have to do some phoning and travelling to and from the property. Otherwise the only costs will be materials if you do some or all of the repairs yourself.

TRAINING AND QUALIFICATIONS

You don't need any training or qualifications, but if you are a trained and qualified electrician, plumber or other building professional this will really help.

PROS

There is a big demand for this, especially in large cities, and if you undertake the maintenance work yourself you could make some reasonable money.

CONS

It can be very annoying work, particularly if one is rung up in the small hours of the morning by a resident complaining about burst pipes and so on. If you don't undertake the maintenance work yourself it can be hard to make much money. You may have to spend a lot of time supervising others and arguing with residents about non-payment of service charges.

USEFUL CONTACTS

The Association of Residential Letting Agents, 0845 345 5752, www.arla.co.uk

Inventing

For some reason, Britons are particularly inventive. A large proportion of world inventions were thought up by Brits, although we are less good at manufacturing and marketing them – it's the Americans and Japanese who do that! If you have a good idea for a gadget, game or even a new food, you could make money out of it.

HOW TO DO IT

If you have a brilliant idea for a new gadget or similar, you could make a lot of money – eventually. But although inventing something could bring in thousands in the long run, you will have to spend a lot of money at the start. The most important thing is to patent the idea so that no one can steal it from you. 'Once you're sure you have an idea that no one has come up with before, you will have to patent it in Britain and probably in the US, Europe and Japan too,' explains marketing executive Jeremy Philpott at the Patent Office. 'In Britain it will just cost you around £2,000, but it will cost about £50,000 to cover all the other countries.'

If you think you've got a brilliant idea, get in touch with the Association of Patentees and Inventors. They will help you through the many stages you need to go through to get your invention considered by manufacturers, including finding a proper patent agent, where to go to get a prototype of your invention made, and how to get manufacturers to look at it.

It may also be possible to get a grant to cover the development, manufacture and marketing of your prototype. How much you might get depends on where you live, what your product is and whether the local grant provider has any money left! Selling an invention can take years, so don't lose heart.

HOW MUCH CAN YOU MAKE?

Anything from nothing at all (in fact, it could cost you money) to hundreds of thousands if it really takes off.

COSTS

Setting up the patents can cost from £2,000 to £50,000. There may be costs involved in creating a prototype, which could be anything from £1,000 upward. You may also have marketing and sales costs to get the idea off the ground. It's possible that you could get a grant to cover some of your costs, however.

TRAINING AND QUALIFICATIONS

You don't need training or qualifications for this.

PROS

If you have an idea that works you may never have to work again – just sit back and enjoy the royalties!

CONS

It can take years of frustration, hard work and high costs to get an invention off the ground, and even then you are not necessarily guaranteed success.

USEFUL CONTACTS

Association of Patentees and Inventors, 020 8541 4197, www.invent.org.uk

Institute of Inventors, www.newgadgets.freeserve.co.uk – a voluntary, non-profit inventors' club, run by unpaid volunteer professional engineer inventors

The Patent Office, 01372 363386, www.patent.gov.uk

www.workingmodel.co.uk – provides feasibility studies, first-prototyping services and promotional opportunities to inventors and small businesses

---

Case study

Full-time mother Kerry Williams, who lives in Wales, won second prize in the 1999 Female Inventors Awards for her seat-belt safety clip. 'I got the idea when I was driving on the M5 and my two-year-old son kept undoing his seat belt,' she explains. 'I had to stop twice to do it back up, and after the second time I had a head-on collision. If I hadn't bothered to stop and strap him in again, I know he would have gone through the windscreen. I then looked for a device to stop this happening and I couldn't find one anywhere so I made my own, quite simply, out of things – a cardboard box from Sainsbury's and Sellotape! – I had in the house.'

It took three years between coming up with the design and actually getting it into the shops. Now, six years after the initial idea, and having spent £6,000 on patents, making prototypes and other costs, Kerry says that whatever she earns from now on will be pure profit.

Work abroad

All right, this isn't exactly a 'bit on the side' – more of a full-time commitment. But if you're serious about needing to make some reasonable money in a short amount of time, there are many jobs abroad that pay high rates and don't give you much opportunity to spend.

HOW TO DO IT

There are various jobs abroad that you could consider. If you are a nanny or a nurse and have experience of babies you could work as a maternity nurse for a family. This means you will be working, or at least 'on call', for 24 hours a day, six days a week, caring for all the baby's needs. Maternity nurse jobs are typically anything from two weeks to three months long. The money is good – you can earn between £600 and £1,500 a week depending on who you work for and how many babies are involved (twins and triplets will earn you more, of course). Nanny agency Top Notch Nannies regularly places nannies and maternity nurses in temporary and permanent jobs abroad. 'Many foreign jobs are far better paid than those over here,' says Leanne Royeppen from the agency. 'We have some maternity nurses who do a highly paid job in, say, the Middle East, and then take a month or so off because they can afford it.'

There are also highly paid construction, engineering and other types of work all over the world, particularly the Middle East. Just a quick glance at the jobs on the website www. expatsdirect.com shows that there are many and varied jobs abroad, particularly for those with high levels of qualifications or experience in construction, engineering and management.

The publisher of the website, Dave Smith, says, 'The majority of the vacancies that we receive are for professionally qualified and senior personnel within the petrochemical/ engineering, construction and mining industries or positions that require extensive experience and qualifications.' At the time of writing jobs advertised on the website include, for example, an operations and maintenance manager in Indonesia, a quantity surveyor in Libya, a push-pull pickling-line supervisor in Saudi Arabia, a contract engineer in Japan, a weld inspector in Qatar, and an instrument supervisor in Egypt.

For these kinds of jobs you will need a very good CV (the website has advice on how to create a good CV) and a willingness to leave home and work in countries that can be dangerous or, at the very least, culturally very different from your own. Jobs tend to last at least six months and many posts require you to sign a contract that will oblige you to stay one or two years minimum.

HOW MUCH CAN YOU MAKE?

It can be thousands a month if you get the right job, and usually there is little time or opportunity to spend it where you are living so this can be a *very* good way of making a lot of money relatively quickly and experiencing a new culture.

COSTS

Mainly your travel costs and possibly accommodation and subsistence, although many jobs include all this.

TRAINING AND QUALIFICATIONS

You will need to be at least experienced, if you are going as a nanny or construction worker, and in many cases training and qualifications in your chosen field are essential to getting the job.

PROS

You can often make significant amounts of money in these foreign jobs. Also, often you are not tempted to spend what you earn, so you can accumulate money quite quickly.

CONS

It can be lonely, boring and tiring doing these jobs. You are away from your family and friends for long periods of time and you could find yourself in difficult or dangerous situations. You can also be treated without respect or kindness in many of these positions.

USEFUL CONTACTS

Expats Direct Limited, Stockton Business Centre, 70 Brunswick Street, Stockton-on-Tees, TS18 1DW, 01642 730822, www.expatsdirect.com

Top Notch Nannies, 020 7244 6053, www.topnotchnannies.com – regularly has work abroad for experienced nannies and maternity nurses

CHAPTER EIGHT

Could You Teach?

'THOSE WHO CAN'T, TEACH,' they say, but actually those that can, also teach. If you have a lot of knowledge in an area that other people want to learn about you could make money teaching them. And you don't necessarily need a teaching qualification to do it.

Computer training

If you have knowledge of anything computer-related you can teach. Computer whizzes are needed to train people at home and also to troubleshoot for those experiencing problems with their computers.

HOW TO DO IT

There are a couple of ways you could go about this – either teach in other people's homes or have them come to you in your own premises. For the former, the best place to advertise is probably local publications such as *Loot* and the *Friday Ad*, while if you're offering a more formal service from your own home you might get more of a response from adverts placed in schools and colleges.

Advertising in a college, school or adult education centre will be a great way of targeting your audience, so it's worth going to these places, finding out the areas in which pupils generally need help, and tailoring a course to meet these requirements. In fact, if a school or college is really behind in one area of computer science you might actually be able to come to an agreement with the head teacher that he will help publicise your course (through letters home, for example) in return for low prices – and of course the promise that you'll improve the pupils' competence with computers.

If you're targeting an older age group you can set up some adult learning courses at your local college (see 'Adult evening classes', p. 227).

HOW MUCH CAN YOU MAKE?

Depending on your area, and the amount your prospective customers can afford, you could realistically charge between £7 and £30 an hour per student for a class of pupils. You can obviously put your price up a bit for one-to-one training. Another approach is to charge a fixed price of anything between £40 and £300 for a comprehensive guide to a specific area of computer training. Guides to more specialist software such as Photoshop or Cubase are currently being advertised at around £300 pounds for a couple of days' training!

COSTS

To make your service stand out, you will probably have to go beyond the free adverts in your local press and take out something more eye-catching. It would also be useful to produce a course guide and some notes for students to use at home, so don't forget to include items such as paper and ink in your expenses.

TRAINING AND QUALIFICATIONS

Computing is an area in which a lot of people with an aptitude for technology seem to learn more on their own than they would from formal training. Thus, you may feel that although you have no qualifications in the area, your line of work, or even simple enthusiasm for what you're teaching, has itself led you to become highly proficient. It is, however, worth going on some kind of course to make sure that your own knowledge is as comprehensive as you think. After all, it's better to discover the gaps in your knowledge before you start teaching than to find out as you go along.

PROS

Our sudden dependency on technology means there are a lot of older people who are in need of training to make up for missing out in their school years. You can work from home, and it's something you can teach in classes if you want to make more money.

CONS

In addition to good communication skills, you need a lot of patience to teach – some of your students may not even know how to switch a computer on!

USEFUL CONTACTS

www.best.co.uk – a good site for finding computer training centres, should you want to brush up on your skills

To stay abreast of the latest computer news, problems and advice, it's great to speak with other computer experts on forums that you'll find on sites such as www.geekstogo.com, www.msfn.org and www.tech-forums.net

Fitness

Yoga, fitness or dance tuition can all be done either at local fitness clubs or dance centres or in your own home if you have room.

HOW TO DO IT

Leading a class of people requires more than energy and fitness alone – it takes confidence, leadership skills and a deep understanding of the particular exercise you're teaching. Yoga, for example, is a dynamic exercise, encompassing many different genres, and you can teach it in a variety of settings and for a range of purposes. For instance, teaching the elderly to increase their mobility will require a very different approach from teaching Ashtanga yoga to people wishing to lose weight. It is difficult to generalise about the types of practices to be used, as it depends greatly on the age and capacity of the class.

Once you've established your own area of expertise, and the type of people who would benefit from it, you can advertise in shops with cards or posters. The best place is probably health food shops in order to target more health-conscious people.

Alternatively you can approach establishments such as colleges, health centres and gyms to negotiate a deal from which you can both benefit. A gym, for example, might offer you some good publicity and a rent-free space in return for a percentage of the profits you make.

HOW MUCH CAN YOU MAKE?

While your fees will vary in different areas according to what locals are willing to pay, it's reasonable to ask for £3–£5 per student per session and £10–£20 for a one-to-one session.

COSTS

In addition to advertising costs, you may be paying rent or a hiring fee within a gym, for a hall, or for your own studio. Alternatively, you might like to set up your own home studio. While yoga requires only appropriate space, an even floor and some mats, other fitness classes such as aerobics really call for a studio on the ground floor (or strong floorboards) and a location in which fairly loud music would be feasible.

TRAINING AND QUALIFICATIONS

If you're considering teaching, you'll probably already be competent in yoga, fitness or dance – but proper training is essential. In addition to knowing how to do it yourself, you've got to be able to communicate effectively with others, assess their levels of flexibility and avoid anyone injuring themselves.

PROS

It's a worthwhile cause, and if you enjoy yoga you can stay fit yourself at the same time.

CONS

Even the most well-trained professionals can be held responsible for causing injury to their students, should they hurt themselves during a class.

USEFUL CONTACTS

Atayananda Yoga Centre, Satyananda Yoga Centre, 70 Thurleigh Road, London SW12 8UD, 020 8673 4869, www.syclondon.com

Kevala Centre for Holistic Health, 1 Courtenay Park, Newton Abbot, Devon TQ1 2HD, 01803 215678, www.kevala.co.uk – their yoga teacher's course has been designed for students with at least intermediate-level experience of yoga who wish to formalise their knowledge

Case study

TV producer Amanda Robbins, teaches yoga in central London at evenings, weekends and even lunchtimes.

'Because I work in central London I can just pop out to Covent Garden and teach a lunchtime class quite easily,' she explains. 'I also teach at a health club some evenings.' Teaching at a private gym, Amanda can earn £30–40 for an hour and a half. At local authority gyms she gets £17.50 an hour. There is quite a lot of work available in gyms, but if she wanted more work she would simply increase her advertising and set up more classes.

'Once I get a really loyal following, I'll set up private classes at home,' she says. 'I have friends who have converted their loft or spare room into a studio. You only need to be able to fit in five or six students and that would be enough for a good class. I could clear £50–£60 for an hour's teaching that way and I wouldn't need to go anywhere.'

Tutoring

What do you know that others need to know? Perhaps you're bilingual and could give language lessons, or you're a musician and could teach others to play. Whatever your subject, you can teach people in groups or one to one and charge by the hour. The amount you can earn will vary depending on the subject, the number of people in the class and where you live, but can be from £10–£100 or more per hour.

HOW TO DO IT

Anyone can put themselves forward as a tutor of anything. Just a postcard in the window of your local newsagent or library could attract interest. Whatever your specialist area, you could be a tutor in it: musical instruments, languages, fitness or alternative therapies are all popular.

But if you want to do it through an agency or local adult education centre, you may need a teaching qualification. 'Most of our tutors have at least one teaching qualification and are often teachers or professors right now,' says a spokeswoman from tutoring agency Gabbitas. Trained tutors are often needed by families for help with reading or enabling children to get up to speed in a subject they're poor at.

If you have a knowledge of a subject such as English or maths, you can approach schools and colleges with an outline of a revision course that relates to their curriculum and ask them to make their students aware of it. With the pressure of league tables in mind, they may be very grateful for the additional help. It may even be that they will provide you with a classroom from which to work. If, however, you will only be teaching a few people who are struggling in a particular subject, you could easily work from home or offer to go to the students' houses. Tutors with strong maths and science are particularly in demand as fewer people go into teaching these subjects.

If you want to do private tutoring in the evenings or at weekends, advertise your services in local libraries, newsagents' windows, local papers and even parenting magazines.

HOW MUCH CAN YOU MAKE?

Prices range from around £10 to £20 per hour, with the most common hourly rate being around £15. For more comprehensive courses, though, where you're effectively offering to teach a complete subject (revision of the entire year's syllabus, for example), you could set up a day at a fixed price of, say, £20–£30.

COSTS

Your costs are likely to be fairly minimal since you can teach a lot of subjects from your own home, or by going to your clients' homes. Don't forget, however, to take paper, ink and so on into account if you intend to make up your own revision notes or books.

TRAINING AND QUALIFICATIONS

While you really do need a qualification in the subject you're teaching, to sell yourself if nothing else, it is also very important to understand the syllabus that the students are studying at the time. You can get a clear idea of this by liaising with schools or even from simply studying past exam papers, which are available in most bookshops.

PROS

You make money from the worthwhile cause of helping people learn new skills.

CONS

You need a lot of patience and you might get into disputes about whether or not your course is worth doing or lives up to students' expectations, and so on. Some people love to complain.

USEFUL CONTACTS

Gabbitas, Carrington House, 126–130 Regent Street, London W1B 5EE, 020 7734 0161, www.gabbitas.net

Personal Tutors, Cheadle House, Cheadle, Cheshire SK8 1AH, 0161 428 2285, www.personal-tutors.co.uk

www.2utorsearch.co.uk – the UK's private tutors' directory, worth registering with

Adult evening classes

If you have expertise in something that you know other people want to learn, why not make some money out of it?

HOW TO DO IT

Your first step is to find a suitable location from which you can work. Working from home might be a possibility, but you will obviously come across as far more professional if you can get a space within a school, college or university.

The best way to do this is by approaching these directly, perhaps by doing a mailshot to all the educational institutions in your locality, detailing your expertise, experience and qualifications, together with a brief plan for the course you want to teach. It is often the case that if you are accepted by the college or university you will only be able to teach your class if enough students are interested.

228 • A BIT ON THE SIDE

If successful, you could end up with some free publicity through a listing in their prospectus, but because class numbers are usually crucial to even getting started it's a good idea to advertise through posters and cards in shop windows around the time you need to sign people up.

HOW MUCH CAN YOU MAKE?

While this does vary depending on how in demand your skill is, it would be reasonable to charge around £10 per student per session for smaller classes; £5 would be more realistic if you're teaching quite a few people at one time. In any case, you need to research the costs of other evening classes in your area to make sure you don't under- or over-sell your own services. If you are working under the auspices of a university, however, the chances are that they will simply pay you an hourly rate of around £15–£20, taking a profit from the students for themselves.

COSTS

While you may think your main costs will be advertising and hiring a room, don't forget about the course materials you'll probably have to produce. Keep track of all the paper, ink and folders you use in the process.

TRAINING AND QUALIFICATIONS

It's always a good advertisement if you actually have a relevant qualification that you can quote. In some areas, such as art, acting or music, relevant experience and proof of your own success are sometimes better.

PROS

You're utilising your expertise to make money and helping others at the same time. Because all the students are also likely to be employed, you can do this out of normal working hours.

CONS

Because you will be designing the courses yourself, you've got to take the flak if anyone wants to complain that it isn't worth the money.

USEFUL CONTACTS

Floodlight, www.floodlight.co.uk – a listing of all the adult education courses in London

www.nightcourses.com – an Irish website that includes a section where you can submit the details of the course you're running

Case study

Marc Blake is a writer and comedian in West London. He teaches comedy and sitcom writing at the City University during term times on Monday and Tuesday evenings.

After years of working as a sitcom writer, Marc felt that he wasn't getting enough advice within the industry owing to the time pressures on script editors. Seeing a niche in the market, he sent his idea for a course to guide upcoming scriptwriters to as many colleges and universities as he could find.

Gaining interest from City University and later Kensington College, he was offered a teaching spot, including a prospectus listing and assistance with course materials and handouts.

'While you can get some people who react badly to criticism of their work, the job is very rewarding the majority of the time', he says. 'It's a great feeling to know you're helping people get started in the competitive industry of scriptwriting.'

Dog-training

Who says you just have to stick to teaching humans? If you love animals and you can handle people too, there's a whole world of possibilities in the animal-training area.

HOW TO DO IT

If you are knowledgeable about dog-training and have a good success rate in the field, you can either run classes that teach owners how to train their dogs, or simply offer to train the animals one at a time yourself. The first step is obviously to gain some experience, but once you are confident there are many ways in which you can advertise to reach a target audience.

As well as skills in handling dogs, you also need to be an excellent people person, as a lot of your business will come from word of mouth, through vets and existing customers. You will also have to be insured – both personally and professionally – and keep your health and safety info up to date. You should have human first-aid training and also basic dog first-aid abilities.

While you can simply hire a hall, it's best to have your own premises since it conveys a more professional image and also allows you to advertise other services, including pet accommodation while people are on holiday.

HOW MUCH CAN YOU MAKE?

You can charge dog owners something in the region of £4–£8 per session if they just want to come along to the odd class, or you could charge them a membership fee for a few months which would allow them to attend any class free of charge. A reasonable price for training a dog for an entire day would be around £15.

If, however, you intend to offer a more intensive course that includes accommodation and food for the dogs, you could ask for about £100–£150 per week. Carolyn Menteith, a professional dog-trainer and one of the *This Morning* programme's 'Barking Babes', says, 'Like all jobs working with animals, dog-training is a labour of love! There is little money in animals (in this country anyway) unless you are a vet.'

COSTS

Professional insurance for one person running classes or giving private lessons will be around £500 a year. If you are also insuring the premises, it will be more. If you are using your own facilities, you will have to approach the local council about potential change of usage. In other words, the setting-up costs can be substantial!

Online shopping can save you money if you're buying a lot of dog-training equipment; www.doggiesolutions.co.uk, for example, has specialist training tools such as bark control collars and training toys that can be delivered to your door at very reasonable prices.

TRAINING AND QUALIFICATIONS

Because dog owners are paying for someone who knows what they're doing, you do need some kind of training. The Academy of Dog Trainers, for example, offers a range of courses, along with advice on how to start up as a dog-trainer yourself.

While there is no requirement for any formal qualifications as yet, this is something that seems likely to change in the near future, with the introduction of the Kennel Club Accreditation Scheme (www.the-kennel-club.org.uk).

PROS

It's a great job if you love animals. You'll be helping dog owners cultivate better-behaved animals.

CONS

There will be difficult animals to deal with at times. As Carolyn Menteith says, 'We are not just talking cute cuddly puppies or nice family dogs, we are talking slavering Rottweilers and defensively aggressive German shepherds, etc.' (because ultimately these are the sorts of dogs people decide to bring to training classes).

USEFUL CONTACTS

www.dogtraining-online.co.uk – offers a range of courses in dog-training for those who want to brush up on their skills

Academy of Dog-training and Behaviour – 7 Chillingham Court, High Grange, Billingham, Cleveland, TS23 3UT 01642 860265, www.dogtrainingonline.co.uk

The Kennel Club – 1 Clarges Street, London W1J 8AB, 0870 606 6750, www.the-kennel-club.co.uk

English as a Foreign Language

You speak the language – or your version of it anyway – so you might be able to teach it. Some do it without training or qualifications although it's much harder to get into without some relevant certificate now.

HOW TO DO IT

Your first step is to go on a course, such as the well-known Teaching English as a Foreign Language (TEFL). Although it is very common for students to then go on to teach abroad, there are a lot of opportunities at colleges and community and language centres within the UK.

Alternatively, you could also teach children in primary and secondary schools who may need support in the classroom or individual tuition. In recent years there has been an increase in the provision of instruction on a one-to-one and small-group basis, sometimes in the home, for adult migrants.

Typical activities include planning, preparing and delivering lessons and workshops for groups and individuals and carrying out assessments of students' needs.

Once you are qualified, the best way to get started is to simply apply for jobs on websites such as www.tefl.co.uk or advertise in your local press or in colleges and shops, letting people know that you offer an informal class in your own home for locals keen to brush up on their English. If you live in a seaside town or a large city you probably have several schools that teach English to foreigners so just walking in and offering your services could be all you need to do to get regular work.

HOW MUCH CAN YOU MAKE?

This is best for people who are looking to travel the world, as a lot of schemes will offer you board and lodgings with fairly minimal pay to allow you to travel without having to save up for a long time in advance.

Working in the UK, you are likely to receive an hourly rate of about £6–£10 from your employer; if you run your own classes, you could charge about £5 per hour, per student.

COSTS

The cost of a TEFL or TESOL (teaching of English to speakers of other languages) course will be between £180 and £260, depending on which one you choose. You then need to sort out your own travel arrangements.

TRAINING AND QUALIFICATIONS

The usual route to teaching English as a foreign language is to do a TEFL or TESOL course which take place all over the country. You can even complete the TEFL course entirely online by going to www.onlinetefl.com. You don't need any other qualifications to actually get on to a course, although you must be over 17.

PROS

An ability to teach English allows you to travel the world and make money at the same time.

CONS

You have to be prepared for difficult students occasionally.

USEFUL CONTACTS

www.englishtc.co.uk – offers advice and resources for going on a TEFL or TESOL course in the UK

ITC, Jabel House, Hurworth, Co. Durham DL2 2AJ, 01325 721066, www.tefl.co.uk – offers intensive training courses in teaching English; here you can find courses, fees, jobs and venues across the world

Exam-marking

Many teachers and lecturers, both active and retired, boost their income by marking GCSE and other exam papers. It's a useful way of squeezing extra cash out of something you already know how to do.

HOW TO DO IT

The exam business is a seasonal one, with exams spread over four main parts of the year. Most marking is done in June and the rest in January, March and November, although the exam boards recruit throughout the year.

The bulk of examiners are employed for the summer. While an examiner might be lucky enough to receive one other batch of marking during the year, the fact that exams are taken at different times means that no examiner will get four contracts in twelve months.

Marking usually takes three or four weeks, for which the examiner will be paid something in the range of £800–£1,000. The number of scripts involved varies from subject to subject, as does the payment per script. Some subjects are tougher to mark, so examiners are paid more for each script but given fewer of them.

Training is provided for new examiners and all examiners have to attend a standardisation meeting for each contract. This is to ensure that they all mark to the same levels.

HOW MUCH CAN YOU MAKE?

Between £800 and £1,000 over three or four weeks.

COSTS

Nothing except your time – assuming you already have your own computer for online marking. Training days are free and most exam boards will pay you if you have to miss a day of teaching. You should get travel expenses too.

TRAINING AND QUALIFICATIONS

You must be fully qualified in the subject you are examining and ideally have teaching experience in it. Computer literacy is becoming increasingly important too, as many examiners are now required to work online.

New examiners aren't thrown in at the deep end without a lifebelt. Most exam boards run training days where new examiners are taught the fundamentals of standardised marking, so that students are treated equally. In addition, examiners are monitored throughout the marking process.

PROS

Three or four weeks will earn you enough to take a holiday! Being an examiner looks good on your CV and will improve your teaching: there's nothing like marking 300 scripts to help you realise what examiners like and dislike. Then you can pass that knowledge on to your students. It also gives you a valuable overview of the subject and how other people teach it, and the training sessions provide valuable networking opportunities. Oh yes, and you can work at home, where the coffee is probably better than at work.

CONS

The work comes in short, sharp, concentrated bursts – 500 pieces of work is a lot to get through in three or four weeks. Self-discipline and effective time management are a must. Don't leave it all to the last minute.

USEFUL CONTACTS

The following exam board websites are good sources of information:

Assessment Qualifications Alliance, www.aqa.org.uk

Council for the Curriculum Examination Assessment: N. Ireland, www.ccea.org.uk

Edexcel, www.edexcel.org.uk (an awarding body that provides academic and vocational qualifications)

Oxford, Cambridge and RSA Examinations, www.ocr.org.uk

Welsh Joint Education Committee, www.wjec.org.uk

CHAPTER NINE

Therapies

THERAPIES OF ALL KINDS are becoming increasingly popular, and 'alternative' therapies are becoming so established that they are even accepted in some doctors' surgeries. There are lots of different sorts to choose, from 'hands-on' therapies to face-to-face mental and emotional help.

Counselling

Incredibly, anyone can become a counsellor. There are very few checks. If you think you have the personality for it, however, it would help to get some training first!

HOW TO DO IT

If you think you have what it takes to help people through periods of change and development, counselling can be a very rewarding occupation. Your aim is to help people change destructive thought patterns and behaviour while also respecting their capacity to find their own solutions.

Although there are no statutory regulations for counsellors, if you really do have the patients' best interests at heart you will do as most others do and work towards becoming an accredited member of a relevant professional association, such as the

British Association for Counselling and Psychotherapy (BACP). Apart from anything else, being a member will help you find paid work.

There is a huge range of courses and books on the subject, so choosing which to follow is just a matter of the time you have to spare and finding the teaching principles that resonate with your own. Many therapists have specialist areas: alcoholism, addiction or depression, for example.

Once you have qualified it is a question of advertising your services on the Net, in specialist magazines and, most of all, through word of mouth. This is definitely a job where personal recommendation works best.

HOW MUCH CAN YOU MAKE?

Counsellors tend to charge around £30–£70 per hour.

COSTS

Once you're trained, costs are fairly minimal, the only real expense being travel, if it's necessary.

TRAINING AND QUALIFICATIONS

Voluntary work is available from a range of organisations, such as Alcohol Concern, the Samaritans, Relate, Cruse and Mind, and in return for your time, many will provide you with free training. Once you are qualified, there are many routes you can take, either setting up your own practice from home or taking on some hours in schools, colleges, organisations for people with disabilities or agencies connected with alcohol, drugs and AIDS.

While there are a lot of part-time hours available, competition for full-time jobs is far higher, and you will normally need some formal qualifications to apply for these posts.

PROS

Pursued well, this is a truly worthwhile profession and one that is very rewarding.

CONS

It can be very stressful to be on the receiving end of negative thoughts all day, and training is needed to deal with people who are emotionally unstable and capable of venting their rage in your direction.

USEFUL CONTACTS

British Association for Counselling and Psychotherapy (BACP), 1 Regent Place, Rugby, Warwickshire CV21 2PJ, 0870 443 5252, www.bacp.co.uk

Confederation of Scottish Counselling Agencies (COSCA), 18 Viewfield Street, Stirling FK8 1UA, 01786 475 140, www.cosca.org.uk

United Kingdom Council for Psychotherapy (UKCP), 167–169 Great Portland St, London W1W 5PF, 020 7436 3002, www.psychotherapy.org.uk

Beautician

Freelance beauty work is fun to do and there's a big demand, particularly for weddings and seasonal parties.

HOW TO DO IT

The services of a beautician are wide-ranging and include offering treatments such as facials, makeovers, manicures, pedicures, hair removal, and various other skin and body treatments. Many will also have some knowledge in other areas, such as hairdressing or massage. In addition to these skills, you'll also need to be good with people to put them at their ease – especially if you offer bikini waxing!

While a lot of beauticians operate in salons, working from your own home has the advantage of privacy for clients and can encourage customer loyalty since it is a more friendly environment.

Another very good idea, to introduce larger groups of people to beauty therapy, is to advertise beauty parties, whereby you go to women's houses so that they and their friends can have their treatments together. You can also offer a special wedding package – some freelance beauticians *only* do weddings – in which for one all-in price you make up the bride, bridesmaids and bride's mother, as well as perhaps offering a soothing massage.

For most beauty work you will need qualifications, but there are some aspects, such as manicures and pedicures, that need very little training, so if you have done your own and others' nails for years to good effect you could make money doing them for strangers, particularly if you undercut the normal commercial rate. If you have skills in manicuring you can make a big profit on fitting people's false nails.

HOW MUCH CAN YOU MAKE?

Beauticians coming to your home tend to charge between £35 and £75 per hour, depending on what the treatment is.

COSTS

It'll take some time to get an idea of the products you'll be using most, so get some advice on stock. If you're working from home, rather than spending money on premises, you'll actually be able to save money by claiming back some tax to pay for a proportion of your rent or mortgage, heating and electricity.

TRAINING AND QUALIFICATIONS

Courses in the area of beauty therapy are widespread, ranging from nail technology to henna hand-painting. By having a qualification such as a BTEC or National Diploma, you'll feel more confident and be far more aware of potential problems and how to cope with them. For instance, it's important to know about various skin conditions for which you may have to refer your customers to a doctor.

PROS

You can work from your own home during hours that suit you. The bond you build with customers means that they are likely to come back if they feel at ease and you get on well.

CONS

You have to be careful who you let into your house – especially if you're living alone. You may need to keep advertising for work as beauty clients are not always that regular.

USEFUL CONTACTS

British Association of Beauty Therapy and Cosmetology Ltd, BABTAC House, 70 Eastgate Street, Gloucester GL1 1QN, 01452 421114, www.babtac.com

Hairdressing and Beauty Industry Authority (HABIA) Fraser House, Nether Hall Rd, Doncaster DN1 2PH, 01302 3800 00, www.habia.org.uk

International Therapy Examination Council (ITEC), 10–11 Heathfield Terrace, Chiswick, London W4 4JE, 020 8994 4141, www.itecworld.co.uk

Case study

Jo Lear used to be a make-up artist for MAC and other companies before becoming a full-time mother in South London. Now she just offers two services: wedding make-up and individual make-up lessons. 'It's easier to just do those two because I know I can organise childcare,' she says. 'I can't just drop everything at two minutes' notice and do a photo-shoot any more, but doing weddings or individual lessons is fine because they're booked in advance and I know where I am.'

Jo charges from £150 for wedding make-up, which involves her helping the bride and bridesmaids in the morning and, if

➤

they need it, staying around for touch-ups during the photo-graphs. For make-up lessons she charges £75 for two hours if working from home but more if she goes to the client's home.

'It's perfect, really,' she says. 'I can pick and choose my work, although of course I'm very busy during the wedding season – June to August.' Clients contact Jo by email at nickyandjo@btinternet.com or sometimes by phone. 'I could work through agents but I don't need to,' she says. 'I get enough work on my own.'

Hairdressing

You can only really do freelance hairdressing if you are trained. If you do have a background in it, however, it can be a terrifically flexible way of making money.

HOW TO DO IT

There's more to hairdressing than just cutting hair – professionals can colour, perm, set and style using a range of products and techniques. Another consideration is that you have to be good with people and be able to chat while you're styling customers' hair.

You don't actually need any formal qualifications but you do need training so that you become competent at the basics before going on to specialise in an area such as Afro-Caribbean hair or barbering.

The first thing you need is a well-lit area equipped with mirrors and a basin where customers will feel at ease. Cutting the hair of friends may be fine in your front room, but for a new clientele it's important to look professional, so ideally you will either work from a studio or create one in your home.

Many clients will pay extra for a hairdresser to come to their home. This is a good way of making money because you can charge salon fees – people appreciate having a salon-type level of service without the nuisance of actually going to the hairdresser's.

Advertise your services locally and through word of mouth. If you are good, reasonably priced and reliable, you will get a lot of work.

HOW MUCH CAN YOU MAKE?

While this depends on your experience, where you are and the range of treatments you offer, generally a mobile hairdresser could charge from £15 for a wash and blow-dry to over £100 for a colour and cut in someone's home.

COSTS

Apart from the cost of your premises, you'll need to have a good stock of products.

TRAINING AND QUALIFICATIONS

You can gain NVQs/SVQs in hairdressing by attending a full-time or part-time course at a college or training centre. Courses usually last either one or two years.

Hairdressing trainees working towards NVQ/SVQ Level 1 in Hairdressing could assist qualified salon staff. Most trainees start at NVQ Level 2 in Hairdressing, which is the basic requirement to work as a junior stylist in a hairdressing salon.

NVQ Level 3 in Hairdressing is the industry-recognised standard for hairdressers and covers the more advanced salon techniques. Some colleges offer NVQ/SVQ units at Levels 2 and 3 in barbering or Afro-Caribbean hairdressing. Some colleges offer courses combining hairdressing with beauty therapy.

Once you are an experienced hairdresser, you can move on to train in salon management or even take a degree in beauty therapy. With these kinds of further qualifications you can go on to teach other people.

PROS

People need their hair cut all the time, and if you get on well with your customers and are good at your job you're likely to get a loyal customer base. Many people are happy to have their hair done at night if you work during the day.

CONS

You're on your feet all day and it could be difficult to build up your client base to start with.

USEFUL CONTACTS

Hairdressing and Beauty Industry Authority (HABIA), Fraser House, Nether Hall Road, Doncaster DN1 2PH, 01302 380000, www.habia.org.uk

Northern Ireland Hairdressers' Association, 221–223 Woodstock Rd, Belfast BT6 8PQ, 028 9045 5740

Massage

Massage is increasingly popular and there are now various different techniques to choose from.

HOW TO DO IT

Many massage therapists prefer to use an holistic approach, as they believe that emotional or personal problems lead to physical conditions such as stiffness or tension.

Common forms of massage include body massage (also known as Swedish massage), which deals with the whole body, especially the limbs and back. Other forms include Indian head massage, which incorporates the neck, shoulders, head and face. It is used for relaxation to relieve problems caused by stress or tension.

There are no set entry requirements for massage courses but GCSEs/S grades or equivalent qualifications in biology, anatomy, physiology and pathology are useful. These are often compulsory at higher levels.

Another very important aspect of the work is health and safety, and your own posture when working. This is why it's so important to do the proper courses before setting up on your own.

Once qualified you could work part-time in beauty therapy businesses or offer an in-office massage service. If you have a room in your home that could be converted into a massage studio, then you will need to advertise your services locally. You could also offer a service in clients' homes. Many busy professional men and women find it helpful to have a home massage once a week. If you are good and your prices are right you could get regular clients through word of mouth.

HOW MUCH CAN YOU MAKE?

Most massage therapists are self-employed. Charges will vary considerably – usually from £20 to £45 per hour depending on location and clients. Income is likely to be affected by business costs such as rent and materials.

COSTS

Apart from your possible studio costs, you will have to have a good stock of essential oils and perhaps even a uniform and some branded towels for a professional look.

TRAINING AND QUALIFICATIONS

Because you're dealing with possible injuries and medical conditions, it's very important to be qualified in what you do. While there are no qualifications legally required to work as a massage therapist, there are several awarding bodies offering courses within this field. Training will help you become a member of one of the professional bodies, such as the Federation of Holistic Therapists, the British Register of Complementary Practitioners or the Scottish Massage Therapists' Organisation. The Vocational Training Charitable Trust (VTCT) and the International Therapy Examination Council (ITEC) also offer massage courses at colleges of further or higher education and private centres throughout the UK. Contact the relevant body for further details.

PROS

Interest in massage and other complementary therapies has increased considerably in the last 20 years, and because of the personal nature of the job this is definitely an industry where you can build up a loyal customer base.

CONS

It could be difficult to get regular work until you are well known. You will also have the annoyance of being contacted by unsavoury men thinking you offer 'extra' services.

USEFUL CONTACTS

British Register of Complementary Practitioners, PO Box 194, London SE16 7QZ, 020 7237 5165, www.icmedicine.co.uk

Federation of Holistic Therapists, 3rd Floor, Eastleigh House, Upper Market Street, Eastleigh, Hants. SO50 9FD, 023 8048 8900, www.fht.org.uk

International Therapy Examination Council, 4 Heathfield Terrace, Chiswick, London W4 4JE, 020 8994 4141, www.itecworld.co.uk

Massage Training Institute, PO Box 44603, London N16 0XQ, 020 7254 7227, www.massagetraining.co.uk

Scottish Massage Therapists' Organisation, 24 Ellon Road, Bridge of Don, Aberdeen AB23 8BX, 01224 822956, www.scotmass.co.uk

Shiatsu Society, Eastlands Court, St Peters Road, Rugby CV21 3QP, 0845 130 4560, www.shiatsu.org

Vocational Training Charitable Trust, Unit 11, Brickfield Trading Estate, Chandler's Ford, Hants. SO53 4DR, 023 8027 1733, www.vtct.org.uk

Alternative therapies

There are many areas that fall into the category of alternative treatment. Hypnotherapy, aromatherapy and reflexology are some examples.

HOW TO DO IT

The aim with any kind of therapy is to work on the patient's problem in a controlled environment, often using techniques to distance the person from any fear they may be experiencing. With the best will in the world you will not be able to help people unless you are qualified in the technique.

So your first step should be to gain some kind of comprehensive qualification that is recognised in the industry. There are plenty of courses available. Many practitioners combine treatments, such as offering reiki along with aromatherapy, so it's important to shop around for the course that is exactly right for you.

The best places to advertise your services are in health food shops and local papers. Once you are more established you can take out an ad in the Yellow Pages and set up a website. At this stage, however, most of your work will come through word of mouth and repeat bookings. You could also make money by teaching the therapy once you have enough experience and have gained a further qualification that allows you to teach.

HOW MUCH CAN YOU MAKE?

Charges may be anything from £20 to £70 for a session lasting one to two hours. A lot of practitioners in alternative therapies are self-employed and incomes vary considerably. Most charge either a sessional or an hourly rate, usually ranging from £10 to £60 an hour, depending on the area in which they are working.

A newly qualified hypnotherapist earns from £15,000 to £20,000 a year. An experienced hypnotherapist earns £35,000 or more a year.

COSTS

A large part of your initial outlay is likely to be on acquiring the right training if you do not already have this.

TRAINING AND QUALIFICATIONS

Working with the minds and bodies of others should not be taken lightly, so even though you might not need any formal qualifications it's important to get some good training.

PROS

It's a job where you get to work closely with people on improving their physical and mental health.

CONS

A lot of people are still sceptical about this line of work and you might even attract claims that you're a con artist.

USEFUL CONTACTS

The British Chiropractic Association, Blagrave House, 17 Blagrave Street, Reading, Berks. RG1 1QB, 0118 950 5950, www.chiropractic-uk.co.uk

British Osteopathic Association, Langham House West, Mill St, Luton, Beds. LU1 2NA, 01582 488455, www.osteopathy.org

Institute of Complementary Medicine (ICM), PO Box 194, London SE16 7QZ, 020 7237 5165, www.icmedicine.co.uk

Reiki Association, Cornbrook Bridge House, Clee Hill, Ludlow, Shropshire SY8 3QQ, www.reikiassociation.org.uk

Tisserand Institute [aromatherapy], 01273 206640, www.tisserand.com

UK Council for Psychotherapy, 167–169 Great Portland St, London W1W 5PF, 020 7436 3002, www.psychotherapy.org.uk

UK Reiki Federation, PO Box 1785, Andover SP11 0WB, 01264 773774, www.reikifed.co.uk

Yoga Biomedical Trust, 90–92 Pentonville Street, Islington, London N1 9HS, 020 7689 3040, www.yogatherapy.org

CHAPTER TEN

Can You Write?

BEING A WRITER myself, I know what a satisfying and interesting activity it is. It is also a flexible occupation, something you can fit into spare moments any time of the day or night. But I also know what a competitive and often insecure method of money-earning it can be. If you have, or suspect you have, a talent for writing, however, there are all sorts of possibilities out there.

Articles

You don't have to be a card-carrying journalist to write for newspapers and magazines. Anyone can do it. You just need to be able to write (not necessarily as easy as it looks) and be able to withstand the many brush-offs your ideas might get from editors.

HOW TO DO IT

Apart from an ability to write and something to write on – ideally a computer but, if all else fails, a typewriter – you will need to know what you want to write and who you want to write for. If you have never written articles before it may be best to start with smaller publications, or even Internet websites, which often need cheap – or free – articles as they tend to have very little money.

Start with magazines or websites that publish in areas that interest you. If you are a dog-lover and you read dog magazines, you may have an idea or two for articles for those publications. Ring up the magazines and find out who you should submit to, then come up with a few ideas for them to choose from and send them in. If you have never been published before they may want you to write something 'on spec', which means you won't be paid for it unless they use it. If you have been published, send a copy of an article so that they can see that you can actually write.

Of course, there's nothing to stop you writing for major newspapers or magazines – other than the enormous amount of competition out there and the fact that some editors often don't even look at speculative letters or articles sent from writers they've never heard of. If you are prepared to persist, however, and believe in yourself enough, get a copy of *The Writer's Handbook* (£12.99, Macmillan) which lists all the major, and many minor, publications in this country. Send ideas to at least ten of them and see what comes back.

If you do get a commission, make sure you match your style as far as you can to the style of the publication. Also, try to keep the number of words you write as close as possible to the number asked for.

HOW MUCH CAN YOU MAKE?

It depends who you write for and how many articles you do. Fees vary from a paltry £25 for 1,000 words for small-circulation, specialist magazines and websites (if they pay at all) to £1,000 for 1,000 words for some national Sunday newspapers – if you're a bit of a name already.

COSTS

There are very few costs other than extra telephone calls for research and Internet use and possibly some travel.

TRAINING AND QUALIFICATIONS

You don't need any training or qualifications to write articles, although it can really help! All local authority adult evening classes include various writing classes, including journalism, and it can be useful to go and pick up some tips. If you get really serious about it, there are one- and two-year journalism courses in colleges all over the country, particularly at the London College of Printing and the City University, which have some of the best courses.

PROS

Thanks to the telephone and the Internet, many articles can be written without your ever leaving home. You can often do them in the evenings – if there is no tight deadline – and sometimes, depending on what you're writing about, you can get some rather nice freebies from hopeful PR companies. It can also be very pleasing to see your name in print above your own article.

CONS

There is an enormous amount of competition and it can be very difficult even to get started, let alone write regularly for money. The pay is also not great, given the amount of work involved, unless you are a celebrity or an established writer.

USEFUL CONTACTS

The City University, Northampton Square, London EC1V 0HB, 020 7040 5060, www.city.ac.uk

The London College of Printing, Elephant and Castle, London SE1 6SB, 020 7514 6562, www.lcptraining.co.uk

The National Union of Journalists, Headland House, 308–312 Gray's Inn Road, London WC1X 8DP, 020 7278 7916, www.nuj.org.uk

www.journalistuk.co.uk – a useful site for freelance writers and anyone wanting to know more about the trade

Novels

Everyone has a novel in them, they say, although frankly many should just keep it there and never let it see the light of day. If you yearn to write a romance or a thriller, however, why not have a go? Even if you don't ever sell it, the mere act of writing it should give you pleasure and you will learn a lot.

HOW TO DO IT

Probably the hardest thing about writing a novel is actually getting down to writing it. Apparently the late comedian Peter Cook met an actor friend at a party once and asked him, 'What are you doing at the moment?' 'Oh, I'm writing a novel,' replied the friend. 'Nor am I,' said Peter Cook.

If you have an idea for a story, get down and write it. It's the only way. You may find it helpful to take some classes first (or while you're writing) at your local adult education centre, and also to read some books on writing fiction – of which there are many. For example, you could consult Stephen King's *On Writing* (£7.99, New English Library) or *Research for Writers* by Ann Hoffmann (£13.99, A. & C. Black) or Margaret Atwood's *Negotiating with the Dead* (£7.99, Virago).

Once you have written your manuscript it is best to send it to an agent rather than direct to a publisher. Many publishers now take little or no notice of manuscripts sent to them direct and only take work from established agents. You can find a list of authors' agents in *The Writer's Handbook* or the *Writers' and Artists' Year Book*, or ask the Society of Authors (contact details below). To save time, send the manuscript to several agents, because many of them will take a while to get back to you.

If you're not sure whether your manuscript is good enough to send – or you have had it rejected by a few agents – contact Helen Corner of Cornerstones agency (details below), who specialises in critiquing novels for new authors and will supply a report on your work and ideas on how to improve it.

Cornerstones will also put writers in touch with agents once they feel the manuscript is worth submitting.

HOW MUCH CAN YOU MAKE?

Most novelists make very little from their craft. According to the Society of Authors, the average advance for a new novel is between £3,000 and £5,000. 'The advances are even lower for what we call "genre novels" like historical, romance, mystery or erotic novels,' says spokeswoman Kate Poole.

If you hit on a winner, however, the sky's the limit, as writers like Terry Pratchett, Jeffrey Archer and, of course, J. K. Rowling know. Also, remember that John Gray received a $3,000 advance for his *Mars & Venus* book, and Douglas Adams received even less for *The Hitch Hiker's Guide*, so if your book becomes a cult classic, who knows . . .

COSTS

There are none involved in writing a novel other than possible research expenses and the cost of sending your manuscripts to agents.

TRAINING AND QUALIFICATIONS

You don't need any training or qualifications to write a novel. You may find it very helpful, however, to attend evening classes in novel-writing – or any sort of writing – or, even better, to do the novel-writing course at the University of East Anglia.

PROS

Writing a novel is an enjoyable exercise in itself if you love writing and particularly love writing stories. If you do manage to sell it you could possibly make millions and see all sorts of other spin-offs, such as TV programmes, newspaper articles and speaking engagements.

CONS

The vast majority of novels written never see the light of day – quite often rightly so. Those that do tend on the whole to make very little money unless the writer is a celebrity or very, very good (and perhaps lucky). If you don't love writing but still really *need* to get that novel out of your system it can be a lonely and dispiriting occupation.

USEFUL CONTACTS

Helen Corner, 020 8968 0777, www.cornerstones.co.uk

The Inspira Group, 020 8292 5163, www.theinspiragroup.com – first-time authors should contact Darin Jewell

The Society of Authors, 84 Drayton Gardens, London SW10 9SB, 020 7373 6642, www.societyofauthors.net

University of East Anglia, www.uea.ac.uk

Case study

Anouchka Forrester, 32, from South London, began writing her first novel when she was working as a receptionist. 'It was a really boring job,' she admits, 'but I had to do it because I had no money.' She wrote under the desk in reception for a year before sending her manuscript to four publishers – who promptly rejected her. She decided to get an agent. 'An agency called Curtis Brown got me a two-book deal for £50,000 almost straight away!' she recalls.

Anouchka's first novel, *Ringing for You*, came out in 1999, and her second, *Darling Daisy*, appeared in 2000. She's now working on a third while she teaches creative writing courses and is a story consultant for a film company.

TV or film screenplays

If you thought that writing a novel was hard, try writing a screenplay! The competition is fierce and there are far fewer outlets for your work. Many complete unknowns have got their work on to the big screen or, more often, the small screen, however, so if you have a yen to do it too, go for it!

HOW TO DO IT

Again, get your idea down on paper. That's the hardest part. If you haven't seen a film script before, it's important to read through a few samples and some books on the subject before even attempting to write your own. You must use the standard industry format for writing screenplays or it just won't get read. You can either learn this or buy professional writer's software such as Final Draft (available online at www.finaldraft.com), which as well as being a fast writing tool will also format for you as you go.

Also, think about taking a few classes in script-writing. The more reading and training you get, the less time you will waste learning from your own mistakes.

Once you have written your script (like it's that easy!) you will need to sell it. Again, it is best to contact an agent first as many production companies, whether TV or film, will only take submissions from agents. Look in the writers' directories mentioned above for agents who deal with film scripts. If you want to approach production companies direct, many are listed in *Contacts* (£10.99, The Spotlight) – also, contact the BBC (www.bbc.co.uk) to find out about the new writers' projects that they often run.

HOW MUCH CAN YOU MAKE?

Anything from a few hundred for an 'option' on a TV script to millions for a Hollywood film that does very well.

COSTS

Apart from the cost of classes (which can be hundreds a time) and books, your only outlay will be the paper and ink you print on.

TRAINING AND QUALIFICATIONS

You don't need either, but it's really helpful to get as much training as you can before and during the time you are writing.

PROS

It is enormously satisfying to have your own work produced on the screen, and it can be lucrative, particularly if it is repeated and you get royalties for years afterwards.

CONS

It is an incredibly competitive, difficult and often nasty business. Also, it is hard to write a script – particularly for the big screen – and even harder to sell it. You need determination, a thick skin and genuine talent to get anywhere.

USEFUL CONTACTS

www.mckeestory.com – you can find out about famous script-writing tutor Robert McKee's classes here

The Screenwriters' Workshop, 1–8 Whitfield Place, London W1, 020 7387 5511, www.lsw.org.uk – a membership organisation for screenwriters

www.scriptfactory.co.uk – a very useful website for film and TV writers; they offer master classes in many aspects of the craft

www.shootingpeople.org – a good source for jobs, contacts and training in script-writing

www.ukfilmcouncil.org.uk – the official site for the UK Film Council

Create a TV game show format

TV companies are always looking for game show formats. Really successful ones, such as *Who Wants to Be a Millionaire?*, can make millions for the TV company, and they'll pay top dollar for an idea they think will run and run.

HOW TO DO IT

Think up an idea and sell it! There, how easy is that? No, really, a good TV game show format is a remarkably difficult concept to come up with. Some people try for years before breaking through.

Essentially, the idea should be simple but fun. You should be able to fit its description on to one A4 sheet, so it is up to you to come up with an idea that is not already being aired, hone it down to some simple rules and a few fun gimmicks and send it to TV production companies or direct to TV channels.

You wouldn't think, to look at them, that it was a hard thing to come up with a winning game show format, but it is amazing how many ideas are submitted to production companies and how few are even tried out. The best thing to do is to study some popular game shows. Watch them regularly and work out what their basic elements are, what, if anything, they all have in common, and what, to your mind, makes them work. Look in the *Radio Times* or on the channels' websites to find out which production companies have made the most popular game shows and target them with your ideas. You can also go direct to the channels themselves although, if they like the idea, they will probably go back to a production company to get them to make a pilot.

There are books and websites that will give you some tips and ideas on how to come up with a winning format, and it's worth looking at these. Try http://pub43.ezboard.com/babsolutewrite, for example. Also, see if you can find an 'ideas buddy' with whom you can brainstorm and come up with formats together. Two heads, in this kind of business, are often better than one.

HOW MUCH CAN YOU MAKE?

If you come up with a winning idea, the sky's the limit.

COSTS

There are no costs involved although, this being TV, presentation is everything, so you may need to spend money on this.

TRAINING AND QUALIFICATIONS

You don't need any training or qualifications.

PROS

If you come up with a good idea you may not have to work ever again!

CONS

It could take you years of trying and failing to come up with an idea that is even optioned, let alone bought. There is no guarantee that you will ever come up with a winner. It can be a depressing business!

USEFUL CONTACTS

Action Time TV, www.action-time.co.uk

www.bbc.co.uk/talent – look here for contacts for entertainment commissioners and producers

Celador, 39 Long Acre, London WC2E 9LG, 020 7845 6999, www.celador.co.uk – this production company makes several game shows and quizzes, including *Who Wants to Be a Millionaire?*

Yorkshire Television, www.yorkshiretv.com – makers of *Countdown*

Write a play or a musical

Writing for the stage may not be as lucrative as writing for the screen, but if you write a West End hit it could support you for the rest of your life.

HOW TO DO IT

To write a play you need to be a good writer, obviously, and it can also help to have a background in the theatre as an actor or director, although that's certainly not essential.

There are several books on playwriting around to give you help, and you can take courses at adult evening classes or at certain theatres, such as the Soho Theatre in London, which encourages new theatre writers and performers. Look at *Writing a Play* by Steve Gooch (£12.95, A. & C. Black), *The Crafty Art of Playmaking* by Alan Ayckbourn (£8.99, Faber & Faber) and *Three Uses of the Knife* by David Mamet ($10.00, Random House, USA) for instruction and inspiration.

Do go and see as many plays as you can, or musicals if that is your thing. Read them off the page and look at scores for musicals. One of the best ways of learning how to write anything is to study good existing examples.

If you are writing a musical it is likely that you will be collaborating with someone else – maybe you are writing the words and your partner the music. There is no law to say that you have to write both elements.

Once you have a script it's helpful to have it performed, probably as a 'rehearsed reading' by actors so that you and a director can see what works and what doesn't. Most large cities have a scheme going in a local theatre to encourage new writers. London, of course, has more than others, and it is possible to get help at places such as the Soho Theatre, the Bush Theatre and the Royal Court Theatre, which specifically target new writers.

Send your manuscript to theatres such as these for possible inclusion in rehearsed readings and script-development programmes. If the play is already brilliant (as of course it will be – you're writing it, aren't you?), they will consider it for a proper commercial performance, which is what you are aiming at.

HOW MUCH CAN YOU MAKE?

Anything from nothing at all to millions if you hit on a winning play or musical which plays in the West End and elsewhere, netting you royalties each time it is performed.

COSTS

There are no costs involved in simply writing. There are, however, many and various costs involved in putting on a play or musical.

TRAINING AND QUALIFICATIONS

You don't need any training or qualifications although, obviously, an ability to write is essential!

PROS

If you love plays or musicals and you think you have talent, what better way to spend your evenings than working on a creative project? The fact that you could make money from it – a lot of money – is a bonus.

CONS

It is very difficult to sell plays and musicals and it can take a long time to write them. Once you have written something you then have to try to get it performed, seen and bought by someone. It costs a lot to put on a play or a musical, even in a small theatre, let alone a large one, so you won't necessarily see any return, even if it is performed in the West End.

USEFUL CONTACTS

Equity, Guild House, Upper St Martins Lane, London WC2H 9EG, 020 7379 6000, www.equity.org.uk

New Playwright Network, www.doollee.com – a useful source website for new playwrights

Playwright's Co-operative, www.plays4theatre.com – a not-for-profit organisation for playwrights

The Soho Theatre and Writers' Centre, 21 Dean Street, London W1D 3NE, 020 7287 5060, www.sohotheatre.com

www.stageplays.com – an American website for playwrights and anyone connected with the theatre

www.writewords.org.uk – a marvellous website for writers where you can join a theatre writers' group as well as pick up tips and hints on all aspects of writing

Other types of book

Writing a book doesn't necessarily have to mean writing a novel. There are thousands of non-fiction titles around – including this book, of course – so if you have an idea, why not try it out?

HOW TO DO IT

Books are like any other market – if there's a gap, you could make money by filling it. If you have an idea for a non-fiction book and you cannot find anything like it in the bookshops or online, it's possible that it could be published and you could make money out of it.

First, think about who would buy it. If it is a very specialised subject it may not be of interest to publishers as it wouldn't sell enough. If you think quite a large proportion of the population could be interested, then go for it. Write a page or two describing the book, note any similar books that are in the shops at the moment and explain how yours would be different, and include a chapter breakdown to show how the book would be structured. If you have not written a book before the publishers will probably want to see one or two sample chapters just to check that you can write.

Once you have your description and some sample chapters, you should send it either to agents or direct to publishers. It is better if an agent takes it up for you as publishers take their submissions seriously and often take a long time going through manuscripts sent direct.

HOW MUCH CAN YOU MAKE?

It is the same as writing a novel (see above) in that you can make no more than £1,000 or so or, if your book becomes a best-seller, you could make several thousand and receive royalties for years afterwards.

COSTS

There are no major costs involved other than telephone and travel expenses for research if you need it.

TRAINING AND QUALIFICATIONS

You don't need training although if you are writing an academic or professional book you may need relevant qualifications – although you don't necessarily have to have them.

PROS

If you enjoy writing and you hit on a good subject, you could make a lot of money out of something that is easy to write.

CONS

It is very hard to sell any book, and even if you get published you will not necessarily sell enough to make much money in the long-term.

USEFUL CONTACTS

The Society of Authors (see above, p. 255)

Joke-writing

Writing jokes is one of the toughest types of writing. Only a comparatively small number of people at any given time have really mastered it, although quite a few others make some money out of writing jokes for comedians or TV and radio pro-grammes.

HOW TO DO IT

Any time you have a funny idea, write it down. There is definitely a craft to writing jokes and there are several rules you can learn which will help. Watch and listen to comedy shows and comedy routines and study the way the lines are constructed. Read joke books and comedy scripts and see how they are structured. Try writing them out verbatim and creating your own jokes with similar constructions.

It is useful to read good books on joke-writing, although sadly there are few of them. Gene Peret's book *Comedy-writing Step by Step* (£10.50, Samuel French) is very helpful, although it is American so you will need to buy it online. Another Peret book, *Shift Your Writing Career into High Gear* (£8, Writer's Digest), is also great. You can get a lot of information at the 'Writers' Room' on the BBC website www.bbc.co.uk, and at Robin Kelly's writing for performance website at www.robinkelly.btinternet.co.uk.

Your local adult education centre might run a comedy-writing course. The quality of teaching is not always good, though. In London the best courses are run at the City University and at the City Lit.

The Comedy Writers Association (see below for contact details) holds seminars and local writers' meetings which can give you ideas and support, but on the whole the only real way to write jokes is to write them, either on your own or with a comedy buddy.

You can make money from your jokes by offering to write for established comedians, who often need a continuous supply of topical gags. Pick comedians you like and contact them through their agents. The Spotlight (contact details below) will give you the numbers if you ring them. Also contact BBC Entertainment for information on any radio or TV programmes that accept unsolicited material from new writers. There are never enough good comedy writers around, so if you have talent, there will always be work for you.

If you have an idea for several jokes on one theme, offer them as a book to publishers. They will want an idea of how the book would look and will want to see at least 20 sample jokes first. As with other books, it's best to offer it through an agent, although if you prefer you can contact publishers direct.

HOW MUCH CAN YOU MAKE?

Anything from £5 here and there for a joke or sketch performed onstage to thousands a month as a top joke-writer for a TV show.

COSTS

There are no costs apart from paying for books or courses on joke-writing.

TRAINING AND QUALIFICATIONS

You don't need any training or qualifications.

PROS

If you have a talent for it, joke-writing can be great fun and rewarding, and can get you into the glamorous worlds of radio, TV and stage.

CONS

It can be very hard to sell your jokes, and demoralising to keep having your work rejected. Also, until you are well established, there is very little money in it.

USEFUL CONTACTS

The Comedy Writers Association, www.cwauk.co.uk

The Spotlight, 7 Leicester Place, London WC2H 7RJ, 020 7437 7631, www.spotlightcd.com

Copywriting

Ever wondered who writes the 'blurbs' in brochures and for websites and the direct mail shots that come through the door? Well, someone does, and they get paid well for it. It could be you.

HOW TO DO IT

Copywriting is essentially about putting together the glowing words you find in catalogues, brochures, adverts and other printed – or online – materials. It's not journalism, it's more sales-type writing – words that attract people and make them buy. If you have a good understanding of human nature and what makes people tick (especially the psychology of buying), know how to sell and 'have a way with words', then you're well on the way to becoming a good copywriter. Some people have the ability to write like this naturally, others need to learn the skills, but anyone will benefit from some sort of training.

Freelance copywriter Tracey Dooley, who markets her work at www.mediaminister.co.uk, says there are many different ways of becoming a copywriter. 'Perhaps the most direct and obvious route is to do work experience for, or get a junior copywriting job at, an advertising agency,' she says. 'You'll soon learn the ropes there. Alternatively, study the successful advertising and direct marketing campaigns written by the pros and read books like *Freelance Copywriting* by Diana Wimbs. Hers is a great hand-book for learning the ropes, and she gives some good advice and examples of various campaigns.'

The Institute of Copywriting runs a distance learning course which you can find out about through their website (contact details below). It will cost you, but you are assigned your personal, real-life, working copywriter to mark and comment on your assignments, and this is particularly helpful as you can learn a lot by having someone else reading and reacting to your copy.

According to the institute's website, there is work for freelance copywriters: 'Unlike the world of book writing,' they say, 'there's little competition – because there are few copywriters. A few people work for big city advertising agencies; but most of us work freelance. We tend to do the smaller jobs that the big ad agencies don't want to tackle. They'd charge too much. And they can't respond quickly enough. That's when a freelance copywriter is needed.'

Many copywriters work through agencies or they get work by networking with other writers and with people from ad agencies and catalogue publishers. Others have their own websites and spend a lot of time selling themselves to get work. The Internet, as well as providing you with a place to market yourself, is a great place for researching potential clients and networking with companies that could provide work, such as PR and marketing agencies. There are also many sites springing up online that allow you to bid for work (see below for a few).

HOW MUCH CAN YOU MAKE?

'It really does vary,' says Tracey Dooley, 'not just from job to job, but from copywriter to copywriter. And then some copywriters charge by the word. Others charge by the hour, day or job. Some estimate, some give flat prices.' The National Union of Journalists suggests a minimum day rate of £300, but well-established writers can charge from £500 a day.

COSTS

As this is basically writing, once you have trained in some way, which is likely to entail spending money, you shouldn't have any major costs.

TRAINING AND QUALIFICATIONS

You don't have to be trained or qualified but it helps.

PROS

This can be a straightforward way of making good money from writing – if you have a way with words and you know what will entice people. There is work around and if you do a good job companies will keep coming back to you.

CONS

Advertising and other sales activities are very dependent on the economy. When it is bad, there is little work around. It also takes some effort to get work in the first place.

USEFUL CONTACTS

The Advertising Association, www.adassoc.org.uk/ – the association also runs copywriting courses

www.contracted.com – look here for copywriting jobs

www.freelanceuk.com/index.shtml – lots of information on becoming a copywriter and getting work on this website

www.guru.com – usually some copywriting work here

The Institute of Copywriting, Honeycombe House, Bagley, Wedmore, Somerset BS28 4TD, 01934 713563, www.inst.org/copy/

Also consider . . .

● Writing ads for lonely hearts. Seriously, people in the USA are paying around $150 a go for someone to write their lonely hearts ad. After all, these are adverts, so it makes sense (in a slightly odd way) for a professional to write about you in a way that makes you sound desirable! If you think you can do it, put an ad near the lonely hearts sections of your favourite magazines and newspapers and see what comes in.

● Writing poems, jokes and little epithets for greetings cards. The greetings card industry is huge and very lucrative. It's highly competitive but well paid if you can get into it. Find contact details for greetings card companies on their association's website – www.greetingcard.org - and send off your witty and fabulous jokes, sayings and poems. You never know!

● Writing press releases for small businesses. It helps to have been a journalist or have some background in PR or copywriting, but if you know a news story when you see one – or know how to make something look like a news story – you can charge for writing and sending out press releases to the media. Get together a database of media contacts (you can simply create one by ringing up all the newspapers, TV stations and so on that you want to target) and email or ring them with stories that could get coverage for your client. It's a skill that only a few have – if they are not trained – but if you have it it can be very lucrative for you and your clients.

Competitions

Anyone can do them. You see them on the back of soup packets, on chocolate bars, on tissue boxes and attached to cars. Coming up with a witty and appropriate line to finish off a sentence can be a great way of winning money, a car or household goods.

HOW TO DO IT

Scour the supermarket shelves for items that have competitions attached to them. Don't go mad and buy things you would never eat or use – unless you just *love* doing competitions – as there's no guarantee that you will win a prize anyway. If you are really into it you can subscribe to a special magazine that has lists of current and upcoming competitions. It costs a whopping £72 to subscribe for the year, but you can get a free sample by sending £1 to cover postage to Intacomps trial magazine, Dept WWL, PO Box 11, Skegness, Lincs. PE25 3QH.

When you have bought your competition product, make sure you keep the till receipt and staple it to your form. Also, have a good supply of blank postcards (those are often required by companies) and sheets of paper with your name, address and phone number on them. Do search around the shop for an entry form if there is one, because apparently these competitions have fewer people entering them, so you are more likely to win.

You might like to invest in a rhyming dictionary and pull out any of the joke or quote books you have in your downstairs loo – these will help with silly rhymes, funny phrases or well-known statements that you could use in competitions. Practise different lines and combinations of words in your spare time and enter as many competitions as you can. You are unlikely to win your first one. The level of entries is probably much lower than you would expect, particularly for the slogan competitions, just because they require a little effort. This knowledge, and a little practice at slogan-writing, allows hardened 'compers' (as the real enthusiasts call themselves) to do well.

Professional comper Lynne Suzanne (website details below)

gives many tips on her site, including: post your competitions at least a week before the closing date; be positive and believe you can win; learn the skills required for success and read, study and practise.

HOW MUCH CAN YOU MAKE?

It could be anything from a £5 voucher for cat food, a new car, a luxury holiday in the sun or a year's supply of toilet rolls to thousands.

COSTS

Usually just the cost of buying the item (in theory you don't have to buy things in order to go in for the competitions, but you are more likely to win if you do) and the cost of postage.

TRAINING AND QUALIFICATIONS

You don't need any training or qualifications.

PROS

If you are good at coming up with pithy, clever lines, this can be a fun way of spending your coffee break.

CONS

You are not guaranteed to win and you could find your kitchen cupboards full of food you don't really like that much with not a prize in sight.

USEFUL CONTACTS

www.competitions.com – a very useful site for anyone interested in comping, with lots of tips, rhymes and contacts

www.wincompetitions.co.uk – this is the website of writer, author and fanatical 'comper' Lynne Suzanne, who has written a number of books on how to win competitions; includes tips, slogans and ideas for winning all kinds of competitions

Poetry

This really is the hardest type of writing from which to make money. Poetry has always been badly paid and is unlikely to make you rich. Writing poetry is good for the soul, however, and you could strike it lucky and make money out of competitions, readings or by publishing your work.

HOW TO DO IT

You write it! Read as much good poetry as you can, go to poetry readings and attend a poetry-writing evening class to give yourself some ideas. Immersing yourself in poetry will help you write your own.

Quite a few poetry reading evenings allow anyone to perform their own work, and once you have enough confidence this can be a good way of finding out what others think of your work. If you are serious about poetry you should join the Poetry Society (contact details below), which costs £35 a year, including four issues of their magazine, *Poetry Review*, and also their newspaper, *Poetry News*. The society also offers discounts on events and all sorts of useful services for poets and would-be poets.

It is also important, if you're serious, to try to get your poems published in one of the many poetry magazines. 'Most poetry publishers wouldn't look at you until you've had a few poems published in magazines,' says the Poetry Society's Sophie Heawood. It is quite hard to get published in the society's magazine, but there are many others, such as *Ambit*, *Smiths Knoll* and *Rialto*, which you can try. All the poetry magazines are stocked at the Poetry Library on London's South Bank (see below for contact details), and it is worth visiting if you are in the area to see what's available.

Sadly, most poetry book publishers have very little money to pay writers, if any at all, but the largest poetry publisher, Faber & Faber, pays a reasonable amount. It is a very competitive area, though, and it will often take years to get to the stage where you have a whole book of poems published. You may be paid for doing poetry readings at clubs or arts events and, for established poets, this often brings in more money than being published.

There are several poetry competitions held around the country which have cash prizes, so it would certainly be worth trying some of these. The prizes are usually small, although the most prestigious one, the National Poetry Competition, run by the Poetry Society, has a first prize of £5,000. The prestigious T. S. Eliot prize for a book of poetry pays £10,000. Most competitions charge you to enter your poems, so if you are keen to make money out of your work, rather than just enjoying the writing of it, you should consider your chances of winning before sending it in. Contact the Poetry Library for a list of all the competitions around the country.

If you become really good you could receive bursaries from organisations such as the Arts Council, the Society of Authors or the Royal Literary Fund, or you could become 'Poet in Residence' for a forward-looking company with money to burn! You could also consider offering your talents to greetings cards manufacturers. See p. 268 for information on how to go about this.

HOW MUCH CAN YOU MAKE?

Not a lot! A new poet would be doing well to make £100 in a year, but if you do a number of readings, win a competition and have a book of poems published you could make £5,000 or more.

COSTS

Entering competitions often entails costs, and you should join the Poetry Society, which would set you back £35 a year. Apart from that, though, there are no major costs.

TRAINING AND QUALIFICATIONS

You don't need any training or qualifications to become a poet, but taking classes and reading up on the subject would help.

PROS

If you love poetry you will love writing poetry. Even if you never make any money out of it in your life it will give you pleasure.

CONS

There is so little money in poetry it cannot realistically be done for financial gain. It can also be demoralising to have your work unappreciated.

USEFUL CONTACTS

The Poetry Library, Level 5, Royal Festival Hall, London SE1 8XX, 020 7921 0943, www.poetrylibrary.org.uk

The Poetry Society, 22 Betterton Street, London WC2H 9BX, 020 7420 9880, www.poetrysociety.org.uk

Being a reader

If you can write, it stands to reason that you can read too. Well, by 'read' here I mean reading manuscripts for publishers or theatre, TV and film producers. All of them have 'slush piles' of unsolicited material from writers all over the country, and they don't have time to go through it all themselves. This is where 'readers' – who are usually experienced writers themselves – are needed.

HOW TO DO IT

If you already have a proven track record in some sort of creative writing – plays, sketches, books, articles – you could be a reader. 'Readers can play a vital role, if they're good, because most publishers receive hundreds, if not thousands, of unsolicited manuscripts and proposals every year, and in-house editors are often too busy to consider them properly,' says Alan Brooke, senior editor at Piatkus. 'Only one or two "unsolicited" manuscripts will get published every year, but there's always the chance you'll miss out on a best-seller if you don't treat the slush pile with respect! The sort of person who would make a good slush pile reader is obviously somebody who can read very quickly, and come to a judgement after reading a few pages. It would help to be an avid reader with a broad taste in books.'

Contact as many publishers as you like (you can find a list of publishers in Britain in the *Writers' and Artists' Year Book* (A&C Black, £13.99) and offer them your services. They may have a form for you to fill in, or it may be best send a letter enclosing a CV and contact details to whoever sends out manuscripts to readers.

HOW MUCH CAN YOU MAKE?

A publisher's slush pile reader would be paid from £100 to £150 for a day's work.

COSTS

There are no costs involved as most work is sent to you or you read it in the office.

TRAINING AND QUALIFICATIONS

Ideally, you need to be a published author or established writer of some sort. A degree-level qualification – ideally in English or similar – is also helpful.

PROS

If you enjoy reading and you can read quickly, this can be a pleasant and flexible job.

CONS

You have to wade through an awful lot of dross before you come across something decent. It can be depressing to see just how bad so many people's writing is!

Songwriting

Songwriting, as you might expect, is a hit-and-miss affair. You could come up with one big hit and retire to Spain on the royalties. Or you could spend your life quite happily churning out songs that nobody hears outside your own bathroom.

HOW TO DO IT

Many people write songs for their own amusement. While few of them hit the musical jackpot there's no harm in your trying. Who knows, you could turn out to be the next Diane Warren. The undisputed queen of the power ballad, she has written thousands of songs, including Cher's 'If I Could Turn Back Time', Celine Dion's 'Because You Loved Me' and Christina Aguilera's 'I Turn To You'. One of the world's most prolific songwriters, she rakes in annual royalties of over $20 million. While not many people manage that level of success, with a little hard work and research there's no reason why any budding songsmith shouldn't have a go.

Lin Cremore from Eastbourne has been writing songs since she was about seven. She's come a long way from that first carol, and now the 46-year-old mother of three has four CDs of her jazz-influenced 'trip hop' under her belt and shows no signs of stopping.

'It's a passion,' she says simply. 'I do it because I can't help doing it.'

A qualified teacher, Lin uses a specialist computer software package to compose and arrange her work. The equipment started to take over the lounge, and now she has a whole room set aside as a studio.

Writing the song is only the first step. Once you have recorded your material it is worth bringing in a professional producer to polish it up. The fee will depend on the producer. Then there's duplication. Lin paid around £1,000 for a thousand copies of her last album. Depending on the packaging you can pay a lot more. The more you order the better the deal gets. But remember, the more you order, the more you need to sell to make a profit.

Once you have got your CDs then you can start trying to sell them. Sending copies to record companies and radio stations can be a thankless task. But one of the most effective ways of getting your music on to the market is via the Internet. There are a number of websites that will sell CDs in return for a percentage of the profits. Trawl the Net to find them. Or you can set up your own website with a system for selling online. Depending on how much you want to spend, you can design a site where visitors can actually hear some of your music.

Lin is under no illusions about making a fortune from her music but she sold 100 of her CD *Vulnerability* in its first month of release.

HOW MUCH CAN YOU MAKE?

The sky's the limit, but only if you are very, very lucky.

COSTS

At its most basic, songwriting won't cost you more than the price of a pencil and manuscript paper. A basic computer software package can cost around £200. If you get a little more ambitious you can end up spending a lot more. Plus, you will need a computer with a lot of memory to store your material.

TRAINING AND QUALIFICATIONS

It helps to play an instrument such as the guitar or keyboards. And being computer literate is an advantage.

PROS

It's creative, fun and you can work at home.

CONS

It can be heartbreaking if you expect too much. Remember that musical talent isn't always the deciding factor in the entertainment business.

CAN YOU WRITE? • 277

USEFUL CONTACTS

www.cdbaby.com – independent music website

www.practicespot.com – loads of free tools to download such as manuscript paper, tutorials and support

www.vocalist.org.uk – lots of songwriting competitions from all over the world on this website

CHAPTER ELEVEN

Are You Fun?

ARE YOU THE LIFE and soul of the party? Are you a bit of a
drama queen or, let's be honest, a show-off? Good. People
like you are always in demand to entertain, run parties or functions, sell things in a lively way or just stand around looking
attractive (yes, really, people do get paid for that!).

Party planning

If you're a good organiser and you like people, this can be a good
thing to do in your spare time – you get to go to parties too!

HOW TO DO IT

Some people cannot organise parties or functions to save their
lives, while others thrive on it. If you are in the latter category
then you can get work organising private or corporate parties
and even weddings. It would help to organise one or two for free
for friends to start off with. Get them to put the word about that
you will do it for a fee, and that should start you off. Also, get
them to write you a letter of reference which you can use later
to get more work from potential clients.

Organising a party is rather like producing a show or TV programme: the more organised you are ahead of time, with every

't' crossed and 'i' dotted, the smoother the whole thing will run. Merely 'liking people' and 'enjoying a good bash' is not good enough. You need to be, first and foremost, an organiser. If you are to do it regularly and make some reasonable money from it, you will also need to have good contacts with caterers, entertainers, venue managers, flower arrangers, employment agencies and others, so that you can get the best service for the cheapest prices (on top of which you will charge your commission, which is where you make your money).

Set out a time schedule with deadlines for finalising the various aspects of the function. Then set a time schedule for the day itself, making sure that everyone involved knows exactly what they are to do, when and where.

On the day, you need to be like a swan: all calm and smiles on the outside but paddling like fury underneath! You need to know that everyone is doing what they should, when they should, and you need to be able to fix anything that goes wrong. At the same time, though, you should exude bonhomie and jollity to your clients and their guests. Not everyone can do that!

If you do well with parties you may be asked to organise weddings too. These are often larger, more complicated and more emotionally fraught than parties or even corporate functions. However, they are also usually well paid. You need even more military precision when organising even an average wedding, and you will be required to do a lot more hand-holding too. Many wedding planners will choose the bride's and bridesmaids' dresses with them, will help organise the right clothes for the bridegroom and ushers, and will even counsel them on the day if they get cold feet or the wedding jitters. It is not a job for the faint-hearted or immature, and it is certainly one where you need to charge over and above what you might initially think is reasonable, because whatever you do charge you will earn it!

HOW MUCH CAN YOU MAKE?

Anything from £100 for a small do to thousands for a big posh function or wedding.

COSTS

You will have phone costs and some travel expenses and you will need to look good, so invest in a few party frocks! You will also have general admin costs and advertising fees, unless you get all your work through word of mouth.

TRAINING AND QUALIFICATIONS

You don't need any training or qualifications.

PROS

This is a fun way to make some money, particularly if you already have good contacts in catering and entertainment. You could also find yourself being wined and dined by hotels and other party venues if they find out that you have influence over where people hold their do's.

CONS

This can be very labour-intensive and frustrating work. You are dealing with people who can often be demanding and quixotic, so if you're not careful you could end up working twice as long as you should. Big do's can also be very stressful, and you may feel it's not worth the extra effort. Also, this tends to be a job in which people with posh friends and contacts in high places can make money. If your friends tend not to hold big functions it could be harder for you to get started.

USEFUL CONTACTS

www.ukdirectory.co.uk – possibly a useful directory to advertise in as they have an event planning section

www.partydelights.co.uk – a useful source of all kinds of party accessories and decorations particularly for children's parties

www.confetti.co.uk – a source for party accessories

Children's entertainer

There's a huge demand for fun and charismatic people to entertain at children's parties. You'd be amazed how much work there is just in your local area.

HOW TO DO IT

Obviously you need some sort of act. It helps if you are already skilled in magic, balloon-modelling, juggling, crafts or comedy, but even if you don't have any of these skills, if you love children and know how to keep them enthralled for half an hour or more you will be able to find work in your area.

Children's entertaining is a business like any other and, once you have an act you think works (try it out for free at family parties or for children of friends first), it's important to advertise in the right places. Your local Yellow Pages is a very good place to start. Local website directories can also be helpful, as can local magazines for families or, if you have more money, some of the national parenting magazines. It may also be helpful to have a website of your own with a photo of you, a description of your act and a few comments from happy customers. If you are good, however, you will increasingly get jobs through word-of-mouth recommendation, which is the best form of advertising.

It's a really good idea to improve your skills as you go on, particularly if you get repeat bookings. You don't want to do the same act twice for the same kids. Do some classes in something that takes your interest, such as balloon-modelling or different types of clowning. Look into your local adult education classes or contact Circus Arts (contact details opposite). If you are good at art you could simply do face-painting or arts and crafts, giving the children things to make that they can take home with them.

You could also include give-aways in your act. Children love having 'party bags' to take away and, as an added extra, you could give each child something that fits in with the theme of your act.

HOW MUCH CAN YOU MAKE?

It depends where you live and how many gigs you get. In London the going rate is around £15 per child with a minimum of, say, 15 children. Outside London it is about £10. It's useful to get your clients to sign a contract before the event, to ensure that you get paid on the day. Take an invoice with you and arrange beforehand to get paid immediately after performing.

COSTS

You will probably need to buy props, a costume (or costumes) and theatrical make-up. You will also have travel costs, and you may need to pay for materials if you do crafts. Then there are the usual business costs, such as advertising, printing of leaflets, and website admin expenses.

TRAINING AND QUALIFICATIONS

You don't need any training or qualifications, but it would help to have some entertainment training or experience.

PROS

Children's parties can be a fun way to make some extra cash, particularly if you like children and enjoy mucking about.

CONS

These parties usually happen in the afternoons, so they are no good if you are already working during the day.

USEFUL CONTACTS

www.circusarts.org.uk – everything you ever wanted to know about circus skills training

Case study

Actress Sally Elsden has been running her children's party business, Madfairy Craft and Dance Parties, for about four years. It grew from the children's drama classes she runs in her home town of St Albans. 'Mothers started asking me if I would help entertain the children at their birthday parties,' she says, 'and after a while it just went crazy! There's a huge demand and much of the work I get is by word of mouth. It's so busy I'm now looking to franchise it.'

Sally charges £10 per child with a minimum of 15 children and works in Hertfordshire, Bedfordshire, Buckinghamshire and North London. The parties last for two hours and include teaching the children a dance, which they perform to the parents at the end, and two crafts. 'With the four-to-six-year-olds we have story time and dance and they make a simple heart-shaped box or a sparkly wand. The older ones decorate picture frames or make jewellery – that kind of thing. At the moment I provide some bits for the party bags but I'm looking into bulk-buying little presents and offering a full party-bag service for extra money.'

Sally says she gets a lot of work through Yellow Pages and also through her website, www.madfairy.co.uk. Other children's entertainers in her area include the usual magicians and clowns but also some who offer hair and make-up parties for little girls, pop star parties, where they get to do karaoke and dress up as pop stars, and a go-karting party service.

Tour guide

Do you like the sound of your own voice? Do you like the idea of a captive audience? Do you have an interest in local history? Then you would make an ideal tour guide.

HOW TO DO IT

In practice, anyone can set themselves up as a tour guide. Simply mug up on an area you are interested in, get a good patter together and advertise in local papers, tourist offices and hotels. It is often a good idea to come up with a theme for your tour. Ghost walks or murder walks are often popular. Walks that follow Jack the Ripper's murders, for example, are particularly popular in London, but you could pick a theme that makes sense for your area – perhaps one connected to local artists or writers, or a popular soap opera or geographical or geological areas of interest. If your tour is good then word will get around, although as your main client base will be tourists, who, by nature, are a transient group, you will need to keep advertising your service to each new crop of people coming into the area.

If you want to do it properly, you should take a course accredited by the Guild of Registered Tour Guides. Primarily they accredit the main 'Blue Badge' course, which can take between seven and 13 months to complete (part-time) and can cost between £1,000 and £2,500. If you get a Blue Badge qualification you can do tours all over your region. For less time and money you could get a Green Badge, which takes just three or four months, part-time, and costs around £500. This would qualify you to run tours in, say, one city. Below this you could get a Level 2 qualification to conduct tours in a specific tourist attraction, such as a castle or cathedral. Generally these courses are run by the people who manage the building.

No one *has* to have these qualifications but on the whole councils, tourist offices and most attractions won't bother with you if you haven't. If you are qualified, you could make between £75 and £100 a day guiding people round buildings, through towns or along a particular route in a bus or car. Of course, the work is generally seasonal, and the amount you can earn depends on the tourist opportunities in your area and the number of other guides around. The Blue Badge courses don't happen very often for this reason. Only London has one every year – no one wants to flood the market!

If you decide to run your own tour, however, and you are good at marketing and publicity, you could certainly make some regular money in the evenings or at weekends – even on week-days – doing this.

HOW MUCH CAN YOU MAKE?

Between £75 and £100 for a day, or even more if you run your own event and you get 20 or more people at, say, £5 each.

COSTS

You should have no costs other than advertising if you are running your own event, except possibly costumes and props if they are a part of it. If you decide to go for a qualifica-tion then you will have the fees and possibly course books to pay for.

TRAINING AND QUALIFICATIONS

You don't need training and qualifications for every type of tour, but more possibilities are open to you if you are qualified.

PROS

If you are an entertaining sort of person, this is a great way of making money, meeting people and, often, getting a lot of fresh air. If you love your subject it can also be very satisfying to make other people see how interesting it is too.

CONS

If you are running your own events it can be very hard to get enough people. You may have to cancel several, particularly in the winter. You will also need stamina and a good voice if you do several tours a day. You are generally on your feet for hours, often dealing with annoying requests from tourists, so be pre-pared to be worn out!

USEFUL CONTACTS

The Guild of Registered Tourist Guides, The Guild House, 52D Borough High Street, London SE1 1XN, 020 7403 1115, www.blue-badge-guides.com

Institute of Tourist Guiding, Lloyd's Court, 1 Goodman's Yard, London E1 8AT, 020 7953 1257, www.institute-of-tourist-guiding.org.uk

Entertainer – functions

We can't all be Elton John or Ali G, but if you think you've got enough talent to entertain a roomful of people, why not get paid for it?

HOW TO DO IT

If you are a singer or musician there are all kinds of entertainment jobs that you could do. Large hotels often need a pianist or harpist to play in the lounge in the afternoons. Local clubs or pubs often want singers, bands or single musicians to entertain, and then there is the wonderful world of corporate entertainment to get into. For comedians, impressionists and magicians, the options are really comedy clubs, magic nights and corporate entertainment.

Probably the hardest thing about this kind of work is getting established in the first place. If you are just starting out as a musician or singer, it can be really worthwhile busking for a while, because there have been genuine cases of people being 'spotted' by agents and record companies simply through busking. Not only that but you can make some money, get some practice and establish what numbers really work with the public.

You should certainly try to get yourself gigs in local clubs and pubs. You may have to perform for free quite a few times before you can start charging, although some club owners might give you a gig just on the strength of a demo tape. Many singers and musicians get on by going in for competitions and talent searches. There are talent competitions going on all over the country throughout the year. Check out www.vocalist.org.uk for ones near you.

Comedy is particularly hard. You will need to get together about five minutes' worth of material that you think is funny and perform it at clubs that offer 'open mike' nights – in other words, you perform for free and see how it goes. There are also comedy competitions which are worth entering as they can lead to paid work if you do well. Work at your craft if you really want to do it. Take classes if there are some near you or if you are willing to travel to London – the City Lit does a stand-up course (see below). If you manage to crack the comedy 'circuit' you can make up to £900 a gig in London, particularly if you are taken on by one of the two main comedy agencies, Avalon and Off The Kerb, which have most of the large comedy gigs, including student union shows, sewn up between them.

You can also make good money by offering your services to corporate and entertainment agencies. There are hundreds of these agencies around the country, from speaker bureaux that deal with blue-chip companies to small businesses that offer entertainers for stag nights and weddings. Look on the Internet for agencies and send them your details – a photo of yourself, a video or DVD of your act and reference letters from one or more former clients. Keep sending them updated information as you get it – a more up-to-date showreel, new reference letters from clients, etc. – perhaps once every three to six months.

Remember, though, that, even more than actual talent, qualities such as determination, confidence, persistence and toughness will really help you get on. The entertainment world is hard and you will probably need to develop quite a thick skin to cope with the pressures and rejections and to make a success of it.

HOW MUCH CAN YOU MAKE?

It can be anything from nothing if you are at a poorly attended gig that is paid through a 'door split', to thousands for a corporate gig.

COSTS

Travel and accommodation expenses (if these are not paid for by your client), costumes, make-up and props are the main costs for entertainers, as well as the usual expenses for advertising and admin.

TRAINING AND QUALIFICATIONS

You don't need training or qualifications to do any of these jobs but the more training and practice you can get in your skill the better!

PROS

This is a great way of using your talents and, possibly, making money from them. If you get really good you may be able to give up your day job to do what you love doing full-time.

CONS

It can be a hard slog trying to entertain ungrateful, difficult audiences in miserable little pubs in nasty parts of town for very little (if any) money until you get established and can pick and choose your venues and charge a reasonable amount.

USEFUL CONTACTS

www.bbc.co.uk/talent/ – the BBC's own talent section

Jillie Bushell Associates, 020 7582 3048,
www.jilliebushell.com – one of the many corporate entertainment agencies in Britain

Paul Farris Entertainments, 020 8334 9905, www.paulfarris.tv
– another entertainment agency

City Lit, 16 Stukeley Street, London WC2B 5LJ, 020 7405 3347, www.citylit.ac.uk

Comedy People, 01727 867454, www.comedypeople.com

www.vocalist.org.uk – lists the many talent competitions around the country, including ones that lead to TV talent shows

Master of ceremonies

If you have a strong voice, a good presence and you enjoy formal occasions, this could be a great way of earning some extra money. You will be needed to shepherd people to and from dinner, to announce guests, introduce speakers and generally make sure an event runs as it should.

HOW TO DO IT

Professional toastmasters (and the majority are men, although there are some women) tend to have taken a course before even attempting to do this for money. There are various approved courses around the country. For example, the London Guild of Toastmasters (they tend to be grouped regionally) runs a three-day residential course in Chicheley in Buckinghamshire which costs £980. 'Once you have taken this course you may apply for association to the London Guild for up to two years during which period you are assigned a mentor who will generally ease you in to that crucial stage before you become a full member if you so wish,' says toastmaster Brian Sylvester.

Ivor Spencer, who runs a butlers' school and agency in London, also runs a toastmasters' course and agency. His is a 13-day course, run on a one-to-one basis. He says, 'You will be taught everything that has to be known about the profession, from officiating at a cocktail party to a royal banquet.' The course costs £3,500 plus VAT, which has to be paid a month before the course commences. At the end of the course you gain a diploma from the Ivor Spencer School for Professional Toastmasters.

Once you have taken a course you will need to splash out on the right clothes. The traditional red jacket costs around £350, and you will also need some proper shirts, a white bow tie, good trousers, patent-leather shoes and a gavel. 'When you start off you get work through colleagues,' says toastmaster John Grosse. 'They just pass on jobs they can't do. There's a lot of work out there, mostly weddings and masonic ladies' nights, but we also enjoy doing corporate work because that tends to be during the day.'

Some toastmasters will travel all round the country to jobs; others prefer to stay in their local area. There is no age limit for this job; some toastmasters are still going strong into their eighties. So long as you have the strength and a good voice there is nothing to stop you. Quite often the confidence of age can help you do this even if your voice is not quite as full as it once was.

As well as the regional groups you can join, there are the National Association of Toastmasters and the Institute of Toastmasters, which are both members of the Toastmasters General Council. There are also some agencies that find work for toastmasters, such as the Glen Grant Entertainment Agency (contact details below); they also find bands and other entertainers for private and corporate events.

HOW MUCH CAN YOU MAKE?

Professionals tend to charge between £200 and £350 a session.

COSTS

Your main cost will be the clothes and gavel, which should set you back around £1,000 altogether. After that there are your travel expenses, unless you charge your clients for these, which many do.

TRAINING AND QUALIFICATIONS

You need to take at least one approved course in being a toastmaster.

PROS

If you're a show-off, have a good, strong voice and enjoy formal occasions this is a great way of making money in the evenings and at weekends. You also get to meet people – quite often celebrities or royalty – and enjoy complimentary posh meals.

CONS

The uniform can be very hot and uncomfortable in some venues.

USEFUL CONTACTS

The Federation of Toastmasters and Masters of Ceremonies, www.federationtoastmasters.fsnet.co.uk

Glen Grant Entertainment Agency, 3 Kinross Avenue, Worcester Park, Surrey KT4 7AJ, 020 8337 9018, www.glen-grant.fsnet.co.uk

Guild of International Toastmasters, www.ivorspencer.com

The Institute of Toastmasters, www.institutetoastmastersgb.fsnet.co.uk

London Guild of Toastmasters, 020 8570 6977, www.toastmastersguild.org.uk

National Association of Toastmasters, www.natuk.com

Busking and street entertaining

You may not believe it but some buskers and street entertainers make a good full-time living. Proper street entertainers with a big and impressive act move from street festival to street festival around the world, collecting serious money! Many buskers, though, just use it as a way of supplementing their income and getting some practice on their instrument or their act at the same time.

HOW TO DO IT

Buskers and street entertainers are different things, as street entertainers, particularly, will tell you. Street entertainers often have a full, theatrical-type act which can last half an hour or even an hour; they tend to perform at specially organised festivals and are paid by the organisers, usually through an agent. Many get this kind of work through the agency Fools Paradise (contact details below).

Buskers perform in a more ad hoc way, either legally or illegally. Quite a lot of buskers start off illegally – they just pick a pitch and do their act until they're told to move on – then they find themselves legal ways of making some cash once they have a good act. There's nothing to stop you playing your guitar or saxophone or bagpipes in the middle of your high street with a cap on the floor for the coins (well, nothing until the police come along and move you on). Some places are more lenient than others, but you will need to get used to being moved from one area to another.

There are now special busking festivals, however, and public places where you are specifically encouraged to busk. Covent Garden in London, for example, has a very organised system for buskers. They don't take everyone, though, and you have to be accepted by the busking authorities there. You can find out about performing here at http://streetperformers.arecool.net/. Also, the London Underground now admits regulated buskers in certain stations. Again, you have to do an audition to be accepted, but you can find out about this, and fill in a form online, at http://tube.tfl.gov.uk/busking/.

'There is a loose network of buskers who follow the sun,' says street entertainer Jason Maverick. 'They go from country to country while the good weather's there. They can make good money because it's cash in hand but it's hard work. Sometimes you can wait for hours to get a good time slot in a tourist area. There's often a lot of hanging around for them during the day.'

You can find out about all kinds of festivals, conventions (such as the European Juggling Convention!), world events, agents and props suppliers at the comprehensive street performers' website, www.performers.net.

It may seem obvious, but whether you are a busker or a street entertainer, the better your act and the more professional your attitude, the more successful you can be. And it is possible to be very successful, particularly if you happen to be seen and heard by a record company executive or top agent.

HOW MUCH CAN YOU MAKE?

From pennies here and there to thousands a year, depending on how good you are, how much work you do and where you do it.

COSTS

Travel is the main cost, as well as props and other kit if you use them in your act. If you get really professional you may start paying agents' fees too.

TRAINING AND QUALIFICATIONS

You don't need any training or qualifications, although it helps to be able to play your instrument or do your act properly!

PROS

If you love entertaining, like people and enjoy the outdoors this is a great way to make a living – mostly in cash too!

CONS

You really need a lot of energy and drive to be able to make this work. It can be very demoralising to be entertaining for hours on end in the cold with just a few coppers thrown into your hat. Street entertainers often have highly physical acts which can be very tiring.

USEFUL CONTACTS

www.foolsparadise.co.uk – the main agency for street entertainers

Performers' Network, www.performers.net – an online community for international variety acts and street performers

www.vocalist.org.uk – go to the busking section on this

website and you'll find all kinds of busking organisations and street festivals around Britain and throughout the world

Disc jockey

Got no talent as a musician or performer? Don't worry. If you have a box of records and a flair for spinning them, go and be a DJ!

HOW TO DO IT

If you're even thinking of becoming a DJ it's likely that you will already have a large vinyl record collection – at least 100 records but probably more. You will also have been practising at parties or in the privacy of your own home, mixing, scratching, experimenting with sounds and beats, and you probably go to bars and clubs where good DJs are working to get inspiration.

If you are confident that you can do the job, go to local bars and nightclubs and offer your services for free for a night. Most savvy bar and club owners expect DJs to do their first session for free anyway.

The kind of work you get generally depends on the type of music you love. Industrial-strength garage or drum-and-bass is not generally wanted by bars and laid-back clubs and parties, so you would get work only at big clubs and special events. If you have an extensive collection of sixties, seventies or eighties music, though, you could get work at parties, wedding receptions and pubs. For these kinds of gigs you will really need a car or van as you will usually need to supply the equipment as well as the music itself. Most venues don't have their own mixer desk, speakers and so on, and anyway, it is better to use your own stuff with which you are familiar.

To get this sort of work you should advertise locally, set up a small website telling people what you do and work to get yourself on the books of entertainment agencies that place bands and other entertainers for parties and functions. You can also do a lot with word-of-mouth advertising if you're good!

HOW MUCH CAN YOU MAKE?

Anything from a tenner in expenses for a first night to thousands if you become a 'name' DJ who punters will follow from club to club.

COSTS

You will need to spend money each week on new records, although you may get some sent to you free once you become a name, and you will also need your own equipment for places that don't already have decks, plus, of course, transport to take it from place to place.

TRAINING AND QUALIFICATIONS

You don't need any training or qualifications.

PROS

If you are passionate about music but can't play it yourself, this is a great way to make money from it and have a good night out at the same time.

CONS

It's a highly competitive area and you may find it hard to get yourself established. It's also very easy to get sucked into the drink and drugs scene that often goes with DJing, so stay strong!

USEFUL CONTACTS

www.decks.co.uk – DJ accessories of all kinds here

www.djsource.co.uk – a comprehensive website for DJ accessories, chat with other DJs and all kinds of information

Case study

Matthew Plummer, 26, is a PR executive, but once or twice a week he works as a DJ in a couple of trendy London bars. 'DJing is the *best* way of making good money doing what you love,' he enthuses. 'Last night I made £120 playing my favourite records for five hours in a cool club. How much better can that be!'

Matthew favours house and lounge music and has a collection of nearly 700 records which he started in the mid-nineties. 'You don't have to have that many records,' he says. 'If you are starting now and you buy two or three a week, you would have enough by the end of the year. But it's only worth it if you love the music. To me, it's my passion so I'm happy spending the money.'

He says he always offers to do the first night for free to prove himself, but adds that once you get regular work in one club or bar you can get lots more as word spreads. 'If you and your music increase the bar takings then you're on to a winner!' he says.

Currently Matthew doesn't have a car but he is saving up for one to help transport his records. 'It's really heavy to carry the stuff and I don't want to spend my earnings on a taxi. At the moment I'm taking the bus but I'm saving hard for a car. It'll be so much easier with that.'

Product demonstrating/selling

You may have come across product demonstrators in department stores, trying to show you how wonderful something is. If you are good at selling and you are a bit of an entertainer on the quiet (or the loud!), you could do this too.

HOW TO DO IT

There are all kinds of product demonstration and commission-only jobs around. Kitchenware is often sold in this way, as are cosmetics and perfumes, but now loan and credit card companies are also using commission-only salespeople to sign up potential customers.

You have to be confident of your ability to engage with the public and sell to them to do this kind of work. Generally you get paid commission only, which means that if you don't sell you don't earn – a daunting prospect for most.

It may take a while before you make any serious money. You have to gain experience and confidence and begin to understand different types of people and what makes them buy. There is a very large drop-out rate in this job owing to the difficulties in making a success of it.

There are often adverts for product demonstrators in *The Stage* newspaper, as resting actors make some of the best demonstrators. You can also get work through ads in local papers or through promotional agencies.

HOW MUCH CAN YOU MAKE?

Depending on the product line, the amount you sell and the level of commission, you could make a fair amount. But you may not make much in the first few weeks while you get your confidence up.

COSTS

There are no costs involved other than your travel expenses.

TRAINING AND QUALIFICATIONS

You don't need any qualifications, although the company whose product you will be selling will give you some training at the start.

PROS

If you are good and you get a good commission rate you could make some serious money. You can also have fun if you engage with shoppers in a friendly way.

CONS

This can be very soul-destroying work. Many product demonstrators give up after a few weeks when they find they cannot sell their product. It is also tiring and you need a lot of stamina to keep positive, energetic and entertaining all day long.

USEFUL CONTACTS

IFM Events, 020 8524 7111, www.ifmevents.co.uk – often have work for product demostrators.

Promotional work

If you look good and you know how to be friendly and polite, you can get regular, reasonable work at exhibitions, conferences, shows and all sorts of events.

HOW TO DO IT

There are agencies all round the country that supply people for promotional events. You can find one in your locality by looking in the Yellow Pages or, better, on the Internet. You will probably find some listed under model agencies and others under marketing, PR or promotions.

The agencies will want a CV and, importantly, some good photos of you, both head and shoulders and full-length. Many agencies will arrange their own photos and they may charge for this. Make sure that the agency is well established and gets regular work before you pay for this service.

The work you get may include handing out leaflets or manning stalls at exhibitions, looking after guests at corporate events, working on reception desks at conferences, exhibitions or other events, handing out leaflets or products to the public at stations, shopping malls or on the streets, and many other wacky and not so wacky tasks.

You don't have to be a great looker to do this kind of work, although some jobs demand men and women who have model looks and are well dressed and groomed. 'Some clients just want someone who's fun and able to talk to people,' says a spokes-woman from Kreate Promotions (contact details below). 'There's lots of work of all sorts coming in all the time, so even if you're not the best-looking person in the world, you will probably get regular work if you're fun and enthusiastic.'

HOW MUCH CAN YOU MAKE?

It depends how much you work. An average daily rate is about £70–£120 in London and a little less elsewhere.

COSTS

There are no costs involved other than travel, which is often paid for by the client.

TRAINING AND QUALIFICATIONS

You don't need training or qualifications.

PROS

This is a nice, easy way of making some money — largely by being friendly and looking good. If you have free days during the week it can be a useful way of making some cash in between your other work commitments.

CONS

The jobs can be very dull and often involve being on your feet all day and dealing with difficult or dense members of the public. Also, the work can be sporadic, and therefore unreliable.

USEFUL CONTACTS

IFM Events, 020 8524 7111, www.ifmevents.co.uk

Kreate Ltd, 020 7401 9007/8 (London), 0131 553 5007 (Edinburgh), www.kreatepromotions.co.uk

L&G, 020 7481 1475 – deals with royal functions, fashion shows, movie premieres, etc.

Tony Page, 020 8830 4000 – a recruitment agency with an events department

Voice-overs

If you have a good or, better still, a versatile voice that can do accents and imitate celebrities, you could make a lot of money out of it.

HOW TO DO IT

Not everyone can become a voice-over artist, but many try! The first thing you must do if you are serious about getting into this is to put a voice showreel CD together. The Showreel.com in West London offers a comprehensive service to anyone wanting to produce a voice-over showreel (see their excellent website below), but many production companies will also do one for you if you know what you want.

The showreel should show you off to your best advantage with snatches of ads you have voiced (or pretended to voice), accents and character voices you can do, and straight corporate 'reads' or narrations for TV documentaries. It doesn't matter if you haven't actually done any of these – you can pretend quite easily using scripts and sound effects.

Once you have a good showreel you should send it round to as many voice-over agencies as you can find. Look in *Contacts* (£12.99, The Spotlight) for a list of voice-over agencies. Most serious voice-over work comes through professional agencies, and it is hard to get work without them. You could also contact TV, radio and ad production agencies direct, however. *Contacts* has a list of some of them, as does the *Writers' and Artists' Year Book* (A&C Black, £13.99).

HOW MUCH CAN YOU MAKE?

Anything from £50 a go doing some ads for local radio to hundreds of thousands for top cartoon series or TV and radio ad campaigns.

COSTS

You will need to make a voice-over showreel which will cost at least £350 to produce and then, if you get the work, you will need to pay for your own travel.

TRAINING AND QUALIFICATIONS

You don't need any training or qualifications but most top voice-over practitioners are trained actors, singers or comedians. It also helps to have a presenting or broadcasting background.

PROS

This can be a great way of making a lot of money by having fun with your voice.

CONS

It is an incredibly competitive area and it's far more likely that you will never get work than that you will. The level of work is very much dependent on the state of the economy – if there is very little advertising around even well-established voice-over artists get little work.

USEFUL CONTACTS

www.jinglebiz.com/vocourse.htm – a US course on becoming a voice-over practitioner

www.ohms.com/vohowto.htm – a cyber-book on how to get into the voice-over business

The Showreel.com, 229 Acton Lane, Chiswick, London W4 5DD, 020 8995 3232, www.theshowreel.com

Club nights

Have you seen those adverts for special club nights in your local papers? Maybe it's an eighties theme night or a drum-and-bass night with specialist DJs, or it could be a singles night or an over-30s night. Someone organises these and it could be you.

HOW TO DO IT

There are four main elements to running a club night: the venue, the theme, the marketing and the organising. If you are a 'together' kind of person, have a flair for marketing and you enjoy going out at night yourself, this should be easily do-able.

First, find your venue. That's almost more important than the theme itself. A nightclub or restaurant, bar or hotel with a party room that is central and easily accessible is a good place to start. If you already have somewhere you like going to – and so do your friends – this would be the best place to ask at first. Otherwise, go and talk to the managers of a few venues that look possible, tell them what you want to do, how many people you think you could bring into their club, and see what they say.

Obviously Friday and Saturday nights are the best for going out, but many venues, particularly clubs, may be booked up then, or they might charge too much. For specialist nights, however, you could get away with a Sunday or Thursday night, or even Monday to Wednesday if yours is a happening town and the theme is really popular. Different places will do different deals. Some will want to charge you an up-front fee for the venue after which you take all the money for the tickets; others might do a door-split so you don't have to put up money beforehand. For most clubs and hotels, the money they make on the bar alone will make it worthwhile for them to allow you to keep the door money, so if you're clever you could even negotiate a percentage of the bar profits. Worth a try!

Once you have decided on your date and your venue, work on getting the word out. Whether it's a singles night, a sixties theme night or a celebrity DJ event, you will need to let people in the area know about it. Use the Internet as much as you can – create a good Internet flyer (which will double up as the design for a printed flyer) and send it out to all your friends, asking them to forward it to all theirs. This can bring in a lot of people on its own. Also, try to get the word out on newsgroups and local websites for free. Put printed flyers up in any hotel, club, restaurant or shop in your area that will take them, as well as on student union noticeboards and anywhere where your target audience is likely to be.

Do as much as you can with PR, which doesn't cost anything, unlike advertising. Try to start this three months before the event, if possible, because many magazines have a three-month 'lead time' (in other words they go to print three months before the magazine is published). Local radio stations would be particularly useful. Send information in to any listings programme they do and offer free tickets for a competition through the station. You could even offer to do the event in conjunction with the station, which would allow them to promote themselves for free on your flyers and at the venue itself. This is a win-win situation as you get free advertising for the event while they get a free marketing opportunity.

Talk to local restaurants and shops to see if you can get some free prizes for competitions at the event. You can mention their business on your flyers and in the press release, which would give them free advertising. You could offer prizes for best costumes or for a raffle or other competition at the event, which should also attract punters.

You need to be organised from the start with an event like this. It's a good idea to set up a simple website with information about the event, a contact email address for you and information about how tickets can be bought online. If you don't want to set up an account with Paypal (www.paypal.com) and you don't have the facility to take credit card bookings online then you could either offer to take cheques or, if the venue is willing, sell tickets through their booking system. You may lose a percentage in administration costs, particularly if you do it through the venue, but it is often worth it just to make it easier for the punters to pay.

You will need to keep a record of ticket sales and liaise with the venue, entertainers, caterers (if you're doing your own food, etc.) and bouncers if this is your responsibility. Get to the venue early and oversee everything and, of course, be at the venue during the event so that you can make sure it is all running smoothly.

HOW MUCH CAN YOU MAKE?

It depends how many events you run and how many come. It could be anything from losing money on a bad night to making thousands if you get a big venue and a percentage of the bar takings.

COSTS

You may have to pay for the venue, which could cost you hundreds, and you will probably have to pay for flyers and possibly posters and other types of advertising. The venue may not have its own door security so you may have to pay for bouncers too.

TRAINING AND QUALIFICATIONS

You don't need any training or qualifications for this.

PROS

This is a fun way of making money – and it could be big money if you run a sizeable event that is popular. It could also get you good contacts in your area for running other money-making events elsewhere.

CONS

This kind of thing can go badly awry if you choose the wrong venue or the wrong night and few people come. If you don't sell enough tickets beforehand you might lose all the money you put into hiring the venue in the first place.

USEFUL CONTACTS

NoChex, www.nochex.com – a popular method of paying online. However, as with PayPal, both you and the payee have to be registered with them to enable the transaction

PayPal, www.paypal.com – the most used method of paying online; if you are setting up an e-commerce site you should sign up with them

Selling stories to newspapers

With the media positively gagging for celebrity trivia, there has never been a better time for making money by selling stories to the papers. Keep your eyes and ears open – and think carefully about what newspapers really want. Just spotting a celebrity in the street won't net you much cash. Spotting a celebrity beating a traffic warden around the head with their shopping, however, could earn you a tidy sum.

HOW TO DO IT

Rule one is research your market. Find out who wants what. That means reading the papers and seeing what sort of gossip column prints what sort of story. The back page of the *Sunday Telegraph* is looking for something very different from the *Mirror*'s 3 a.m. girls. Certain people are regulars in certain columns. Read and learn.

Once you've done this, then keep your eyes and ears open. When you think you have a story, gather as much information on it as you can, then approach the most appropriate column. Most of them make this easy by providing a contact email address. Don't give them the whole story right away – just enough to get them interested. But *do* remember to give a contact number. And when they call, ask about payment before you spill the beans. Don't worry – they're used to it.

Get your facts straight. It's no good saying you think you may have seen 'that bloke from *Corrie*' falling out of a taxi cab. Journalists are busy people. They don't like their time being wasted. And don't think you can get away with making things up. Despite their dodgy reputation, journalists do actually check things out. If you're caught out telling porkies then the story won't get printed, you won't get paid and you won't be trusted again.

HOW MUCH CAN YOU MAKE?

From £50 for a simple tip-off to six figures if you are Rebecca Loos, the PR girl who had textual relations with England soccer captain David Beckham.

COSTS

How much does a phone call or an email cost?

TRAINING AND QUALIFICATIONS

Absolutely none required – except the ability to spot a good story when you see one.

PROS

How else can you earn £50 just by picking up the phone?

CONS

In most cases you won't be paid unless the story is printed. And if you spill the beans on a friend you risk losing them.

USEFUL CONTACTS

News International (for the *Sun*, *The Times* and the *News of the World*) – 020 7782 5000

Associated Newspapers (for the *Mail* and the *Evening Standard*) – 020 7938 6000

Express Newspapers (for the *Express* and the *Star*) – 020 7928 8000

CHAPTER TWELVE

Buying and Selling

G IVE YOUR HOME a good spring clean – whatever the time of year – and create a pile of things that you don't want any more. Sell them in a car boot sale, to a rag-and-bone man, on eBay or Amazon, in local freebie advertising sheets or by advertising them on a postcard in a local shop window. If you really like buying and selling, consider importing to sell to shops or on the Internet or through word of mouth. Also, export if you have access to goods that are wanted abroad. Selling things – particularly things you have in your house already – is probably the quickest way of making some instant cash. So if you need an injection of funds, look round your home for stuff you don't want *now*.

Selling on the Internet

It's amazing what you can sell on the Internet, and lots of people are doing it. According to research from NatWest FastPay, Britons are hoarding in the region of £3.5 billion worth of 'stuff', with 20 per cent of people having at least one item that's worth more than £500. More than 10 per cent have over £500 worth of books and old clothes stored away. Go on, make some cash out of it!

HOW TO DO IT

eBay

You can sell pretty much anything on www.ebay.co.uk (or the original US version, www.ebay.com) and people do! Some make a good regular living out of it; others just use it to sell stuff they don't want any more. Buying and selling on eBay or Amazon has grown in popularity in recent times but, of course, it doesn't always work out if you get a bad customer. The Office of Fair Trading has seen an increase in the number of complaints about failed transactions, ranging from late or non-delivery of items to buyers and non-payment to sellers to goods being of lesser value than or substantially different from the description sent to the buyer. So it has now published tips on safe trading via Internet auctions on its website (www.oft.gov.uk), which are worth reading before you launch into any sort of sales.

Once you have got used to it, selling on eBay is not hard, but there are a few tips to remember to ensure that you get the best price. eBay has all sorts of tutorials to guide you through the selling/buying/bidding process. It is definitely worth studying the ins and outs before you start using it. Look for an item that is the same or similar to what you are selling and see how much it is going for. Read listings to get a feel for the way it's done and try to improve upon them with your own listings.

The words you use in the title are crucial. There is a vast number of items listed on eBay at any one time, and most people do not simply wade through all the items listed in a specific category – they search using a particular term, usually confined to words likely to be in the title. Get the right term in your title and you'll get the maximum number of people seeing your item.

It is crucial to give a full (and honest) description of the item. Most buyers assume the worst if no description has been given and just move on. Note that honesty is vital on eBay. If there is a fault in the item, then make sure you say so, although there is no reason why you shouldn't cast it in as positive a light as possible.

Always include the cost of postage and packing. If you leave that box blank, people might assume that you are going to sting them for a high fee after the auction ends, and may avoid you. Always include at least one picture of your item if you can. Buyers are usually happier to have a picture to look at so they know what they're getting. If you can't include a picture, then make the description extra detailed.

When you sell an item, you have the choice of selling by auction (with a variety of cut-off dates to choose from – up to ten days) or as a 'buy it now' category, where the price you list is the price you get when it sells. Be careful with your pricing on eBay – sometimes if you price an item too low it sells for the minimum, and if you price it too high you don't get any bidders. It is a real skill getting the pricing right.

You can start your auction at any price you like, and you can also set a reserve, i.e. a price that is your lowest acceptable limit – if the bidding doesn't go that high, you're not obliged to sell. The end time of your auction is absolutely crucial. Make sure you get this right. It is a fact that the vast majority of bids on eBay come in the first 24 hours of the listing and in the final 12–24 hours. Indeed, many items attract a flurry of bids in the last few minutes or even seconds. Always consider when your target market is likely to be using the site, and set your auctions up so that they end when most people are likely to be browsing.

If you specialise in one area, say dolls or football memorabilia, you may be able to make money by buying things at a cheap rate from the US eBay site then selling them on for more money on the UK site, or vice versa. Many people go to car boot sales at the weekends looking for specific items, then sell them on eBay during the week. If you know your stuff, go for it! If you are an artist, jewellery maker or clothes designer, or if you have an excess amount of stock, then eBay offers the facility of having your own store for just £6 a month. This is an excellent low-cost solution for anyone who doesn't want the hassle or high cost of setting up their own online store.

Amazon, etc.

Many people just like to sell old books, videos, DVDs and CDs, and www.amazon.co.uk is the most popular site for this. Another website that is also gaining in popularity is www.abebooks.co.uk. Books sell particularly well on these sites as they are known best for reading materials. It takes very little time to advertise your books, film or music here. Simply log on to Amazon and search for the book, CD, DVD or whatever item it is you're selling, click on the box that says 'sell yours here', choose the condition of the book and set a price that is lower than or the same as the lowest price there at the moment – after all, you want to sell it, don't you? The whole process takes about two minutes. You will be notified by email when someone buys the book and you will need to send it off by first-class post within two days. Postage and packing are added on to the price automatically. The money will be put into your account electronically within a couple of weeks.

You can also register with www.abebooks.co.uk and follow their instructions for selling books online. This website also has connections with Amazon, so if you like you can advertise with them both at the same time. Check out the fees charged by both and see which suits you better.

Setting up your own e-commerce website

See the 'e-commerce' section in Chapter 13 for lots of information on how to set up your own selling website.

HOW MUCH CAN YOU MAKE?

The sky's the limit! Some people make a fantastic living simply buying and selling on eBay. It all depends on what you have, how much time you want to spend on it, and how much you know about your products.

COSTS

None, unless you want to buy a digital camera to take pictures of your items. If you are buying in order to sell, then you will of course have to factor in the cost of paying for the goods first.

TRAINING AND QUALIFICATIONS

You don't need any training or qualifications.

PROS

This is a nice, easy way of making money from junk in your house. It is also a good way of buying and selling goods you know about with almost no overheads – no market stall or shop to pay for, just postage if you decide not to include that in the price.

CONS

You need to know what you are doing with these kinds of sales. If you are not clued up you could find yourself losing money if you don't set a lower limit in auctions.

USEFUL CONTACTS

www.abebooks.co.uk

www.amazon.co.uk

www.ebay.co.uk

www.fool.co.uk – look at their discussion board, called 'Living Below Your Means', for useful discussion 'threads' on selling online

www.nochex.com – a popular method of paying online

www.paypal.com – the most used method of paying online; if you are setting up an e-commerce site you should sign up with them

Case study

American Thea Newcomb, who lives in Glasgow and runs her own websites, www.soyouvebeendumped.com and www.stopbigamy.co.uk, has been buying and selling on eBay for years. 'I've sold everything from postcards to a car!' she says. 'In the States I sold a '68 Roadster for $13,000. It didn't even run – the guy had to come over and tow it away, but it was a beautiful car, a classic.'

Now she sells anything she has around the house that she doesn't want, and she also keeps her eyes open in charity shops and at car boot sales for anything cheap she could sell for more on eBay. 'I've just sold a mobile phone for £150. I got it as an upgrade and hated it. I've sold loads of memorabilia for bands because I used to work for a record company. You can make good money on posters, programmes, CDs and T-shirts if they're the right ones. Not everything sells, and you need to learn from your mistakes. I sold a fabulous, canvas-backed poster of U2 once for about £40, and I know it was worth close to £100. I should have put a reserve on that. On the other hand, I sold a sealed CD single I got for free from a record-plugger for $25 once. You just never know!'

Recently Thea has started to sell more things on Amazon. She finds it easier as you don't have to photograph the item – the photo is already on the site. She keeps a box in her home into which she puts anything she finds around the house which she wants to sell. 'It's a good system,' she says. 'It's tidy and I know where to lay my hands on the stuff when I sell it.'

Car boot sales

Car boot sales have become almost a religion for Britons! Some just do them once or twice a year to get rid of junk; others do them every week and make serious money out of them.

HOW TO DO IT

Search every room and every cupboard in the house and gather up everything you don't want. You really can sell *anything* in a car boot sale, so just put as much as you can fit into your car the night before the sale. Don't take anything you know to be valuable, however. People who go to car boot sales expect to pay no more than a few pounds for anything, so save anything good for eBay or local second-hand and antiques shops.

Car boot sales are advertised in local papers and on the walls or gates of the places where they are held. If you ask around, you should be able to find out which are the biggest and most popular in your area. The *Sun* newspaper also publishes a list of all the car boot sales in the UK each week, so you could simply pick the one nearest to you in this list.

Make sure you get to the site very early – ideally as soon as they open the gates. You will find that at popular sites there will already be a queue of cars lined up outside long before it opens. When you get in, set up your table (a wallpaper pasting table seems to be best) and, if you have it, your clothes rail, but don't put anything on them yet. Dealers, and other stall-holders, will crowd round you long before the public are allowed into the sale, and they will try to buy your best bits off you for a knock-down price. To avoid this annoyance – and often nastiness – just don't put anything out until the last minute.

When you do, make sure everything is priced and laid out in such a way that people can easily see what you have. Small items such as jewellery, CDs and perfume often go most quickly, so put these at the front and don't just take the first offer you get. Others may offer more. Be prepared to negotiate on most things, though, and don't expect to make more than a few pounds on anything.

Take a bum-bag or other type of purse with lots of change and small notes in it, and also take food and drink with you. You will be there for a few hours. It is also very helpful to do these sales with a friend. If there are two of you then one will always be able to go off and look around or go to the loo while the other watches the stall.

Whatever you have left at the end can be put back in boxes and dropped off at the charity shop on your way home. If no one has bought these items this time round, it's likely that no one will next time either.

Another way to make money from car boot sales is to hold or help organise them, rather than simply going along to them. If you know of a school playground or easily accessible piece of wasteland that could host a sale, get in touch with the owners and offer a price for one day a week or a month. After this it is just a question of advertising the event – if you arrange it, people will come.

HOW MUCH CAN YOU MAKE?

Usually somewhere between £20 and a few hundred, depending on what you have and how good a salesperson you are.

COSTS

Petrol and the cost of setting up a pitch – usually between £5 and £10, depending on where you are.

TRAINING AND QUALIFICATIONS

You don't need any training or qualifications for this.

PROS

This is a nice, easy and often interesting way of making some money out of your junk. You might also find some bargains on the other stalls!

CONS

The vast majority of car boot sales start at unearthly hours of the morning, and it can be particularly demoralising to get up at 5 a.m. on a winter's morning and lug your stuff to the sale only for it to be rained off within hours. Some people can get nasty if you don't give them something for a knock-down price. You may be disappointed at how little you get for your stuff.

USEFUL CONTACTS

www.carbootcalendar.com – the website of the £1.50 publication Car Boot Calendar, which you can buy at several car boot sales, featuring lots of information and upcoming sales

Garage sales

These are more popular in the States than over here, but that doesn't mean to say you can't make some good money out of selling your junk this way in Britain.

HOW TO DO IT

First, go through every cupboard and every room in the house and gather up a pile of stuff you want to get rid of. Then pick a date and time for your sale and advertise it. If you're feeling energetic, and you don't mind the neighbours seeing just what kind of junk you have, make some cheap flyers (black-and-white ones printed off from your computer will do) and post them through doors in the surrounding streets. Otherwise, put a card up in the newsagent's window and put signs up on your front gate – you could even consider putting an ad in the local paper, if it's not too expensive. Make it very clear on all the advertising that you don't want dealers (unless, for some reason, you do!), as they will try to offer you tuppence to take your best stuff away and can even get nasty when you refuse.

Get your stuff ready before the sale – ideally the day before. Make it easy for browsers to sort through items: group them together as they do in department stores. Hang clothes, if possible, on a rail, not on hooks or nails on the walls; display things on tables where possible, or on a blanket on the ground; put price tags on everything, but be willing to negotiate; plug in electronics and have batteries in battery-operated items so that people can check they work; put large and more expensive items near the street, or in your drive-way, to attract passers-by.

Have a bum-bag or cash box ready with lots of small change and a few notes in it, and get at least one person (a friend or family member) to help you. If they want to sell things too, use different-coloured price tags for their things so that you know what's what.

Anything you have left over can be put in boxes and taken to the charity shop.

HOW MUCH CAN YOU MAKE?

It depends on what you have and how many people want it! Anything from a few pounds for a bad sale to a few hundred if you're selling off much of your home.

COSTS

The only costs are for advertising and printing your flyers.

TRAINING AND QUALIFICATIONS

You don't need any training or qualifications.

PROS

You can make money out of stuff you don't want and you don't have to travel anywhere to do it. Even if it's raining you can still hold the sale if you have a big enough garage.

CONS

There is no guarantee that anyone will turn up, and if they do you may not get anything like the money you were hoping for for your old treasures.

Auctions

There are auctions and then there are auctions! We're not talking Sotheby's here – but it's amazing what you can pick up at police auctions, bankruptcy auctions and others.

HOW TO DO IT

The point of going to these auctions is to pick up cheaply goods that you can sell on for more. What you pick depends on what you know, what method you have of selling them on and what the competition is. You might want to take a market stall or car boot pitch to sell small, inexpensive items, or you could sell second-hand computer equipment direct to the public if you know your stuff and can pick it up cheaply at auctions. You can use classified ads, particularly free ones such as the service offered by *Loot*, the free ads paper, to sell individual high-price items.

Check out your local phone book for auction houses – some specialise in selling computers, cars or bankrupt stock. Also, ask at your local police station about the next police auction. They sell stolen goods that they have not been able to return to their rightful owners, and you can pick up all sorts of things, from jewellery to bicycles. Lost-and-found auctions are also worth a visit, including those run by the rail networks.

Always look out for other dealers at an auction so that you're not trying to outbid professionals, and try to pick an area without much competition. If everyone is buying up computers and furniture, go for bicycles, for example.

You can get some real bargains at bankrupt-stock auctions. When a business or household goes into bankruptcy a receiver is appointed to sell off any assets to repay debts. Stuff tends to be sold at very low rates. You can find out about this kind of auction in the *Financial Times* or in local and regional daily newspapers. You can also bid online at bankrupt-stock auction websites. Look at www.uk-cheap.com for a list of these websites.

HOW MUCH CAN YOU MAKE?

Anything from nothing to thousands, depending on what you buy, how good you are at selling and where you live.

COSTS

Your main costs will be buying the goods in the first place, transporting them and then advertising them.

TRAINING AND QUALIFICATIONS

You don't need any training or qualifications.

PROS

You could make a lot of money pretty easily if you know what to buy and where to sell it quickly and easily.

CONS

You could end up owing money if you don't buy the right things and can't sell them. Also, it can take a while to get the hang of auctions and learn to pay the right price for the right things.

USEFUL CONTACTS

www.bumblebeeauctions.co.uk – this is an online police auction site; most of the police stations taking part are in the South, which could be a problem if you live in the North and have to pick the goods up from the station

www.government-auctions.co.uk – sign up here to find out about auctions held by the police, Customs and Excise, the Revenue, and so on

Case study

Senh Lou from Kent has often used government auctions to buy cheap goods for himself, but he warns that they can be too much of a hassle to bring in regular bargains. 'They are quite good but not brilliant,' he says. 'Often there is VAT to pay and a bidder's premium to add to the final bid price. These two costs combined can add up to 35 per cent to the total cost. I saw a decent mountain bike sell for £100, but with fees and VAT, it actually cost in total around £133. You must mentally add these costs before bidding or else you could be in for a shock when you come to pay for your items!

'The other issues I have with these auctions are (a) you can't test the products so electrical items may be a bit of a lottery, (b) you may have to wait ages before items of interest to you are called up, and (c) there are just too many people in these auctions these days trying to buy cheap and sell on for profit. There are many experienced traders there, coming back probably every week, and they're on the ball with prices, so real bargains are not too common.'

His advice to anyone thinking of using the auctions either to buy for themselves or in order to sell on for a profit is to ask for a preview booklet of what's up for sale, to take a calculator along to work out what the total costs are before bidding, and not to be afraid to walk away when the price goes above what is the most that you'd expect to pay. He also suggests that you try different auctions in your area as some are much better than others.

Property development

Judging by all the TV programmes on the subject, you'd think this was an easy way to make money. In fact it's nothing of the sort, but if you know what you're doing it is possible to make thousands in a few months.

HOW TO DO IT

Not everyone can think of buying, doing up and selling property for money. For a start you need to have some cash to invest, as you will need to put money down as a deposit. If the property will be your only home then you will only have to put down about 10 per cent – or even less – of the selling price as a deposit. If it is to be on a buy-to-let basis – in other words, it's not going to be your home – you will need to put at least 20 per cent down. Not only that, but if you are going to do the place up you will need cash to pay for materials (if you will be doing the work yourself) and labour (if you won't). Obviously, the more work you need to do, the more expensive it will be. While the work is in hand, you will also need to pay the monthly mortgage instalment as well as other bills, such as council tax and your solicitor's fees, stamp duty and surveyor's fees. It all adds up!

If you *do* have this kind of money to invest, however, then you need to approach this as a business. The most important thing, as everyone now knows, is the location of a property. Ideally you should buy a property in an area that is going up in price anyway so that you can make money without even trying. It is often easier and cheaper, however, to buy in your own area, which you will already know quite well and where you can oversee any work being done on the property.

Once you have chosen your area, get friendly with local estate agents. Tell them what you want to do and get them to show you properties they think could make money. Also, go to auctions, but make sure you get advice from experts beforehand, about how much properties under the hammer are *really* worth. When considering a property, as well as the asking price make sure you factor in what you will have to pay in stamp duty, solicitor's and surveyor's fees and any mortgage interest while you own the property. Also, of course, you should estimate – possibly with the help of a builder – the cost of any building and decorating works and, upsettingly, the capital gains tax you will have to pay on any profit you make, if this is not your main home.

If you do the work on the property yourself you will save a *lot* of money, but you may lose out if you need to take time off work to do it. If you have to employ a builder, your profits could easily be eaten up. This is why most professional property developers tend to be builders – the money stays in their own pockets.

The bank is also taking a gamble. At some point during the renovation the property is going to be in a worse condition than it was when you bought it (for example, when you've demolished the kitchen units and the bathroom suite and haven't replaced them yet). If the bank has lent you, say, 90 per cent of the value of the house (loan to value), they're at risk of not being able to get their money back if, at that stage, you can't afford to finish the job. This has happened often enough for banks to be wary of lending to amateurs these days unless they have a sizeable deposit.

Do also keep in mind what is known as the 'profit pool'. The original vendor wants to make a profit, as does the builder and his workmen, the estate agent, the conveyancer and the Inland Revenue. After taking all this into account, and your own renovation and selling costs, will there be enough profit left over for you after everyone else has taken their share? The gap between the buying and the selling price needs to be wide enough to ensure the project is truly worthwhile.

All in all, property development is something you should not go into lightly. You should certainly research the subject, and the area, as much as possible before even thinking of offering on a property. Read the property sections in broadsheet newspapers, and look at magazines such as *What House* and *What Mortgage* and local glossy magazines from posh estate agents to keep an eye on house prices and what the buying and selling trends are.

HOW MUCH CAN YOU MAKE?

Anything from losing money if you buy badly to several thousand if you do up a property well and it is in an area that is rising in value anyway.

COSTS

Buying and selling a house involves thousands in costs at both ends. You will need to pay solicitor's and surveyor's fees, mortgage instalments if you are taking one out, stamp duty and bear extra monthly costs such as utility bills and council tax. You will also have to pay for the improvements on the property, and when you sell it you will have to pay solicitor's fees again, plus estate agent's fees and probably capital gains tax.

TRAINING AND QUALIFICATIONS

You don't need any qualifications, but it would help if you have training or experience in building, decorating, plumbing and electrics.

PROS

If you are handy and you know something about property, you can make a few thousand in one go by doing up a grotty place in a nice area and selling it at a profit. You will also be helping the community by improving one more home in the area.

CONS

There are so many costs involved that it is easy not to make any profit at all once you have taken out tax, charges, building costs and so on. Also, houses in many parts of the country are not going up in value at all, so you may struggle to find a property that you could make easy money on.

USEFUL CONTACTS

Association of Residential Letting Agents (ARLA) – www.arla.co.uk, 0845 345 5752 – Maple House, 53–55 Woodside Road, Amersham, Bucks HP6 6AA

www.nationwide.co.uk – the Nationwide Building Society has a monthly, regional house price index which it publishes on its website

www.propertyauctions.com – includes a database of property auctions around the country

Also consider . . .

- Doing up properties for others so that they sell more quickly and for more money.

- Offering a service to local property developers whereby you meet prospective buyers in show homes and take them round. Search for local property developers by putting 'property developer' and your area in Google, then phone up and see whether they have any properties that need showing. Most pay by the hour or by the day. Being well presented and well spoken really helps in this work, as does the gift of the gab!

● Offering your services to local lettings agents as a compiler of inventories for the properties they let. You will need to put together a list of all the items in a property new to the lettings market, and also make a note of the condition of all furnishings. There is also work available checking the inventories when tenants move out of a property. Agents pay either per hour or per job for this service, and the amount varies depending on where you are in the country. Just go into lettings agents on your local high street to see what the work prospects are and how much they will pay.

Property finder

If you are interested in property and you have contacts with estate agents in your area, you could earn money looking for homes for people who don't have the time or energy to do it for themselves.

HOW TO DO IT

You need to build up contacts and, in particular, a reputation as someone who knows their way around the property market in your area, and who understands their client's needs well enough to find the perfect property for them.

Having a background in estate agency or property management or other property-related work will be very useful for this. Your contacts in the property world will be vital to the health of your business, as will your ability to generate contacts among those looking to buy – cash-rich, time-poor businesspeople, often foreign, who don't have the leisure or interest to spend looking for their own place.

Get friendly with mortgage brokers, relocation agents and

human resources departments in large, multinational companies which might be grateful for outside help. Also, keep an eye on property movement in your area by reading the property sections in local papers and magazines.

HOW MUCH CAN YOU MAKE?

A few thousand every time you find the right house for a client, so it depends how many clients you get each year.

COSTS

Advertising, travel expenses, including the cost of a good car to impress your clients, and phone charges will be your main outlay.

TRAINING AND QUALIFICATIONS

You don't need any training or qualifications.

PROS

If you are good at this, and you have lots of property contacts as well as contacts abroad, you could make quite a lot of money with relatively little effort.

CONS

You can find yourself traipsing around lots of properties with clients only to find that they don't buy any of the places you show them. It can be time-consuming and frustrating if sale after sale falls through.

USEFUL CONTACTS

www.propertyfinder.co.uk – a useful website to start your research of properties all over the country

www.findaproperty.com – another useful research site

www.upmystreet.co.uk – all kinds of information about property, facilities and social structure of all areas of the UK

Case study

Australian Livio Bonollo manages some properties in London and also helps to let flats through a Soho agency, but his great love is finding property for people. He has set up his own business, James Oliver (www.jamesoliver.net), to do this. 'I get most of my clients through word of mouth,' he says. 'Some mortgage brokers send me clients too and I'm now actively going for more foreign buyers because they're the ones that need the help. I'm putting ads in Russian newspapers, contacting Italian media – because I'm originally Italian – building up my contacts in the States and all over really!'

When he finds a property for his clients, Livio charges them a finder's fee of 1.2 per cent of the property's value, with a minimum of £3,500. 'I have very good contacts with estate agents and quite often they'll tell me about a new property before it goes on the market, which is very useful. I also track auctions because some useful stuff comes on the market that way sometimes.'

Market trading

You can sell all kinds of things at different markets. If you're free at weekends you can make some good cash by setting up a stall for the day, or even selling out of the back of a van in some places!

HOW TO DO IT

You can either do it properly, paying for a proper market stall on an occasional or regular basis, or you can do a bit of fly-pitching! One unlicensed trader who doesn't want to be named says he makes a lot of cash on a Saturday simply selling furniture out of the back of his big van. 'I get moved on a lot at Brick Lane market,' he says, 'but at Portobello market I can usually stay there all day and just keep selling. You can make a lot of

326 • A BIT ON THE SIDE

money if you sell the right things and have a lot of charm. I sell furniture, and the amazing thing is that people often buy it and then don't bother to collect it! I once sold the same nasty table for £40 to three different people before one actually picked it up!'

If you want to do this on a regular or semi-regular basis, however, you would be better off paying to rent a stall at a market you like. Rents seem to vary from £3 a day in cheaper markets across the country to around £32.50 a day in London. Some markets don't allow casual traders, but most do. If you want to know how to get into your local market, check the database on the website of the National Market Traders Federation, www.nmtf.co.uk. That lists prices, amenities and phone contacts for markets of every type all around the country.

What you sell is up to you, and also depends on what is selling at your market. You might sell things you have made (see Chapter 6) or things you have bulk-bought or picked up at auctions (see p. 316). If your area is quite touristy, then you could sell gift items or things connected with your locality that tourists might like to take home.

Whatever you sell, make sure you have a lot of change with you and, ideally, someone to help you for at least part of the day. Most stall-holders are friendly and will watch your stall if you have to nip off to the loo, but it's better to have a friend to share the work throughout the day.

HOW MUCH CAN YOU MAKE?

Anything from nothing to hundreds a day, cash in hand, or even more if you are selling expensive antiques.

COSTS

You will have to pay for the market stall and also, of course, for the goods you are selling.

TRAINING AND QUALIFICATIONS

You don't need any training or qualifications.

PROS

This is a fun, outdoors occupation. You get paid immediately in cash and you can make a good amount of money if you have the right goods and a winning way of selling.

CONS

It can be back-breaking lugging your stuff around and setting up the market stall. It is not fun when the weather is cold and wet and there are few shoppers around. On some winter days you could make very little money for standing around in the cold for hours.

USEFUL CONTACTS

National Market Traders Federation, www.nmtf.co.uk

Also consider . . .

● Selling hot dogs, burgers, ice cream, flowers, fruit or other fast food in high streets, by the side of the road or at festivals and open-air events. You will need a licence from your local council and you will also need to have your vehicle checked by them for health and safety purposes. You may also need to go through some sort of council training. If you intend to trade from one specific place for some time you will need to get permission from the landowner as well as the council. What you pay for the licence will depend on the size and location of the site. For example, Salford City Council announces on its website that the current fee to trade is £450 per annum (1 April to 31 March); however, this fee is proportional to the time of year, so you would pay less if you applied in November, for example. You can find out about food trailers and mobile catering units for sale at www.startinbusiness. co.uk, in your local *Exchange and Mart*, in the Yellow Pages and on the Net.

Bulk buying and selling

With so many factory outlets and discount cash and carrys around, it's quite possible to buy a load of some items at knock-down prices and sell them for a profit elsewhere.

HOW TO DO IT

If you enjoy rummaging around factory outlets and cash and carrys, you will know where you can buy things really cheaply. If you happen on closing-down or end-of-line sales, you could find really good things going for a song.

Some people specialise in buying certain types of goods and make contacts with producers so that they can get even better offers. You might specialise in certain cosmetics, for example, or candles or rugs or sweets. Pick out things that you know you could sell at a discount but still make a profit on.

The question then is where to sell your goods. Some people take a regular stall at one or more markets in their area. Some simply sell them at local car boot sales and others sell direct at special sales that they set up in a hired room – more expensive goods such as cashmere or jewellery do well in this environment. You could even sell through adverts in newspapers and magazines such as *Exchange and Mart*, or through the Internet.

You could also sell things privately to friends and neighbours. For example, if you are a keen gardener, and your friends and neighbours are too, you could bulk-buy bulbs, fertiliser, pots and other essentials at a discount from a wholesale garden supplier or nursery or market garden, then sell them on. You would get products you personally need for your garden at a cheaper price and you could undercut local gardening stores and make a profit. Make sure you deal in products that people have to restock on a regular basis – these will obviously be easier to sell than something bought once or twice in a lifetime.

HOW MUCH CAN YOU MAKE?

It depends on what you buy and how much you sell. If you have good contacts and you are good at selling you could make hundreds or even thousands a month.

COSTS

You will need to pay for the goods in the first place, then there are the costs associated with hiring a market stall or room for a special sale. You may have advertising and transport costs too – you will certainly need a car or van to carry the goods to and fro.

TRAINING AND QUALIFICATIONS

You don't need any training or qualifications.

PROS

If you enjoy buying and selling and you hit on a good product, you could make some reasonable money without too much effort.

CONS

If you buy the wrong things and you can't sell them, you could find yourself out of pocket and out of sorts with the world!

USEFUL CONTACTS

www.ciao.co.uk – listings and reviews of factory outlets around the country

www.shoppingvillages.com – listings and description of factory outlets around the country

Import/export business

You don't have to be a big company to do some importing or exporting. A lot of individuals do it quite successfully.

HOW TO DO IT

Importing goods to sell in this country or exporting goods to foreign climes can be lucrative if you get it right, but can also be much more than a part-time occupation if it becomes successful. 'My advice is to consider three things,' says spokesman Hugh Allen from the Institute of Export. 'What is the product? Who can you sell it to? And is it appropriate? If you get it right you could earn several thousand a year.'

You may be considering importing goods from a country you visit a lot or where you have family contacts. First you need to work out whether there is a market for the item, or items, you want to bring over. Do some research to see whether anyone else is already bringing over the same or similar products. If not, work out how much it would cost you, per unit, to bring over, and try some shops or other outlets to see what they would be prepared to pay. If, taking all the costs into account, you think you could make a profit and that the product would sell here, start by bringing a few samples over and trying them in just a few shops first to test the water.

Exporting is a harder business. You need to know the countries you want to sell to very well and have good and reliable contacts there. You also need to do a lot of research, in the country you want to sell in, to be sure there is a market for your goods. If you do not speak the language yourself, make sure you get good professional help so that there are no misunderstandings. Also, get yourself thoroughly clued up on the importing and retail laws of the country in question so you don't make expensive mistakes.

If you think you have good contacts and a great product, you can get cheap – and sometimes free – help and advice from your local business link. Look in the Yellow Pages under 'Business Enterprise Agencies', or go to www.businesslink.co.uk. Get as much help and advice as you can. You will need it!

HOW MUCH CAN YOU MAKE?

The sky's the limit if you hit on something that everyone wants – either here or abroad. This could become a full-time job or it could just earn you some nice pocket money each month and give you a good excuse to visit one or more countries each year.

COSTS

There could be huge costs involved, as with any business. You will certainly have travel expenses, all the usual business admin costs, customs and excise fees, transport charges and all the costs connected with marketing your goods.

TRAINING AND QUALIFICATIONS

You don't need training or qualifications but you would probably find it helpful to do some short courses in business management, import/export and basic bookkeeping, which you can get through most Business Links.

PROS

You could make good money at this, particularly if you have sound contacts in one or more foreign countries and speak their language. If you have family who can help you at the other end it will be even easier.

CONS

The amount of work involved in this kind of business – particularly as it involves a lot of transport, customs payments and red tape, and long-distance communications – could make the whole process too much effort for too little money.

USEFUL CONTACTS

www.bizhelp24.com – lots of information here for importers and exporters

Business Link, www.businesslink.co.uk

The Institute of Export, Export House, Minerva Business Park, Lynch Wood, Peterborough PE2 6FT, 01733 404400, www.export.co.uk

Network marketing/direct selling

Network marketing got a very bad name – rightly so – in the 1980s when pyramid schemes were rife. The industry has cleaned itself up a lot recently, however, and it is possible to make a very good living at it *if* you are good at selling.

HOW TO DO IT

There are two main ways of doing network marketing, or direct selling. You can either become an agent for a company like Avon or Betterware and simply sell their products direct to customers, or you could make money by recruiting other sales agents – as well as selling direct yourself – in which case you get a commission for every sale your agents make.

Companies that operate in this way – and there are several, including the well-known Amway, Ann Summers, Kleeneze and even the Body Shop – sometimes run recruitment drives where they will tell you that this is a way of making money easily so that you can spend more time with your family without having to work all hours. For a few who are good at selling and feel no embarrassment at recruiting friends and family to make money for them, this is true. But the money you make will depend very much on the amount of time and effort you put into selling and on your actual ability to sell. In other words, don't imagine you can do a little work then sit back and watch the money flooding in. Once you have put in the work – often over a few years – then you will see the money coming in from other people's efforts, but it doesn't happen overnight.

If you *are* good at selling and you have a wide network of friends you could sell to, and who would introduce you to others, then this can be an excellent way of making money. There are many products available to sell, and it goes without saying that you should choose a range or a company that you believe in, because that will make it much easier to sell. Also, make sure that there are not already several agents for this company in your immediate area, which would make it very difficult for you to achieve reasonable sales.

Most companies that operate in this way belong to the Direct Selling Association (check out their website, contact details below). 'We are rather proud of the fact that very few direct selling companies require more than £100 investment for the basic kit,' says director Richard Berry. 'The only time you might need to buy stock is if you are running a party and you need extra items to sell then and there.'

Once you have picked the company you want to sell for, you will be given some training, and then it is up to you to make contacts and sell through friends, friends of friends, your hairdresser's clients, your dentist's clients, and anyone who will let you leave a catalogue in their office for passers-by to order from or through which to join your network as another seller.

If you want to make reasonable money at this you will need to work quite long hours, at least for the first few years. You could be simultaneously selling products and recruiting people and training them. They will want information, stock, help with their own recruitment, and a bit of encouragement from time to time. You will probably need a car – though not necessarily – and you will also need energy, resilience, a thick skin (for the many rejections you are likely to get) and a good sense of humour.

Some direct selling companies advocate parties to sell their goods, such as the well-known Tupperware parties. Although there was a slump in interest in these events in the 1990s, they are now gaining in popularity again. Ann Summers is known for its 'naughty' parties, often for women only, and some other ranges tend also to be sold to groups rather than individuals.

HOW MUCH CAN YOU MAKE?

Anything from a few pounds here and there to tens of thousands a year, depending on how much effort and time you put into it. Richard Berry of the DSA says, 'Some people with a big network make £100,000 a year without much effort, but the average annual earnings are just £4,000 to £5,000. It depends what people want from the business.'

COSTS

You should not have to buy the goods you sell on, although you will probably have to pay for a few samples of the products to start off with at around £100. Apart from that your only real costs will be telephoning and, possibly, advertising yourself in local magazines and through a leaflet drop.

TRAINING AND QUALIFICATIONS

You don't need qualifications but you will need to be trained to sell the product you choose. The company will give you the training you need. It will also help if you have experience and training in sales generally.

PROS

If you are good at selling and have friends you could persuade to sell too, you could make some really good money, particularly in terms of what your friends make on your behalf. It is also a way of meeting new people, your working hours are quite flexible, and you could have fun evenings at other people's homes.

CONS

You cannot make the promised huge profits unless you put a lot of time and effort into it. You could find yourself losing friends if you try to push products on them or try to make them become agents too.

USEFUL CONTACTS

Amway, Snowdon Drive, Winterhill, Milton Keynes MK6 1AR, 01908 298050, www.amway.co.uk

The Body Shop at Home, Hawthorne Road, Wick, Littlehampton, West Sussex BN17 7LR, 01903 731500, www.thebodyshop.com

The Direct Selling Association, 29 Floral Street, London WC2E 9DP, 020 7497 1234, www.dsa.org.uk

Kleeneze, St Ivel Way, Warmley, Bristol BS30 8WB, 0117 975 0350, www.kleeneze.co.uk

Telecom *plus* plc, Dryden House, The Edge Business Centre, Humber Road, London NW2 6EW, 020 8955 5000, www.telecomplus.co.uk

Case study

Colin Bowman has been an independent distributor for Telecom *plus* for over four years and says he has no plans to stop. 'The number one thing I like about it is flexibility,' he says. 'When I'm not so busy with my job I can work at building up my network, and then when I am busy, as I have been for the last six months, I'm still earning money! I also like the fact that it's a British company and the fact that not only can you earn through selling and developing a network but you can also earn share options in the company. That's very valuable.'

Telecom *plus* provides fixed line and mobile phone services and electricity and gas supplies for the home. Those of Colin's contacts who are interested in becoming distributors for Telecom *plus* just go to his website, www.colinco.co.uk, where they can get all the information they need to become a distributor.

He says that so far he's been able to pay for some good family holidays thanks to Telecom *plus*, but in the long-term he looks on it as his pension fund. 'I've been freelance for years,' he says, 'and like a lot of freelancers I've got no pension. This will definitely look after my future. Ideally I'd like to get to the point where I do it full-time. Apparently the company's just had its first millionaire, which is good news!'

Private swap shops

There are quite a lot of things you can't sell at car boot or garage sales (or if you do, you don't get much for them), such as cosmetics, clothes and accessories. So get your friends round and trade with them for things you want with people who don't mind half-used pots of cream!

HOW TO DO IT

Choose a few friends who have similar tastes to you and, ideally, are a similar size. It's probably best to stick to friends who are the same sex (it's mostly women who go for this type of thing, anyway) as you will have more swap possibilities.

Tell them to bring round any clothes, accessories, cosmetics or bric-a-brac that they don't want any more. Make it into a party – a weekend afternoon is good, or a weekday evening – with food and drink, and get everyone to put their 'swap goods' in a pile in front of them in your room. It's up to everyone to look at everyone else's goods and decide what they might swap for things they like. If they don't have anything the other person wants, they can negotiate a price for it.

At the end of the party you should have got rid of a few things, found a few new treasures and had a good time with your friends.

HOW MUCH CAN YOU MAKE?

Not very much, but you could get some free clothes, cosmetics or other bits, which can be just as good.

COSTS

Just the cost of feeding and watering your guests – which you might do anyway.

TRAINING AND QUALIFICATIONS

You don't need any training or qualifications.

PROS

This is a fun way to get rid of bits you don't want and pick up for free things you do want.

CONS

You may end up not getting rid of any of your things but spending money on other people's.

Selling your own perfume

Believe it or not, you could make and sell your own perfume and perfume-based products. It's not that hard or expensive to do, and you can almost always find what you need at a health food store.

HOW TO DO IT

First, decide how strong you want your fragrance. Perfumes are the strongest, containing 15–30 per cent essential oils diluted in a base of alcohol, with a small percentage of distilled water. Less potent toilet waters contain 5–10 per cent essential oils, and colognes and body splashes may have 1–2 per cent.

You will need: your favourite pure essential oils (such as rose, lavender or sandalwood); alcohol for cleaning; fixatives; eyedroppers; small vials, bottles or jars.

The best alcohols are the highest-proof ones, as they contain the greatest concentrations of ethyl alcohol: use 95 per cent grain alcohol (190 proof) or vodka (the highest proof available). Fixatives prolong a fragrance. They are ingredients added to a composition to lend their own unique scent and to 'fix' the other ingredients, retarding their overall rate of evaporation. Commonly used fixatives are sandalwood, benzoin, myrrh, vanilla and balsam of Peru. Other fixatives, particularly useful for oil and bath blends, creams and lotions, are tincture of benzoin, grape seed oil, castor oil, and liquid from vitamin E gel capsules.

You should use glass containers (rather than plastic) for preparing and storing perfumes. Make sure you record, date and name each blend and be prepared to wait for days or weeks once you have made your perfume as ageing is necessary to smooth out and mellow the raw-ingredient smell – allow your blend to age in a cool, dry, dark area. When you are constructing a formula, after adding each new essential oil be sure to smell the result to get an idea of how each added ingredient changes the formula and how you might like to modify it in the future. Clean the eye-dropper in alcohol or vodka between each addition of a new essential oil.

'You can do what you want, of course, but when I'm working with new oils or new combinations, I usually start with equal amounts – for example, two drops of ginger, two drops of jasmine, and two drops of sandalwood,' says American Sherill Pociecha, who mixes her own perfumes (see her article about it at www.nature-helps.com/agora/perfumes.htm).

If you have a background in chemistry and like technical books, *The Chemistry of Fragrances* (£19.95, RSC Paperbacks) by D. H. Pybus and C. S. Sell is a useful sourcebook for would-be perfume-makers.

But the actual fragrance is just a very small part of the total perfume package, as all the big perfume-makers know. You will need good packaging – attractive bottles, pretty printed labels and possibly extras such as ribbons, dried flowers or coloured plastic wrapping and boxes. If you are artistic, or you know someone who is who will help you, this can be the really fun part of it.

It's important to work out your marketing concept before you make your final selection of a fragrance. You want the concept – the image of the fragrance – to work in tandem with the scent. Don't go overboard on frills. Try to find a simple theme and express it in a simple yet creative way – it's easier and usually much cheaper, but is still likely to sell as well as more fussy things.

If you learn to make soap, candles and creams (none of them

too difficult), you can supply a range of products in one particular scent which you can also market as gift boxes.

You will need to market your product to gift shops – in the high street and online – and possibly independent chemist's shops and toiletry stores. You could also sell at craft fairs, local markets and gift fairs such as Top Drawer, which takes place annually at Earls Court in London, or set up your own website and sell your products direct to the public.

HOW MUCH CAN YOU MAKE?

The mark-up on perfumes is very high, so if you are successful you could earn thousands a month, but it will take a while to build the business up to this kind of level.

COSTS

You will have to spend a lot on raw materials, bottles, labels and packaging. There will also be advertising, travel and marketing costs, including the cost of Web design and hosting and the cost of exhibiting at fairs or markets.

TRAINING AND QUALIFICATIONS

You don't need any training or qualifications, although a background in chemistry, aromatherapy and/or marketing and design would help.

PROS

If you love perfume and are creative this can be a delightful hobby. Also, if you get it right you can make a lot of money just by selling a few units, as the mark-up can be high.

CONS

To make any serious money you will have to spend a lot of time developing the fragrance and packaging and marketing it. It could take months before you start selling anything. It also involves a lot of up-front costs.

USEFUL CONTACTS

Top Drawer – www.topdraweronline.com – the big gift trade show that happens at Earls Court in London

Telesales

If you see ads in the 'Media' sections of newspapers that talk about 'getting on the fast track' or 'dynamic opportunities' or similar, you can bet your bottom dollar it's a telesales job!

HOW TO DO IT

It's very easy to get a job in telemarketing. It has a very high turnover of staff, and there are always ads for salespeople in *The Stage*, media sections of national newspapers and the jobs sections of local papers. Many of these jobs can be done in the evening or at weekends as the people they want to target are at home at those times, so it is a useful extra occupation if you work during the day. The money is often very bad, however, and you can make reasonable cash only on commission. Try it only if you are good at selling, project a lot of confidence on the phone and have some belief in the product or service you are selling.

Selling successfully over the phone requires good interpersonal skills, excellent selling skills, an in-depth knowledge of the product or service on offer, a massive reserve of persistence and confidence, and a hide like a rhino's. You will be given some sort of training by the company you join, but ultimately it is up to you. Some companies allow you to call from your own home but the majority will want you to work from their office or call centre. Many will offer no basic pay but will ask you to work on commission only. If you are very confident of your ability to sell and you believe in the product this may be worth doing, but *only* under those circumstances. On the whole it is best to go for jobs that offer at least some sort of basic pay.

HOW MUCH CAN YOU MAKE?

Anything from nothing at all to thousands if you are good (and lucky!).

COSTS

There are no costs involved other than your travel expenses.

TRAINING AND QUALIFICATIONS

You don't need any qualifications although some companies hold in-house training sessions for their employees.

PROS

If you are good at selling and you have a product that people actually want, you could make some serious money this way.

CONS

This can be a truly mind-numbing, depressing way to spend your time. Some jobs will only pay you if you manage to sell, and it is often very difficult to sell over the phone, so you could find you earn nothing at all. You will also get some abuse from people who are angry at being cold-called when they are at home or busy, and hassled businesspeople who are annoyed at being bothered in their office.

USEFUL CONTACTS

The Call Centre Association, www.cca.org.uk – the official body for telemarketing companies and call centres

Hammond Marketing Services, PO Box 2943, Warwick CV35 9ZF, www.hammond-marketing.co.uk

The Telemarketing Company, 26–27 Regency Square, Brighton, East Sussex BN1 2FH, 01273 765 000, www.ttmc.co.uk

CHAPTER THIRTEEN

Got a Computer?

TIMES ARE CHANGING, and with an older population more at ease with mobile phones, laptops and the idea of UK call centres in foreign countries, many of us are starting to become familiar with the idea of working from home. In fact, thousands of people already do so, and many more should be seriously considering it; new mums, OAPs (millions of whom are already known as 'silver surfers'), the disabled – all have much to gain from using their periods of virtual house arrest more productively.

Key to this earning potential is the Web, which allows you to promote your services or products, check out the competition and take payment at the click of a mouse and the cost of a local telephone call. So, if you're not already online, buy a PC magazine and start shopping. You can get a perfectly adequate PC, modem and Internet connection for under £500, so consider it an investment that should pay for itself within weeks if you're determined and well organised.

Once you've done that, here are some ways you can make money without ever leaving your house.

CV and letter-writing

This was once a profitable service, uniquely suited to the Web, but there are now so many copycats it can be hard to get noticed.

HOW TO DO IT

You take garbled messages or notes and turn them into professional-looking documents. There are hundreds of agencies and individuals now specialising in this area, although the average state of their websites suggests that this is far from being a pot of gold. So, what does the work involve?

CVs are among the most important documents we ever send out, and everyone thinks they know what makes a good one. So if you're trying to persuade someone that you can be trusted to write one for them, you'd better have *lots* of examples. See ivillage's excellent guide to writing a CV for both information and inspiration (www.ivillage.co.uk/workcareer/findjob/cvs/articles/0,,185_162720,00.html).

Just as important as the content and style is how the CV is presented. Increasingly clients want their standard A4 paper CV available in digital format, on CD-ROM or posted to websites. For a full concise guide to popular file formats for both letters and CVs, see www.economics.ltsn.ac.uk/formats. You won't need to know how to produce them all – most people are happy with a simple Word document – but it's best to know the most important jargon. After all, you *are* supposed to be the expert!

HOW MUCH CAN YOU MAKE?

Small amounts for single documents (say £10–£25 each) but once you establish a reputation the figure can climb dramatically. Established agencies charge £250 per CV and £50 per hour for letters.

COSTS

Office accessories (papers, printer cartridges, etc.), phone calls, and software such as Microsoft Word.

344 • A BIT ON THE SIDE

TRAINING AND QUALIFICATIONS

Obviously, you'll need to be very good with word processors and have experience of what makes a good letter or CV. This is work best suited to those with human resources experience or ex-secretarial/journalist types.

PROS

Money for old rope, if you're well organised and professional.

CONS

Quick turnaround rewarded by usually slow payment.

USEFUL CONTACTS

www.alec.co.uk/cvtips – an informative site, and a prime example of how to promote your services persuasively without breaking the bank

www.netmasters.co.uk/directories.html – includes a hyperlinked index of all Web search engines (e.g. Google, Yahoo, etc.)

Case study

Paul Mason worked in a busy personnel department until retiring last year. He now edits CVs and proof-reads as a hobby, blaming the difficulty in generating business for not taking it more seriously.

'Once you've persuaded someone to produce a CV, don't expect to see them again for a couple of years. You have to keep generating new customers, all the time – which is down to advertising, reputation and above all a good listing on any search engine you can find.

'I know that if I put more effort into it I would generate more leads and make more money, but I get by on what I do at the moment. You can make a living out of it but I'm happy to cover my living expenses at the moment!'

Online research

There are two types of online research, both of which can make you money, but involving very different levels of work. Let's deal with them quickly in turn.

1. Market research. Every day in the papers or online you'll notice some headline such as 'One in four women thinks sex is less important than cake'. Ever wondered who these strange people are? People just like you, actually.

2. Private research. Individuals and companies often need in-depth information about particular subjects or places. For instance, a novelist might need to know something about a particular profession, or a business might need to research a local area for the purposes of building a new depot there. Needless to say, this type of research pays better but involves a lot more work and is a great deal harder to find. See Chapter 5 for information on academic research.

HOW TO DO IT

Finding online questionnaires and surveys is relatively easy – simply type 'online research' into a search engine and it will fill up with potential offers. This is one of many areas where con-men operate, however – making you fill in tedious online questionnaires and then forgetting to pay, or passing your name on to spammers. So don't fall for every offer you see – the more lucrative or tempting it sounds the more likely it is to be a waste of time. At the time of writing, reliable online research companies include www.yougov.com, www.ciao.co.uk and www.drdosh.com – but you simply have to shop around and keep your eyes peeled.

HOW MUCH CAN YOU MAKE?

Online research pays least well (between 10p and £2 per questionnaire), while face-to-face research or focus groups can pay as much as £100 per session. Be careful, however – the Web is full

of agencies offering non-existent survey work at $200+ per hour
... in exchange for a modest registration fee, of course! (See
Chapter 14.)

COSTS

Standard telephone and ISP costs.

TRAINING AND QUALIFICATIONS

Some research outfits will be seeking people with specific experience or interests; most, however, just want average consumer
experience.

PROS

Easy, occasional work that will increasingly rely on instant messaging or webcams. Get in early.

CONS

Hardly a reliable source of income, and watch out for the con-
men!

USEFUL CONTACTS

www.freemoneyresource.co.uk – a big site with links to
online surveys and much more

The Research Buyer's Guide Online, www.rbg.org.uk – another
good place to check for background info and reputable agencies

⌐ Case study

> Pamela Castel, 34, is on the lists of four research companies and
> averages around ten surveys or focus groups per week. 'Phone
> or Web-based research is poorly paid,' she explains, 'but it's just
> ticking boxes and having an opinion – so no prob. Focus groups
> can be a laugh, but they take the whole afternoon and you really
> need to be close to the agency to make them worthwhile.'

Desktop publishing

The beauty of modern software is that, once purchased, all you have to do to become proficient at it is to keep practising. Consequently, although desktop publishing (DTP) is a vast area covering the full range of word-processing, graphics or photo-editing packages, if you become skilled at even one of them you too are a DTP professional.

HOW TO DO IT

It depends on your current level of skill. If you're already good at knocking up tasty presentations and documents in programs such as Adobe Acrobat (www.adobe.com) you're halfway there – because thousands of businesses need exactly such skills every day and are paying PR agencies thousands more to supply them. All you have to do is persuade the client you could do these jobs better, cheaper or faster – this is the essence of seeking and keeping any kind of freelance work.

But what if you're not a software junkie, just a gifted amateur with design or writing skills wanting to test your potential? Well, that's not a problem either, because as long as you have natural aptitude, hands-on experience is the only training you need, and software skills do improve the more you use a particular package. Most programs contain extensive tutorials for you to follow and there are bulging websites full of hints, tips and support groups to answer your queries or help solve your problems.

For novices there are courses, clubs, books and teachers aplenty to help you improve; the BBC, for example, provides a range of assistance, including the elementary Bite-Size study guides (www.bbc.co.uk/schools/gcsebitesize/ict/software/0wordprocessinganddtprev3.shtml), and the Open University offers courses covering DTP and other aspects of IT (www3.open.ac.uk/courses).

So, after a few months you should be confident enough with a single DTP package to move forward. Small companies often need small jobs done – newsletters, testimonials, business cards, case studies, etc. This is bread-and-butter DTP work, and shouldn't pose much of a problem *if* you can find the clients in the first place. And this is one area where having a kick-ass website of your own is crucial.

As the proud owner of a website, all you have to do is email your client the address (URL) and they can check out your graphical skills at their leisure. For more on website design, see the section below.

HOW MUCH CAN YOU MAKE

DTP is usually undertaken on an hourly basis for a bare minimum of around £20 per hour, rising sharply according to the job, your experience, the package you're working with, etc. It is important to consider the client relationship as well as fair compensation for the work. A small business might pay a trifling £50 for a newsletter or flyer, but do it well and you might get their next annual brochure or direct mail campaign – where your fee could run into hundreds or thousands.

COSTS

DTP packages are frequently upgraded and rarely cheap (the Professional version of Acrobat, for instance, costs around £350). So you'll need to invest before you can start honing your skills.

TRAINING AND QUALIFICATIONS

In the multimedia age, an impressive website showing off your abilities is worth a dozen letters after your name. Specialise in one application so you can produce your best results on demand.

PROS

Learning how a software application works is a skill easily practised at home.

CONS

Given that it is so software-based, novices and technophobes will find DTP an uphill struggle.

USEFUL CONTACTS

http://desktoppub.about.com – not a bad introduction to the world of DTP, but if you're after the applications themselves you'll need the excellent CNET, whose download site, http://download.com, provides a one-stop shop for downloading shareware (30-day free trial) or full-priced software: search under the intitals 'DTP', or indeed for any other type of software you like

---

Case study

Caroline Staunton, 27, works from home, specialising in Power-Point and Adobe presentations, and makes a healthy £1,500 a month from a couple of regular business clients.

'IT skills are the modern equivalent of carpentry or lock-picking,' she explains. 'Only certain people can do it, and if you can do it well, there's no shortage of people prepared to pay for it. But software keeps evolving and so must you. Nobody wants an expert in last year's version, although they'll expect you to be that as well.

'If you do a reasonable amount of networking and putting your name around in the right places you can get regular, good work in this sector. I've picked up a lot of work through word of mouth, and that's the best way to do it. If you do a good job the other work does come in.'

Web design

With so many of this chapter's suggestions requiring a website, the ability to design one is a very valuable skill indeed.

Admittedly, the costs of corporate websites run into the tens of thousands of pounds and are usually beyond one person's skill to design, but individuals and smaller companies tend to need more manageable and affordable sites.

HOW TO DO IT

Like everything to do with programming, there are dozens of CD-ROMs, books and websites offering a broad introduction to HTML (Hypertext Mark-up Language) – the language used to make up most Web pages. It's best to check out some of these study aids as soon as possible; programming is not for everyone, and older adults find it especially hard to pick up. So before you sign up for evening classes, check out the following free alternatives:

http://build-website.com – admittedly, a beginner's guide to website design, but a very helpful one.

www.321webliftoff.net – looks horrible, but a surprisingly useful introduction to HTML, Java and basic design concepts.

Still keen? OK, you now have plenty of choices, all with the aim of helping you improve your skills. A quick search under 'website design' on the government's 'Learn Direct' site, for instance, turned up an impressive 173 regional and online courses in the subject (www.learndirect-advice.co.uk/finda-course). You could also look in the Yellow Pages under 'Business Enterprise Agencies' (or click on www.businesslink.gov.uk) for government-sponsored help and advice agencies for small businesses.

As with desktop publishing, however, there is no substitute for hands-on experience. Find a Web design package you feel comfortable using, practise doing so until you know it inside out, and then start promoting yourself to the wider world. Obviously, as a budding website designer you must have an impressive and original website of your own – so put your money where your mouth is.

Once you know how to design websites, you can advertise your services on the Web or through friends. Get in touch with small businesses in your area, offering a cut-price website. This is an area where word of mouth can really work, so be prepared to do your first two or three websites for little or nothing just to get the word out.

HOW MUCH CAN YOU MAKE?

Depends on your own skill and the complexity of the work. Freelance designers get at least £150 for designing a basic home page, rising to literally tens of thousands for bigger designs. Don't be greedy or take on projects you subsequently struggle to complete.

COSTS

Only the software, which admittedly can run to thousands of pounds per application. Clients incapable of designing their own website may also be incapable of running it, finding the right Web address or organising an ISP to host it – all of which presents you with business opportunities *and* potential overheads.

TRAINING AND QUALIFICATIONS

Apart from HTML, ideally you will need a smattering of other programming languages such as Java and XML, or familiarity with one of the common Web creation packages such as Dreamweaver, GoLive or Flash MX. These days, however, even word-processing packages let you save documents and presentations in a Web format – so you can start practising with simple layouts almost at once.

PROS

A skill much in demand and very well paid for.

CONS

As hard to learn as any programming language, although there are plenty of guides and courses to help you. Also, it is a very competitive field to break into – which in turn has driven down prices!

USEFUL CONTACTS

www.spellsoftware.com – purveyors of reasonably priced design software

www.adobe.com – the official Adobe site

www.kelkoo.co.uk – a great site for comparing software prices (and prices of all kinds of consumer goods)

Case study

Janet Franks is a new media manager for a business publications company in London but designs websites in her spare time. 'I used to be an air hostess,' she says, 'and in my time off I did a part-time website design course. Then I just fiddled around on a site for myself and started off by doing some designs for friends' websites. After a while, their friends started calling because they liked the first ones I'd done and it just took off from there.'

Kate says she can design a small website in a weekend but larger ones have to be done over a few weeks, working evenings and weekends. 'You don't need to have formal design training,' she says, 'but you need to have an eye for design. Not everyone has it – just because you can master HTML, it doesn't mean to say that you can create a good website.'

Affiliate/partnership schemes

Once you have your own website, there are several ways to make money from it. Online affiliate programmes reward you either for displaying banner ads on your Web page or by encouraging your visitors to frequent your partner's site. It is one of the oldest Web-based money-making schemes.

HOW TO DO IT

Whatever the subject of your website, as soon as it starts attracting visitors it also becomes attractive to advertisers and sponsors. Naturally, big players require seriously big audiences (online ad agency Doubleclick – www.doubleclick.com – demands a million visitors per month) but smaller players – known as affiliates – will reward you for any business you can send their way.

HOW MUCH CAN YOU MAKE?

It depends on how many visitors your site is attracting and the affiliate scheme you choose. Returns are nearly always paid in US dollars (making them harder to chase when something goes wrong) and range from a miserable 1 cent for each ad a user clicks on (known as 'clickthru') to a healthy 5 per cent payback on any items subsequently sold.

COSTS

It costs nothing to sign up with all the major online affiliates. The only real outlay will be your time.

TRAINING AND QUALIFICATIONS

None. The only skill you need is in spotting a partner who won't rip you off or make your precious website look like an advertising junkyard. Fortunately, after years of suffering a bad reputation affiliate advertising schemes are making a comeback, with the likes of Google's Ad-Sense (https://www.google.com/adsense/) combining easy rules with reliable pay-outs.

PROS

A simple means of generating a steady dribble of income.

CONS

It can take ages to add and update links – which you need to do frequently to keep a site looking fresh. The money can be paltry, particularly when you receive payment only if someone buys something on the referred link.

USEFUL CONTACTS

www.homeworking.com – has tested various affiliate schemes: 'Do affiliate programs work? If you earn one cent per banner display, and your Web page is seen by 250 people per month, then you will earn about $2.50 [about £1.50] per month. But if your Web page is seen by 250 per day, then you will earn 250 x 30 x 1 cent = $75 per month, [about £50] or $900 [£500] per year.'

www.iwantmyownsite.co.uk – full of helpful tips about advertising and affiliate schemes

Earn while you surf

You can earn money for surfing the Web? Surely too good to be true? Maybe . . .

HOW TO DO IT

Sign up to one of the better-known schemes, such as www.horizonsurfer.com or www.cashglow.com. You then download a small plug-in which updates your browser to take note of how long you are 'actively' surfing (i.e. clicking on hyperlinks or playing games).

Technically these sorts of programs are like legitimate spyware (because you're opting *in* to letting it spy on your online habits) which records the sites you visit and reports back to a company . . . like market research where the researcher is invisible and follows you around online!

HOW MUCH CAN YOU MAKE?

Virtually nothing, and no, you can't just log on to Yahoo and then go on holiday. You need to be clicking on a link at least once every two minutes to earn, and even then it's only 7–70 cents per hour – that's around £50 for over 500 hours of click-ing!

COSTS

ISP costs, which means this scheme only works for those with free or unlimited Internet access who are constantly on the Net.

TRAINING AND QUALIFICATIONS

For clicking a mouse 20,000 times? Duh!

PROS

Theoretically, money for nothing . . .

CONS

. . . in reality, money for repetitive strain injury.

USEFUL CONTACTS

www.iwantmyownsite.co.uk – an excellent source of advice for making *real* money online

Online auctions

To be frank, there's only one big, reliable player in town, and that's eBay (see Chapter 12 for information on how to buy and sell well there).

E-commerce

With the exception of share dealing, e-commerce is probably the only way to make serious money without leaving your home. Naturally, it also requires the most time, skill and investment to pull off, but why should that deter you? If you've got a good idea, a lot of patience and the will to succeed, the Web *will* make money for you – the only question is how much and how quickly.

HOW TO DO IT

Basically e-commerce is the buying and selling of goods and services through the Internet, or more specifically over the World Wide Web. Although a hugely complicated subject, the basic model is simple enough: you sell – either products or a service; the customer pays (ideally by clicking his mouse a few times); you send (either by post if it's goods or over the Net if it's services); and that's it. The secret is to make this process as swift, user-friendly and secure as possible; and naturally there are a thousand ways to do it.

The possibilities are endless. You could sell food, T-shirts, lawnmowers, CDs or designer bras. The services you offer could be Christian dating, Muslim matches, tarot card reading, song-critiquing or parental advice.

Perhaps the best place to start is with a few blank sheets of paper and your very first business plan. The Online Women's Business Centre has a helpful section on this, so try www.onlinewbc.gov/docs/starting for some free (if female-focused) guidance. A business plan is there to help you focus on four key elements: 1) what exactly are you selling? 2) who precisely may need it? 3) how much is it worth (compared to what else is on the market)? and 4) how can you promote it to your target audience as efficiently as possible? Once you think you know these things, and more importantly can back them up with facts, figures and research, you have a foundation on which to build your business, attract investors or partners and focus your lofty ambitions.

Armed with a business plan, it's time to roll up your sleeves and start building. E-commerce may be no more than a digital version of the old corner shop, but the language can be unfamiliar and the learning curve near vertical. If you want to learn the skills, jargon and principles, there are books, CD-ROMs and websites galore to help, and dozens of full- or part-time educational courses, either sold by private companies or part-funded by local initiatives. The DTI even provides a series

of free, downloadable Best Practice guides (www.dti.gov.uk/
bestpractice/technology/internet.htm).

The beauty of e-commerce, however, is that it's a relatively
new science, and almost anyone who ever made money from it
did so by breaking a few rules. The only way to actually discover
what works and what doesn't is to build your website, set out
your virtual stall, and experiment. Alas, building even a simple
e-commerce website would take a chapter in itself – but fortunately there are half a dozen monthly magazines devoted to just
this subject and plenty of free online resources to help you. Here
are just a couple:

www.tiscali.co.uk/business/sme/ebiz/guide.html – Tiscali's
excellent and concise guide to how e-commerce works.
www.tamingthebeast.net – a more detailed and jargon-heavy
guide to developing and improving your site. As always, read but
don't feel obliged to sign up to anything.

HOW MUCH CAN YOU MAKE?

The sky's the limit; Michael Dell (www.dell.com) made $40 bil-
lion from understanding exactly what makes e-commerce tick,
while Mahir Cagri (www.ikissyou.org) earned considerably less,
albeit by flogging a single dodgy catchphrase. The beauty of
e-commerce is that it genuinely rewards persistence and
ingenuity.

COSTS

At first, you can buy and sell almost anything with little more
than a one-page website and a PO box, but you'll quickly realise
that using a Payment Gateway such as Paypal.com to take the
cash is a lot more practical. Gateways charge a small percentage
of the item price and/or a small fixed fee per transaction; however, they also provide security against non- or late payers. As
your e-business grows you may also need an accountant to make
sure the books are in order.

Also, if you sell products online you may need to add a shopping cart to your website, which you can buy from Actinic

(www.actinic.co.uk) for between £250 and £750, depending on the number and nature of the products you're selling.

TRAINING AND QUALIFICATIONS

None, and there are plenty of companies and ISPs who will fall over backwards to help you buy a basic e-commerce solution. They will even run the commercial side of the site on your behalf (for a percentage of the turnover, of course), although you may prefer a more hands-on approach. It's up to you.

PROS

The only way to consistently make money online.

CONS

Still, a difficult way to make money online unless you hit on a great idea.

USEFUL CONTACTS

Business Link, www.businesslink.gov.uk/bdotg/action/ sitemap?r.l1=1073861197&topicId=1073861197&furlparam= mkt1_it_map – the government's excellent but vast guide to IT and e-commerce

Case study

The last word on e-commerce belongs to the man who made the most out of it, PC-seller extraordinaire, Michael Dell.

'First of all, don't start a business just because everybody else is doing it or it looks like it's a way to make a lot of money. Start a business because you've found something you really love doing and have a passion for. Start a business because you've found something unique that you can do better than anyone else.'

A Bit on the Dumb Side

IF YOU REALLY NEED some extra cash urgently it's easy to be taken in by one of the many scams and bogus money-making schemes now offered online and offline.

To protect yourself against losing a lot of money, use this as a mantra:

'If it sounds too good to be true . . . it probably is.'

Any time you are faced with a money-making proposition that sounds so fabulous you can't believe it's true, let that suspicion stop you putting any money into the venture right there. Always check any business venture thoroughly and never part with large sums of cash on the promise that you will be making a fortune in no time at all. Question why they want to make you rich rather than keeping the idea to themselves.

Also check your greed level every now and then. If there's one thing that can make you vulnerable to really bad scams, it's greed. Another thing that can protect you from dodgy scams is to keep yourself informed.

Make Money Fast schemes (MMFs)

You are bound to have a seen a few of these, either on cheaply produced posters by the side of the road, on leaflets stuck on your car windscreen or in classified ads in your local paper. Whatever the 'product' these schemes offer, they are mainly based on a chain letter. Statistically speaking it is impossible to reach the amount of money promised as this would mean the entire world's population being involved.

In recent years, women have been targeted by an unscrupulous group of people setting up so-called 'Women Empowering Women' and 'Hearts' schemes. Again, these work on a chain letter principle, although there is no letter, not even any product. The idea is for a woman to give £3,000 to someone down the chain, then she has to find eight more women to do the same, who each have to find another eight women, and so on. The theory is that you will make £24,000, but this is only true for the few who start the scam. For most of the others there is no chance.

Home-working schemes

Advertisements for home-work schemes frequently appear in situations vacant or recruitment columns in newspapers, rather than the business opportunities section, and tend to appeal to people who are most in need of legitimate work from home, such as the unemployed, single parents and the disabled. They are often simply exploitative and should be regarded with the greatest of caution. For example, in 2001 the Advertising Standards Authority received 65 complaints about advertisements for home-work schemes, of which nine were upheld. The ASA received 164 complaints in 2000, of which 28 were upheld, relating to 25 advertisements. Common problems include work being persistently returned as sub-standard and no payment being made; exaggerated earnings claims; and advertisements that don't fully describe the work involved, or which refer to a 'one-off registration fee' when subsequent literature demands further payments before any work is offered.

If you are tempted by an ad like this, visit the Advertising Standards Authority's site, www.asa.org.uk, to see whether they are aware of the business and what they know about it. There are some genuine home-working jobs but many are bogus. You will know that they are dodgy if they make you pay to get the work in the first place. For example, adverts asking for money for home assembly kits are simply scams. They say they will pay you for making up the goods or give you your money back but they never do so.

Envelope stuffing

This is definitely one of those home-working schemes that is a highway to nothing. According to the US Postal Inspection Service, 'In practically all businesses, envelope stuffing has become a highly mechanised operation using sophisticated mass mailing techniques and equipment which eliminates any profit potential for an individual doing this type of work at home. The Inspection Service knows of no work-at-home promotion that ever produces income as alleged.'

More generally, you can just about guarantee that any company offering total strangers overpaid work is up to something and is best avoided.

Medical claims processors

This is an American scam, but British people have been targeted too. The idea is that US doctors need to process insurance claims for their patients electronically, and they need people to do it for them. However, surprise, surprise, these people need special software to do it. The software companies (for that is what they claim they are) put together a package along with 500,000 names of doctors and sell it to the public with the promise of easy money to be made out of processing the claims.

People have lost thousands of dollars in this scheme, sending out hundreds of letters to (probably very irritated) doctors with no work coming back. Apparently the companies are doing nothing illegal, so there is nothing to stop them charging between $350 and $500 per package. Don't be taken in!

SMS and 09011 competitions

If you have a mobile phone you have probably had at least one irritating SMS telling you about a fabulous money-making scheme or a message waiting for you at a premium-rate phone number or a hot babe waiting to hear from you on another premium-rate phone number. There are also competitions you can go in for just by using your mobile phone, but these are expensive and the odds on you winning anything are so remote you might as well give the money to charity.

All scratch card competitions should be binned immediately, particularly if you have to call a premium-rate number to find out whether you've won. These are obvious scams.

Similarly TV competitions that ask you to call an 09011 number are largely a waste of money. Not all the results are checked, and they tell you you've got another ten minutes in which to phone, when in reality the producer already knows the winners. The questions are kept laughably simple to guarantee a high call rate, so make sure you're not one of the callers.

Fiendishly, the whole premium-rate scam has now shifted to the Web, in the form of 'dialler programs'. These are tiny down-loaded 'cookies' that instruct your modem to dial a premium-rate number rather than your usual ISP. So, if you use the Web, either buy yourself some anti-virus software and a decent fire-wall or remember *never* to install any program file unless you know exactly what it is.

And that's just for starters . . .

Internet scams

The Internet is a joy and a fabulous tool for making money in all sorts of ways, but it has also spawned scam after scam and, incredibly, hoards of people are falling for them. Britain's Office of Fair Trading, along with organisations in 30 other countries, recently conducted an international sweep of the Internet, looking for dodgy websites offering goods, services and prizes that sound much too good to be true. They found 176 of them operating from the UK alone, and 1,847 websites were found worldwide.

The UK-based websites included 90 working-from-home schemes, 52 get-rich-quick schemes, 20 lottery scams, 15 free prize offers, and four sites offering educational qualifications. More than 234 breaches of UK consumer protection laws were identified, and trading standards officers are now in the process of tracking down the culprits.

The sort of things you should watch out for include promises of instant wealth, free gifts and incredible discounts and bargains, stories from people claiming 'astounding results' but with no verifiable contact details (no phone number is an instant give-away).

Keep your eyes peeled for 'Matrix' or 'MML' schemes (they're like pyramid schemes, only bigger), chain letters, registers and bureaux that ask for a subscription in exchange for finding you work, envelope stuffing work (why would anyone pay a stranger to do something their mates could do more cheaply?) and, of course, anything including the words 'make money fast' or 'risk free'.

You can usually spot scams by the fact that the perpetrators charge registration fees or demand credit card authorisation (for instance, on the grounds of confirming your age). Whatever you do, never divulge personal or financial information except over a secure Internet connection (a little yellow padlock symbol will appear at the bottom of your screen when you're in one).

For more information on online scams, check out these sites:
www.homeworking.com – home-working hints, tips and a few hidden dangers exposed.
www.scamwatch.com – online scams neatly categorised in twelve common areas.

Cyber begging

Cyber begging is a fast track to nothing. If you do it right, it can make you a few hundred quid . . . maybe. But you'll have to work for it. The idea is that you set up an amusing, interesting or heart-rending website, then direct your punters to a PO box or preferably an online payment gateway. The original cyber begging site (www.savekaryn-originalsite.com/) had the goal of raising $20,000 to pay off a credit card bill. Twenty months and two million visitors later Karyn Bosnak succeeded, transforming herself into an author and minor celebrity in the process. She started the whole cyber begging craze, and her original statement proved that honesty was the way to a punter's heart . . . at least, it was in 2002:

'Please help me pay my debt. I am nice. I am cheery. I am the girl at the office that MAKES YOU SMILE. I didn't hurt anyone by spending too much money. I was actually HELPING OUT THE ECONOMY. Give me $1, give me $5 – Hell, give me $20 if you feel like it! I promise that everything you give me will go towards paying off my debt.'

Hmm.

The Lottery (Lotto)

Since it was launched in 1994, the Lottery has taken £40 billion from us. Camelot, the company that runs it, has paid back only half this sum in prizes, which makes it Britain's worst gamble. So next time you're tempted to take a fiver out of your purse to buy five Lottery tickets, take another fiver out and set fire to it – that should give you an idea of what is really happening to your money.

Although it's really worse than this. Your chance of winning any prize whatsoever, let alone the jackpot, is around one in 54, which is a little under 2 per cent. The odds against hitting the jackpot are even worse – 13,983,816 to one!

Some people kid themselves that they play the Lottery

because some (actually very little) of the money goes to charity. In fact you, and the charities, would do far better if you simply made sure you gave regular money through Gift Aid, which enables the charity to claw back the tax you would have paid on that money.

The EuroMillions draw is even worse. This was set up by Camelot to try to entice increasingly jaded punters into buying tickets again. Tickets cost €2 each and can be bought by anyone in the UK, France or Spain. Incredibly, though, the odds on you winning this jackpot are even worse than for the silly old Lotto. They're 76,275,360 to one! You are more likely to die buying the ticket than you are to win!

Free lotteries

These are supposedly a legitimate, fair and harmless form of gambling. Most, however, are linked to other 'gaming opportunities' where money is taken from you and seldom seen again. Stick to the free games and you're safe enough. Online lotteries present you with simple on-screen games; click on the numbers, register an email address and password, and wait for a return email telling you the fortune is yours. Don't hold your breath, though!

The biggest UK game currently offers £1 million per day, based on picking six numbers out of a hefty 64. This makes the chances of winning billions of times worse than Lotto's 14 million to 1, and explains why the biggest online prizes are so rarely won.

Only take part in these if you're bored and you know that they are entirely free – oh, and don't use your real email address. *Never* part with money to take part in online games, competitions or lotteries.

If you're still interested, try these:

www.apennyearned.co.uk – features many free lotteries and schemes; look, but don't feel obliged to buy!

www.thedailydraw.com – the largest prize I could find – two free goes at £1 million per day!

At the time of writing, the most recent online lottery millionaire I could find was Indian hotelier Bimal Kumar Gajmer, who picked up $1.75 million in May 2002. He said he was thinking of getting married, and although there's no confirmation I find it hard to believe he had any trouble.

Gambling generally

'There are two times in a man's life when he should not speculate: when he can't afford it, and when he can' (Mark Twain)

Gambling in whatever form is a mug's game. The odds on winning anything from scratch cards, horses, dogs, football, etc. are extremely bad. Always remember that, on the whole, gambling is a way of whisking your money into a bookmaker's pockets.

In fact, the only sure way to make money out of gambling is to run a racket yourself. In the 2003/04 financial year, gambling companies did very nicely, thank you. Hilton Group, which owns Ladbrokes, made £272 million before tax; Rank Group, which owns Mecca Bingo and Grosvenor Casinos, made £192 million; William Hill made £171 million, Stanley Leisure £42 million and Paddy Power a paltry £20 million. All these millions came out of punters' pockets – your pockets if you gamble at all! This is doubly true of online casinos, which collectively now siphon off more cash than Las Vegas, despite being located in obscure offshore hideaways and monitored by no one you've ever heard of.

'In every bet there's a fool and a thief' (Anon)

Premium bonds

Buying premium bonds (also known as Ernies, from the Electronic Random Number Indicator Equipment) is still gambling but somewhat less of a rip-off than most other forms. In fact, some swear by it as a form of investment. Around 23 million Britons own premium bonds worth a total of more than £4 billion.

Every month, National Savings and Investments pays out over half a million prizes, ranging from £50 to £1 million, to premium bond holders. There are around 23 billion premium bonds in total on the market, and each bond has an equal chance of winning. So, if you have just one bond that means you have a one in 23 billion chance of winning each month – not great odds!

If you have the maximum £30,000 invested, the odds of winning the jackpot fall to around one in 770,000 per draw. On average, then, you could expect to win around twelve prizes per year from this, which would give you an annual tax-free return of 2.15 per cent – much lower than that offered by a good building society account.

If you *have* to gamble (and really, if you still have a yen to bet you need to ask yourself whether you need to get out more), premium bonds are probably the best of all the options. At least you don't lose your money as the bonds stay in the 'pot', giving you chance after chance to win.

Property

Surprised to see property in this section? Well, of course, a lot of people have genuinely made a handsome profit on their properties – usually by accident – and while the stock market was in a slump between 2000 and 2002 property seemed the only sensible option.

Even houses are not 'as safe as houses' when it comes to investing, however. Just because the property market has made phenomenal gains in the last 30 years does not mean that it will continue to do so. Indeed, apart from the fact that demand on our housing stock is likely to continue to increase there are many sound economic reasons why house prices should level off or even decrease in the next ten years. Don't try to jump on the property bandwagon just because everyone else seems to be doing so. When you see everyone else investing in something, that is usually the time to do exactly the opposite.

Certainly any ads you see or hear for seminars on becoming a property millionaire within two years should be regarded with the same level of horror and incredulity as those awful time-share meetings that are advertised all the time. Most of the 'trainee property developers' come away £2,000 or more worse off, and that's just from the fees they are conned into paying to learn these so-called secrets.

If you really want to do a course in buy-to-let then you would be better off taking one of the classes run by the Association of Residential Letting Agents (ARLA). The master classes cost £200 each, including VAT. Contact them on 0870 607 0711, or look on the website at www.arla.co.uk.

Property programmes on TV often miss out or mention only briefly the various costs associated with buying, selling and maintaining investment property. When buying you have to pay stamp duty, solicitor's fees, surveyor's fees, moving costs and usually a few thousand in redecoration and furnishing costs. When selling you have estate agent's fees, solicitor's fees and the cost of moving out. While you own the property you could also be spending thousands fixing boilers, fences, roofs, windows and who knows what else. There is also the possibility that you will have tenants who don't pay their rent or who trash your place.

Certainly there are some very wealthy property developers around – many who have done it on the side – but they usually have a fair amount of money to start off with and know what they're doing when it comes to property.

Only go into this if you really know what you're doing!

CHAPTER FIFTEEN

Being a Business

MANY OF THE IDEAS in this book are things you can do on an ad hoc basis – a bit of selling on the Internet, a bit of medical research, maybe some babysitting or dog-walking or selling some cakes here and there. It's quite possible that you will confine your activities to making a bit of part-time cash.

If you have the time, the energy and the money-making ideas, however, you may find yourself running a whole little business 'on the side'. If you do end up running a proper business – however small – it will really help keep your stress levels down and help you make more money if you are clued up on a few basics before starting (or while doing it, if you've already started!).

Is it for you?

Do you really have the time and energy to devote to a small business? Do your partner and family feel happy about it, and would they help in any way? Can you organise yourself and your time? Are you tough enough to cope with difficult customers and tricky suppliers? Are you willing to do what it takes to make it work?

If the answer to all or most of these questions is yes, then you have a chance of making the business work. If there are a few no's then you should try to find a full-time job that pays more than the one you have now. Either that or confine yourself to doing bits and pieces to make money. (Don't knock it, by the way, as some people make a good living and keep their families going simply doing lots of different bits and pieces throughout the week.)

Make a plan

It helps to do a few costings and make estimates of how much time you would need to devote to a business, how much you could make and so on, before you start. On the whole it is best to try to make money out of something you enjoy, something you do already (gardening, toy-making, yoga, etc.) which you don't need to spend too much time and money on before you actually set up the business.

If, however, you have always wanted to try your hand at singing in clubs or being a dog-trainer, and money isn't your prime object, then go for it. If you make money at it too that will be a bonus!

Try to be strict with yourself and consider worst-case scenarios when you are working out costs, effort and possible profits. It's best to go into a venture with your eyes open! If you have a partner, make sure they are happy with what you are doing and, ideally, could help. There is no point bothering if you won't have support at home.

Decide whether you are going to be a sole trader – this gives you lots of freedom and flexibility but you will be completely responsible for any liabilities you incur in the business, which means that your personal as well as your business assets may be at risk – or a partnership. In a partnership you can share a lot of costs and responsibilities, but you will have to do everything by consensus and you need to know that you can trust the other person absolutely. If you do go down the partnership route, make sure you draw up a partnership agreement with the help of a solicitor – however much you trust each other at the start!

If you are going to do things on a reasonably big scale, make a business plan. This should be brief, easy to read and include all the relevant information that you and any possible financer will need. It should be a useful guide for you as you run your business, and can be as invaluable to a small sole trader as it is to a multinational company. There are many books and websites that offer help on writing a business plan. Go to your local library, or look at Lloyds TSB's free website, www.success4business.com, or www.businessbricks.co.uk or www.entrepreneur.com/business-plan.

Try to test out the market you are going for before launching into the business proper. If you are already involved in this activity in a small way you will be doing that anyway. Also check out the viability of your idea with your local Business Link. They offer a lot of free or cheap one- or two-day courses for business start-ups, and it is often worth attending one of them.

Keeping your books

Many good businesses fail simply because they haven't kept a wary and regular (sometimes you need to do it daily) eye on their accounts. Whatever the size of your business, you need to know your costs and your income exactly to ensure that you are making a profit and not in danger of running into financial problems.

There are several good accountancy packages on the market which you could use, although many small businesses find that a simple spreadsheet set up on Microsoft Excel is quite good enough. Do have a look at Quickbooks (www.quickbooks.com), Microsoft Money or, if you have a big and prosperous business, Sage (www.sage.co.uk). You can find reviews of other accountancy packages at www.accounting-software.qck.com.

Unless you have a background in finance or accountancy you would do well to employ an accountant too. Accountants come in all shapes and sizes, good, bad and totally useless, so go by recommendation if you possibly can. Even those with qualifications up to their armpits can be expensive and hopeless, so be careful.

Bank accounts

If you are working for yourself it is helpful to have a separate bank account for your business's incomings and outgoings. It doesn't have to be an actual business account – most banks charge extra for those – just a separate account, perhaps called your 'Number 2' account. If you would like an actual business account, Abbey National does a special account for small businesses which is free – in fact they even give you some interest if your account is in credit.

So, with your personal account, or joint account if you have a partner, you pay your personal and household bills, but with your 'business' account you pay business expenses, pay in money from clients and perhaps also pay yourself a kind of wage (known to accountants as 'drawings'). Also, if you pay for business-related things out of your personal account you can reimburse yourself later from your business account.

There is no law to say that you *have* to work this way but it makes it easier in the long run for tax purposes if you keep it all separate.

Advertising

You can lose a lot of money buying expensive ads or ads in the wrong places. You can also lose out by having ineffective or misleading ads, so be careful. Many small businesses may need only a listing in the Yellow Pages, a small website (one you could create yourself) and some word-of-mouth 'viral marketing'.

Look at where competitors are advertising and how they are doing it. This should give you an idea of the useful sources. Try an ad in a particular paper or on a website if you're not sure. You will be able to tell from the number of enquiries you get whether it is worth it or not. On the whole, when you start off it is not worth spending large amounts of money on advertising. Keep your costs low until you know you can sustain more expensive publicity.

If at all possible, use PR, which is free, rather than advertising. You will probably need to do both if you have a proper business on the go, but wherever possible fork out as little as you can!

Marketing

Marketing covers all kinds of things – printing, exhibitions, logos, websites, telemarketing and direct mail among others.

If you are a great designer yourself, feel free to design your own logo, website, headed notepaper, etc., but if not it is really worthwhile finding an individual or a small design company that will do it all for you. Brand is important these days, particularly where there is a lot of competition, and the more you push your brand – on your website, your logo, your headed notepaper, gifts, etc. – the more it will promote you.

The best marketing strategy is to allow some time each week to talk to existing, past and potential customers, check out what the competition is doing, consult staff and suppliers, and look for opportunities to promote your service or product.

PR

PR is the best and cheapest form of advertising there is. Gaining column inches or air-time for your product or service for free is incredibly valuable. If you have lots of money you could hire a PR agency to run a campaign for you, but a) they tend to be expensive – even if they are one-man operations, and b) there is no guarantee that they will get you into the media.

If you have a journalistic or any sort of writing background, this can help. Essentially you need to come up with interesting and even exciting press releases that will hook local and/or national media. Try to think from their point of view rather than your own. Your product or service may be the most interesting thing in the world to you, but to others there could be very little that is newsworthy in it.

Think around the topic. If your business is picture-framing, for example, you could find out which are the most popular prints that people have on their walls, send them out to the media as a 'top ten' (journalists love these, particularly 'top ten tips') and mention, in passing, that you can frame any of these prints – or anything else for that matter – for a fraction of the price of high street shops ... oh, and here are your website and contact details.

What annual events are important to your business? Think of a fun story featuring your business for Christmas, Valentine's Day, Easter or the summer holidays. If you offer tours around your town, offer a special deal with champagne and small boxes of chocolates (possibly acquired free from a local chocolate shop) for couples coming on the tour in Valentine's week. You could also research 'lurve' facts about your town and send them to the local media as a fact sheet (journalists love these too) with bullet-point snippets of information about historic romantic happenings in your town.

Just be creative and think laterally. Find out the names, numbers and email addresses of journalists in the local or national media that you particularly want to be featured in. Personal contact goes a long way, just so long as you don't irritate people with constant pestering.

There are several books on the subject of PR, and it's worth reading one to get some ideas. *Public Relations Kit for Dummies* (£15.75, John Wiley & Sons) is nice and clear and there is also *The Public Relations Handbook* by Alison Theaker (£16.99, Routledge) as well as *Public Relations: a Practical Guide to the Basics* by Philip Henslowe (£15.99, Kogan Page).

Insurance

Insurance often seems like such a waste of money that it wouldn't be surprising if you've overlooked it. With some businesses, however, if you don't have certain types of insurance you could actually be breaking the law.

You may need public liability insurance, motor insurance, employer's liability insurance, fire, flood and other perils cover, cover for goods in transit, professional indemnity, cover for computers and other business equipment, and so on.

If you belong to an association or federation for the sector you are in you can get cheaper insurance through them. Otherwise, check websites such as www.insuresupermarket.com, www.the-aa.com, www.moneyfacts.co.uk or www.find.co.uk to compare prices and get the best deal.

Getting paid

For most sales, you will need to invoice your clients for payment. It is up to you to set a date for payment – some businesses insist on payment within 14 days, which is perfectly acceptable as long as your potential client knows this beforehand and agrees to it. The legal limit is 30 days from the date of the invoice and now, thanks to the Late Payment Act of 1998, you are within your rights to charge interest on invoices paid after 30 days of base rate + 8 per cent.

If you are being paid by the hour, keep track of the hours you work each day and include the total on the invoice. This helps your client see what has been done for the money. Many accounting packages offer templates for sales invoices which you could use, or you can make up your own.

Your invoice should include the date, an invoice number, your name (or business name) and address and, if you like, your National Insurance number. It should have the terms of payment (e.g. payment within 30 days) and the name and address of the person responsible for paying. It should also include brief details of the work done or products sold and the total price (including a breakdown of charges if necessary). You may also like to include details of your bank account for BACS payments, as more and more people now prefer to pay that way.

If you are having difficulty getting paid, simple persistence usually works. Close to the final payment date, start ringing your client every other day reminding them, in a friendly way, that they haven't paid yet. Quite often just one phone call will do the trick, but for stubborn non-payers you may need to keep sending new invoices with interest slapped on before they pay.

If you continue to have problems, look into factoring. This is where you sell your debts to raise cash and get a certain percentage – up to 80 per cent – of the value of the invoices. The balance, minus a factoring fee, is paid when the debts are collected. You will probably need a turnover of around £100,000 a year, however, to make this a viable option.

Further reading

Paul Barrow, *Raising Finance*, Kogan Page, £15.99

Patricia Clayton, *Law for the Small Business*, Kogan Page, £14.99

Godfrey Golzen and Jonathan Reuvid, *Working for Yourself*, Kogan Page, £12.99 – a best-selling guide for people going it alone

Michael Morris, *The Sunday Times Guide to Starting a Successful Business*, Kogan Page, £14.99

The Which? Guide to Starting Your Own Business, Which? Guides, £10.99

CHAPTER SIXTEEN

Do I Have to Pay Tax?

WELL, THE ANSWER is yes and no! Yes, you may have to pay tax, particularly if your 'bit on the side' turns into a part-time or even a full-time business, but no, you won't have to pay tax if you are just doing bits and bobs of babysitting or dog-walking or selling on eBay and the amount you make is no more than your personal allowance. So, it depends!

Of course, the other issue is that many of the money-earning ideas in this book could be done on a cash-only basis. Many people do this – in fact it is on the increase – and in aggregate it is called the 'black economy'. It is understandable that people should not want to pay tax on these earnings – who does? Tax is a horrible thing to have to pay, and most people have negoti-ated cash-only payments with handymen, cleaners or other workers at some point because it is cheaper.

If you decide to do your work for cash only that is up to you. You are a free agent. Do take these facts into account, however:

- If you are caught by the Inland Revenue – and people are quite regularly – you will be forced to pay back taxes, which they will calculate for you, as well as a punitive fine and you could possibly face jail.

- In many cases, if you are being paid in cash and, therefore, you do not have a contract with the person paying you (because you don't want the Inland Revenue to find out about it) you will leave yourself in a vulnerable position. You cannot take them to court for non-payment, and if they decide to get nasty they can threaten to tell the Inland Revenue.

- The 'black economy' costs individual taxpayers a lot each year as the Treasury has to put up taxes elsewhere to make up the shortfall caused by non-payers. Obviously, the money for the NHS, education, government and all the other services we share and enjoy has to come from somewhere, and that somewhere is taxation.

- If you are on a relatively low income already, the government has introduced various 'tax credits' that even single, childless people can now benefit from. In some cases, if you have children, you can earn up to £58,000 a year and still get a tax break. Contact your local Inland Revenue office or look on their website at www.inlandrevenue.gov.uk to find out what you could be entitled to, even if you do extra work. There is a calculator on the website where you can input your earnings and find out whether you are eligible.

If you are earning money in addition to your salary from your employer, or you intend to work full-time for yourself, you will need to complete a self-assessment return. You don't have to register as a company but you will need to inform the Inland Revenue of your new status. You have to do this in order to reclaim costs against tax.

You can fill in your tax return yourself but if you have a lot of costs and a fair amount of money coming in you will probably find it helpful to get an accountant. That way you should get the relevant tax breaks. Also, check the Inland Revenue's website for a lot of useful free advice.

Expenses you can claim

When you are paid by your client you are paid a 'gross' amount. This means that it has not had tax or National Insurance deducted from it, unlike when you are employed by a company. If you are an employee you will be taxed through the PAYE (Pay As You Earn) scheme, where the tax and NI money is paid before you even see your money.

Self-employed people and businesses have to pay tax only twice a year, but they have to keep records of their earnings so that the tax office can work out how much they owe. It's a good idea to keep all your invoices in a file once they have been paid so that you have proof of your income. Then, in another file, box or bag, or whatever makes sense to you, keep records of all the expenses connected with your job. Put as much as you can in here because the more you put forward as expenses, the more you can set against your earnings and, therefore, the less you pay in tax! Relevant expenses, depending on the work you do, could include:

- Clothing (special working clothes, protective clothing, posh uniforms)

- Travel

- Part of your phone bill (work out a percentage that you think you could argue is business use rather than personal use)

- Part of the rent/mortgage and utility bills you pay in your home if you use part of it as an office (you could claim, say, 20 or 30 per cent, or whatever you think you could successfully argue if the Inland Revenue questioned you on it). Mind you, if you do this you might put yourself in the position of having to pay some Capital Gains Tax when you sell your property.

- Courses and research materials

- Equipment

- Relevant books and magazines

If you possibly can, always get and keep receipts for any of these expenses. If you can't get a receipt, at least log it in your diary so that you have some sort of proof of the payment.

When you come to do your tax return (or your accountant does it for you), you will use all these records of incomings and outgoings to give you the final amount due in tax. If you need more help and advice on this or any other tax matter, check out www.inlandrevenue.gov.uk, which also lists phone numbers you can ring.

What you *can't* claim

Personal expenditure such as your supermarket shopping bill, a holiday abroad, your everyday clothes, home improvements (unless it is to build an office or workshop), dinner with your partner, your TV satellite package, and so on.

National Insurance

You will have to pay National Insurance contributions if you become self-employed on a full-time basis. Check with your local Inland Revenue office or look on their website, www.inlandrevenue.gov.uk, to find out what your situation should be.

VAT

You will have to register for VAT if your turnover (not profit) exceeds the VAT threshold – currently £58,000. If you find you have to pay a lot of VAT to your suppliers you may decide it is worth registering voluntarily, even if your turnover is nowhere near the threshold. That way, although you will have to charge VAT to your customers, at least you will be able to claw back the VAT you pay your suppliers and the VAT you pay on various goods such as computer equipment, clothing and travel.

Many people dislike the idea of filing VAT accounts once a quarter but others enjoy the money they get back. If you want to find out more about VAT, look on the Customs and Excise website at www.hmce.gov.uk.

CHAPTER SEVENTEEN

Make Money by Saving Money

S AVING MONEY — it has a penny-pinching, reusing-the-tea-bags, drab sort of sound to it, doesn't it? Not at all like the glamorous one-upmanship of making some extra cash without trying too hard.

But think about it. Although there are many ways of making money without much time or effort, most of the activities in this book involve at least one or the other and usually both. Not only that, but when you make money – including when you make it by investing it (see the next chapter for ideas on this) – you usually have to pay tax on it. For every pound you make, unless you are clever with your expenses or you earn less than your annual allowance, you will have to pay a basic 22p in income tax and another 11p in National Insurance contributions (after the £4,000 or so you can earn before paying any tax).

When you *save* money, however, not only can you do it (quite often) without any effort or time, but you won't have to pay tax on it. Every pound you save is ignored by the tax office. They take money off you only if you have *made* money. So you get to keep the whole lot. It's just that saving money doesn't seem as clever and lucrative as making it. But trust me – it is!

Saving money without changing your lifestyle

How would you like to make a few thousand pounds in a couple of days? Because that's all it takes to switch your mortgage, and that's how much you could save over the life of your mortgage. Add to that a few hundred saved each year by getting cheaper utilities and another few hundred by switching banks and you've saved loads without changing your standard of living one iota.

So, be a rate tart – you save lots of money and you don't feel used in the morning.

MORTGAGES

There are currently over 7,000 mortgage products on the market with more appearing every month, so it's quite possible that there is a better deal out there than the one you currently have. Once a year, do a bit of research on the Internet, in the money sections of Sunday newspapers and by talking to mortgage brokers. Go to www.charcolonline.co.uk, www.moneysupermarket.com, www.moneyfacts.co.uk and www.fool.co.uk and get an idea of what is on offer. Don't just go for the cheapest 'headline rate' – the one that's quoted in the 'best of' lists in newspapers etc. Quite often there are expensive catches behind this rate and it can end up costing you more money in the long run.

Don't go for cheap rates that lock you in for years after the discount period has ended. Also, don't be put off haggling with your current lender if you find a better deal elsewhere. Sometimes you can get a cheaper mortgage from your own lender simply by threatening to leave. This is ideal, really, as by staying with them you cut out some costs such as surveyor's fees, solicitor's fees and any penalty charges.

UTILITIES

You can save a lot of money each year just by spending an hour on the Internet or on the phone switching your providers. Don't ever think that you should be loyal to your bank/gas supplier/phone company. They're not loyal to you, so unless they give you fabulous service and are the cheapest – or nearly the cheapest – on the market, check your bills once a year (January is a pretty good time) and switch to someone cheaper.

Useful companies to try are:

www.buy.co.uk; www.switchwithwhich.co.uk; www.uswitch.co.uk (or phone 0845 601 2856); www.switchandgive.com (or phone 0870 922 0353); www.saveonyourbills.co.uk (or phone 0800 083 0808); Simply Energy, 0800 093 9884; www.ukpower.co.uk

BANKS AND SAVINGS

We are still ridiculously loyal to our banks. A recent survey from Alliance and Leicester found that most young adults still open accounts with the banks that their parents use quite without thinking. The problem with this is that you can lose hundreds in a year by being with the wrong bank. If you currently bank with one of the big high street institutions it's highly likely that you could get a much better deal – and make more money – with a former building society, a phone bank or an Internet bank. Whether you're overdrawn all the time and paying charges or you have savings and are making (some) interest, you are guaranteed to do better with a non-standard bank.

Check out www.switchwithwhich.co.uk, www.moneysupermarket.com or www.moneyfacts.co.uk for a comparison of various bank accounts. You could also look directly at what some of the Internet and phone banks offer. ING consistently offers the best savings rates – find them at www.INGDirect.com. Internet banks Egg, Cahoot and Smile are also regularly good value – find them at www.egg.com, www.cahoot.com and www.smile.com. Phone bank First Direct consistently gets first-class reviews from its customers. You can contact them at www.firstdirect.com. Nationwide building society also gets top marks for service and offers some good deals, depending on your circumstances. Contact them on www.nationwide.co.uk.

GET CHEAPER INSURANCE

We're constantly ripped off by all sorts of insurance products, so do shop around. The Internet is a marvellous tool for this, so go to www.find.co.uk for all kinds of insurance websites. You could also look at www.insuresupermarket.com, at the insurance centre at the Motley Fool site, www.fool.co.uk, as well as www.insurancewide.com, www.moneyextra.co.uk or www.moneynet.co.uk.

PAY BILLS BY DIRECT DEBIT

The bank clearing house BACS reckons that a typical consumer can save £169 a year by paying bills by direct debit. Also, paying by DD usually means you get better deals on loans, mortgages, and so on.

BUY THINGS CHEAPER

Right, you like spending, you want to buy things. Fine, just spend less on them! Why buy a DVD player at full price when you get exactly the same thing – the same model even – cheaper on the Internet or in a sale or at a factory outlet shop. Get used to thinking about how you can get something cheaper than the asking price in the shop. Try your hand at haggling – you'd be surprised how many big high street shops, let alone market stalls or small boutiques, will knock off 5–10 per cent if you haggle and offer cash rather than the usual credit card payment.

Also, make friends with Internet sites such as www.kelkoo.co.uk, which compares the prices of thousands of different products and will direct you to the cheapest offer on the Web. Other sites that are useful are www.best-online-price.co.uk, www.checkaprice.com, www.dealtime.co.uk and www.priceguideuk.com.

Also, why not read newspapers for free? Most newspapers are available online, so you might as well read them for nothing. Alternatively, keep up to date with BBC News Online at www.bbc.co.uk or www.ananova.com. Take a book if you need something to read while commuting. As a special treat, you could buy yourself to your favourite Sunday newspaper as a reward for being frugal!

Cut down on your fuel bills *and* save the planet by being more energy efficient. You won't have to forgo anything and you will help the world at the same time. Go to www. saveenergy.co.uk and the Energy Saving Trust's website at www.est.org.uk for tips on cutting your energy costs and what grants are available to you (hey – free money!).

Make sure you're getting all the benefits you are entitled to. Every year millions in benefits payments go unclaimed, so you could have a whole wad of money coming to you that you're completely unaware of! Ring the Benefit Enquiry Line on 0800 88 22 00 for information or go to www.entitledto.co.uk to see whether you are owed anything.

Cut down on car payments. It costs well over £100 a week to run the typical private car – do you honestly need yours? Look at how much you use your car and what for. You may find you could do without it, in which case you could make thousands by selling it. If you do need to keep it, cut down on the running costs. Find cheaper petrol at www.aapetrolbusters.com, and shop around for a cheap loan if you need one to pay for the car. The AA reckons that we waste an average of £1,000 by not shopping around for the best loan deal! If you're borrowing £10,000 over five years, you could save around £2,000 by shopping around. Improve your driving skills and you will reduce your motoring costs and cut your insurance premium. Take the Institute of Advanced Motorists' advanced driving course (www.iam.org.uk). It costs £85 (£75 for under-26s), but teaches better driving techniques that will reduce your risk of an accident and help you drive more economically. Shop around for motor insurance and potentially save hundreds in a year. Go to www.find.co.uk for a list of insurance companies and brokers, or www.theaa.com, www.insuresupermarket.com and Kwik Fit Insurance – www.kwik-fitinsurance.com or 08000 279367.

Cutting back

To be honest, all of us spend more than we need to, and we could all save – or make – a substantial amount of money each year by cutting back on things we really don't need or even want in the long run. According to the latest figures from National Statistics, the average household spends about £2,375 a year on clothes, £5,491.20 a year on recreation and £3,532.88 on restaurants and hotels. There are definite savings that can be made here! It may sound hard, but if you cut back on things you don't really need or desperately want, it gives you a lot more money to spend on things you really do want or, even better, to invest well and make you lots more money later on.

- *Keep a spending diary:* Everyone should do this once a year. For one month write down *everything* you spend, however small. If you buy a latte, write it down; if you pick up a newspaper, write it down. After a week or so you'll start to realise just how much you are frittering away and why you don't have any money left at the end of the week. By the end of the month, you'll work out which things you could happily do without and that's what you can cut back on.

- *Cut back on vices:* Cutting down on vices and reducing your spend on pointless bits and pieces can really add up. A forty-a-day smoker would save around £3,300 a year by giving up, for example, or someone halving their beer intake from 12 pints to six pints a week would save £780 a year. Merely saving that amount each year won't make you really rich but investing it in a good stock market fund (and leaving it there) will. Just put the £780 a year for 25 years in a fund that grows an average of 9 per cent a year (and that is the average before tax for a basic tracker fund) and you have £69,245. Put the £3,300 in each year for 25 years and you will end up with a whopping £292,960. You're also more likely to be alive and able to enjoy it!

- *Cut back on inessentials:* Look through your spending diary and think about your lifestyle generally. What are the inessentials you can cut down on? Do you have a gym membership that you only use once a month? Cancel it. Do you have takeaways twice a week? Cut them out and you will probably save about £20 a week (that's £1,040 a year). Have you got magazine subscriptions, or an expensive TV satellite package you don't really use that much? Cancel them. Wash your car yourself instead of paying an average of £5–£10 for car washes or valeting services.

- *Reduce your mortgage term:* OK, I'll admit, in the short-term this doesn't look like saving money, but in the long-term you can save *tens* of thousands of pounds by reducing the number of years your mortgage will last. For example, if you have borrowed £100,000 on a 25-year mortgage at 5 per cent interest, over that period you will pay a total of £175,377. If you reduce that by ten years to a 15-year mortgage, however, you will pay a total of £142,342 – saving you nearly £30,000! The drawback with this is that in the short-term you will have to shell out more money each month. On the 25-year mortgage your monthly payments would be £584.59 whereas on the 15-year mortgage your payments would be £790.79.

  If you decide that you could manage that extra amount already each month, then go for it. On the other hand, you may find that the best use of the money you make 'on the side' through the tips in this book would be to pay off your mortgage asap. In fact, more and more people are setting themselves the task of paying off their mortgage in five or even two years. If you are really determined and you have the stamina to cut back on all your expenses and earn as much extra cash as you can while you go, you could save yourself tens of thousands of pounds in just a few years.

Freebies

There are a lot of Internet sites now that offer all kinds of free samples of products and give you money-off coupons for super-markets and specific products. Go to www.wishvalue.co.uk and

www.homesolutionsnews.com for coupons on all kinds of products.

Also, look at www.fixtureferrets.co.uk for special offers from
seven leading supermarkets.

Saving tax

According to IFA Promotions (www.ifap.org.uk) we hand over
nearly £6 billion more than we should to the taxman each year,
mainly because we don't use up tax allowances. That's over £130
per person. Now unless you have a close, personal attachment
to the Chancellor of the Exchequer, there doesn't seem to be any
good reason to overpay in tax. So make sure you do the following each year:

- Make the most use of your pension allowances. Yes, I know
  pensions have had a bad press recently – rightly so in many cases
  – but you do get tax relief (well, really tax deferred) on all the
  money you put into your pension pot. If you are a higher-rate
  taxpayer, this means you will save 40 per cent on all the money
  you put in there.

  If you have a company pension, stick with it. If you are self-
  employed, go for a stakeholder pension, not a basic personal
  pension. Stakeholders perform better than the old personal
  pensions as the annual charges are much lower, so you waste less
  money. Find out about stakeholders at the Financial Services
  Authority's website, www.fsa.gov.uk, which has fact sheets on
  pensions. Also, the government's website,
  www.stakeholderhelpline.gov.uk, gives a list of companies that
  offer stakeholder pensions.

- Make use of your ISA allowance. If you have savings in the
  building society or you put money into the stock market, do it in
  an Isa. You can put up to £3,000 per tax year into a cash mini ISA,
  saving you tax on the interest you make (it will go down to £1,000
  a year from April 2006) and up to £3,000 a year into a shares
  mini ISA, which saves you a little tax. If you want you can put up to

£7,000 into a shares maxi ISA each tax year, although that will go down to £5,000 a year from April 2006.

● Use up your capital gains allowance. Currently you can make up to £7,800 a year in capital gains on shares, investment property and other appreciating assets. Also, you can save on capital gains by transferring assets between spouses to make the most of the lower-rate taxpayer.

● Sort out your self-assessment. Make sure your form arrives present and correct by the 31 January deadline or you waste £100 in penalty charges. You may also be liable for other penalties for any errors you make, so stay alert when you fill it in.

● Make a will – plan properly to avoid inheritance tax liabilities, write life assurance policies in trust and keep inheritance tax allowances in mind.

Quick tips

● Make friends with your local library. Don't bother buying new books unless you *have* to.

● Have the occasional 'swap shop' with friends where you swap or buy from each other clothes and other bits that you don't want any more.

● Keep up with the general maintenance on your home. It can get very expensive if problems such as the roof or plumbing get really bad.

● If you can't stop buying clothes, get into charity shop buying. You'll spend less money and, most of the time, you'll get far more interesting clothes than you can find in the shops.

● Buy annual, all-in-one travel insurance rather than individual trip cover, if you take two or more holidays per year. Shop around on www.insuresupermarket.com, www.theaa.com or www.insureandgo.co.uk.

- Never shop on an empty stomach. Use a shopping list and stick to it.

- Regularly check out websites like www.fool.co.uk and www.moneysavingexpert.com for loads of saving tips.

- Get your friends to have more nights out at each other's houses than in expensive clubs and restaurants. You'll probably find that they're grateful to spend less too.

And if things get really tight ...

- Always be the third person to buy a round in the pub. You'll spend less!

- Go away at Christmas to avoid sending presents and cards.

- Become a 'freegan', picking out perfectly edible food thrown out by supermarkets in the evening. You'd be amazed at what you can get for free!

CHAPTER EIGHTEEN

Making Your *Money* Make Money

THE EASIEST WAY to make money on the side is to get your money to work for you. In other words, invest your money and it will grow on its own, while you sleep, without you having to lift a finger.

Does that sound too good to be true? Particularly in the light of recent ups and downs (well, mostly downs) in the stock market? Well, not if you're playing a long game. Investing means that you put money into something for a long time, probably decades, and over that time it grows bigger every year. During the property boom, some people managed to make money by investing in a property they knew would be popular, touching it up a bit and selling it again a few months later. It is still possible to do this in certain parts of the country, but you really need to know what you are doing and have the time to pick the best properties. Many have made money on their own properties by accident. They happened to buy them at least five years ago and they have risen in value since then. This is a form of investment and has been good for some in the past, but there are no guarantees that property will be a rock-solid performer in the long-term. It may be, but if too many people go into the buy-to-let market it could spell misery for many (see Chapter 14).

Ideally, if you invest in the stock market – either in

individual shares or in a fund that includes various shares – and you reinvest any interest or dividends you receive, your money should grow by a larger amount every year, like a snowball rolling down a mountain and gathering more snow with each revolution. The more you save, and the longer you save, the more you'll end up with. You start off just getting interest, but then you earn interest on that interest and then you earn interest on the interest on that interest, and so on. Over a long period of time it really adds up.

Short-term investment – where you buy into a company on the stock market hoping to double your money in a few days or months – is basically gambling, and you'll remember what Chapter 14 revealed about gambling! But over the long-term, particularly if you invest in a tracker fund (see more on this below) that tracks a FTSE index cheaply and efficiently, you will be surprised and pleased at how much money your original investments make you.

How to do it

You should find that once you have paid off your debts and learned to live below your means you are able to save a tidy little sum each month, particularly if you are earning a bit on the side as well. Put this away in a high-interest building society account until you have enough to cover you and your family's living expenses for three months and leave it there. That way you will have some cash to draw on if you hit an emergency or if you lose your income for three months. It might sound like a drag to have all that money in a savings account but it can really help if you suddenly lose your job or get ill. All the big, billionaire investors such as Warren Buffett (the second-richest man in America) suggest you have a 'sinking fund' of three to six months' worth of savings, 'just in case'.

Once you have that, then the fun starts. Well, all right, it's not exactly rib-tickling, get-your-knickers-off-and-wave-them-in-the-air-type fun, but gently, gradually, over time, a quiet glow of satisfaction can grow into a degree of wealthy smugness that even your mother will find irritating!

Investment options

There are various things you could invest in. Broadly they divide up into cash (bank accounts, building society accounts), bonds and gilts, shares (in the stock market), property, pensions and objects (antiques, art, wine, classic cars, Barbie dolls . . . whatever takes your fancy). Of course, you might also be investing in a business, probably your own business, which you hope will grow over time and keep you in your old age.

Cash

Safe, dependable cash. You know where you are with it, don't you? For most of us it's the closest we've ever got to 'investing'. Perhaps your mum and dad opened a building society account for you when you were a kid, and when you've been feeling sensible you've put some money in every now and then and got a bit excited once a year about the extra few quid you got in interest. So why not carry on with that? It's safe, it's guaranteed to bring a bit of money in, and you can't lose, right? Well, actually, in real terms, over time you most certainly can.

Long-term building society returns just about match the long-term rate of inflation after you've taken tax into account, and, if you also consider average earnings growth, cash really is a loser. This means that even if you keep reinvesting the interest you get each year over time the real spending power of your little pot of money will actually decrease. Currently you can get a return of around 5 per cent on the highest-paying accounts (before tax), which is better than a smack in the face with a wet kipper but only really worth having for accumulating reasonable amounts of money over the short-term to put in better-paying vehicles later on. If we're thinking long-term (and we always are, aren't we?), keeping your money in banks or building societies is only slightly better than sticking it under the mattress.

PROS

Cash is dependable, liquid (i.e. you can get your hands on it pretty quickly) and you know where you are with it.

CONS

Over the long-term, because of inflation and the low amounts you earn even in the top building society accounts, you can actually lose money by investing it in cash. In real terms, the amount you will have in 20 years' time will buy you much less than you will need. It's a good idea to have some cash invested at all times, but for serious investments set your sights higher.

Bonds

All right, we're going up in the investment food chain here but not very much. Bonds, like cash, are a nice, safe-ish place to put your money, and you do get a better return than with cash, but it's still not great. That's the trade-off, you see – safety costs and absolute safety *really* costs.

Bonds are essentially loans that can be bought and sold on a market. The most common are government loans, or gilts (see below). But you can also trade corporate bonds, which are loans to large companies. Basically you lend the company a sum of money to use as they will. They agree to pay the money back to you at a specified date in the future, plus an annual amount of interest. Bonds have different safety ratings depending on the risk, but mostly they're pretty safe if you stick to big, solid companies. If you wait until the bond's term is up before cashing it in, you should get your money back in full if you bought it at the right price to begin with. If you try to sell it on in the meantime, however, its value will vary depending on the current yields on bonds and the time remaining to the redemption date.

The capital value of bonds moves up and down in relation to

interest rates, so they are not totally safe as houses, but they do tend to be popular with many investors (and financial advisers) because they give a half-decent yield with very little risk. If you are close to or in retirement, bonds can be a useful form of income, and so they are often favoured by older people. Over the long-term, however, for investment purposes, they return slightly more than cash, but not much, so they're hardly exciting.

Gilts

These are a kind of bonds sub-set. They are also known as government bonds – basically loans to the government. As we are living in a stable country with a relatively stable, democratic government – not in one of those places where the leader has a special salute and a predilection for tight uniforms (although give it time . . .) – lending money to the government is generally considered to be a pretty safe bet. After all, the government does print the stuff! It's certainly safer than lending to companies. Therefore, the return on gilts, though nice and secure, is even smaller than that on company bonds. Hmm . . . worth bothering with for long-term investing? Not unless you're afraid of your own shadow.

Shares (also known as equities)

Ah, now you're talking. Numerous studies have been done about the rates of return that each of the main types of investment have made down the years. Over and over again they've shown that equities (shares) give far and away better returns than cash, bonds or gilts. In the period 1918–2003 the UK stock market returned an average of 11 per cent per annum, or 7 per cent per annum if you adjust for inflation. In terms of spending power, this rate of return means that £10,000 would turn into £38,700 over the course of 20 years.

Anyone can invest in the stock market. You don't have to wear red braces and shout 'buy, buy, sell, sell' into a phone all day. If you want to do it seriously you could invest in a few individual companies, such as Vodafone, Tesco or GlaxoSmithKline. You will need to be prepared to study the companies and investment rules first, though, to stop you making serious and expensive mistakes. The website www.fool.co.uk has lots of very helpful advice and useful discussion boards to guide you through the shark pool that is stock market investing if you want to do this.

On the other hand, an easy and no-fuss way to invest is through a fund that invests in a range of companies for you. There are all kinds of funds to choose from, but they break down into two main forms: managed funds and tracker funds. Managed funds are run by clever human beings who study companies all day every day and decide which are the best to invest in. Tracker funds are run by computer and they tend to invest a very small amount in lots of companies based on a complicated computer program.

Over time, it has been shown that the humble tracker fund consistently outperforms managed funds 75 per cent of the time. Not only that, but tracker funds are cheaper to invest in than managed funds (mostly much less than 1 per cent a year in charges), so you waste less money there too. Again, www.fool.co.uk has information on funds, and in particular tracker funds, to invest in.

The best way to start investing is by putting regular amounts of money – say, £25, £50 or £100 per month – into an index tracker, preferably within a low-cost ISA to protect your gains from tax. Several companies offer tracker fund investments that are already wrapped in an ISA. Here are a few to consider:

- Edinburgh UK Tracker Trust (FTSE All-Share). Annual charges: 0.25 per cent. Minimum investments: £250 lump sum or £30 per month. Contact: www.edfd.com or 0131 313 1000.

- HSBC FTSE All-Share Fund (FTSE All-Share). Annual charges: 0.5 per cent. Minimum investments: £500 lump sum or £25 a month. Contact: www.hsbc.co.uk or 0800 289505.

- Legal & General UK Index (FTSE All-Share). Annual charges: 0.53 per cent. Minimum investments: £500 lump sum or £25 a month. Contact: www.legalandgeneral.com or 0800 0920092.

- M&G Index Tracker (FTSE All-Share). Annual charges: 0.439 per cent. Minimum investments: £500 lump sum or £10 a month. Contact: www.mandg.co.uk or 0800 390390.

- Virgin UK Index Tracker (FTSE All-Share). Annual charges: 1 per cent. Minimum investments: £1 for lump sums or monthly investments. Contact: www.virginmoney.com or 08456 101020.

Property

Property has grown in value so fast over the last 30 years that some people who happened to buy their home in that time have made a lot of money. Property development has also become the pastime of the layman, not just specialist builders, and, as the stock market has wobbled worryingly since 2001, it has seemed the safest and best place to invest your money. Generally the thinking is that as property prices have been rising this fast you should get on the bandwagon quickly before it leaves without you. Or should you?

Well, certainly a lot of other people in this country think so. In 2001 the whole buy-to-let market rose by about 60 per cent and is now worth more than £10 billion in mortgage debt. Around 90 per cent of landlords have just one buy-to-let property, so we're not talking about the big property developer types! It just shows how many people are putting money into bricks and mortar. It has also become easier and cheaper to raise a mortgage for rental property as more lenders have come into the market and are now offering rates that, in many cases, are cheaper than ordinary residential mortgages.

PROS

People will always need somewhere to live, and as the number of single households is predicted to rise in the future, so the demand on the housing stock is likely to increase faster than dwellings can (or will) be built. So in the medium-term, at least, the demand for properties to rent should continue or even increase.

Unlike shares or pensions, you can physically see, feel and touch property. You know it is there and, unless it is blown up or burnt down (and naturally you would have it insured against those eventualities), it is unlikely to crash or dwindle away.

You feel rather more in control of property than you might with shares, and certainly than you would with a pension. It is up to you to maintain it, monitor the tenants and set the rent. If you get the right property in the right area at the right time you could find it rocketing in value over five or ten years.

CONS

Property is an inflexible investment. It has the potential to produce good returns but those looking to make a quick buck should think again. Latest indicators show housing market growth slowing markedly – gone are the days of annual growth rates of 20 per cent plus. So, if you want to buy a second property for investment purposes you should be thinking about investing for the long-term. Also, when you come to sell the property, bear in mind that it could take months to get your hands on the money.

You can't guarantee 100 per cent occupancy. It takes only a month or two of emptiness to knock your annual return down significantly. In extreme cases, you might have your property empty for long periods, which can cause big problems. Tenants who don't pay the rent can be very expensive. Not only can you lose rental income but getting them evicted can cost money too. If it happens to you, you might have to face writing off a whole year's rent.

Even decent tenants will cause wear and tear to parts of the house and furniture. After a few years of ordinary, understandable wear and tear you will have to foot the bill for repair and redecoration. This will cut into your income. Rectifying damage after a tenant has moved out takes time too: time when you're not getting any rent. You also have legal responsibilities in relation to the safety of the building, the furniture and the gas and electricity supplies.

Unless you pay a management company to deal with any problems your tenants encounter, you may have the hassle of midnight phone calls about the boiler or Sunday morning calls to a plumber to fix the drains.

A buy-to-let mortgage is a debt, and debts have to be paid. When you take out a mortgage, be sure to stay well within your means. What will you do if you don't get any rent for six months, or a year, or more (for one of the above reasons)? The answer is to be sure you can cover the repayments from your own income. You may have net outflows each month or, in the worst case, have to sell the property.

House prices can't keep growing faster than earnings for ever, and the rises we've seen in recent years won't continue indefinitely. And when you sell, you'll have to pay capital gains tax if you make a profit. Any decent profit is likely to put you in the 40 per cent bracket if you're not already there. Unlike with shares, you can't put a house into your ISA, although you may be able to put it in a SIPP at some point soon.

HOW TO DO IT

If you are still determined to invest in a buy-to-let property, the important thing to remember when looking for a house or flat is that it is an investment, not somewhere you want to live. Try to keep emotions out of it. This is business, not comfort. First, look for areas where there is likely to be high rental demand. Good local facilities and transport links are also essential. If you want to save money and manage the property yourself, however, you should make sure you buy in an area that is easily accessible from where you live.

Speak to local lettings agents about what kinds of properties let best. Generally flats and small houses seem to be the most popular, particularly in cities. As with buying your own home, location is everything. A property close to transport and amenities will be easier to let and is more likely to appreciate in value as well. But of course this means that there can be a lot of competition for the 'best' properties. Also, ask the local agents whether furnished, unfurnished or part-furnished properties let most readily and follow their advice.

Once you have bought somewhere, decide whether you want to use a local agent to let it or whether you want to save the monthly charge by doing it yourself. To start with it may be wise to let an agent find and check your tenants and collect the rent, but once you have worked out how it is done you should be able to do it yourself using the services of credit checkers and basic contracts from your local newsagent's. You can get lots more information by joining the Residential Landlords Association at http://www.rla.org.uk.

Pensions

Pensions have had a very bad press in the last few years, and rightly so in many cases. Just as piling into property because everyone else is doing it is a bad idea, however, shying away from all types of pensions just because some have had a bad press is also not too sensible. In fact, particularly in the case of the much ignored stakeholder pension, now could be a very good time to start considering pensions as a serious investment plan – at least as part of your investments for the future.

A pension is basically a savings plan. That's it. You sign up for a 'pension' and stuff money in it for 40 years or so and that money is invested on the stock market for you. When you reach 50 or more – it's more likely to be much later now – you are left with a large pot of money with which you can fund your retirement. The general theory goes that in return for their fees the pensions company will have invested your money sensibly, so with a bit of luck your pension fund may have done better than average. Hmm ... maybe.

One big problem with pensions is that when you retire you

will be forced to buy an annuity with 75 per cent of the money you save in your pension fund, which will guarantee you a certain amount of money each year until you die. That may not be an enormous amount but it is something and it is guaranteed not to run out before you die. It is still annoying, though, not to be able to invest it in something you think would give you a better return.

One good part about investing in a pension is that your contributions for personal or company pensions come out of your gross income – in other words you are not taxed on it – although the money you get from it once you retire, through an annuity, will be taxed. On top of this, the government has introduced the concept of stakeholder pensions. Basically this means that these pensions have to meet certain requirements, on costs and terms, in order to call themselves stakeholder pensions. It's a sort of government seal of approval, rather like CAT (Charges, Access and Terms) standards for ISAs and other financial products. Also, you don't have to be working – or earning – in order to have one.

The rules are that stakeholder pension providers can charge you only a maximum of one per cent of the value of your pension fund each year to manage it. The charges are taken out of your fund, and, as well as the one per cent, the law allows pension providers to recover costs they have to bear for certain other things. All stakeholder schemes must accept contributions of as little as £20, which you can pay each week, each month or at less regular intervals.

You can get stakeholder pensions from all sorts of financial services companies such as insurance companies, banks, investment companies and building societies. Other organisations such as trade unions may also offer stakeholder schemes. On the whole, stakeholder pensions are pensions based on tracker funds – they have to be because very few other types of funds have such low charges.

So generally, stakeholder pensions are worth considering as part of your investment portfolio (even if there are just a few hundred pounds in your investment pot, it is still a portfolio!).

Appendix

Useful books

The eBay Book – David Belbin (£9.99, Harriman House)
The Which? Guide to Starting Your Own Business – Anthony Bailey
  (£10.99, Which? Books)
The Freelance Writer's Handbook – Andrew Crofts (£9.99, Piatkus)
*The Daily Telegraph Small Business Guide to Starting Your Own
  Business* – Michael Becket (£10.99, Pan)
The Complete Guide to Being a Cheapskate – Mark Miller (£10.95,
  Alpha Books)
A Girl's Best Friend Is Her Money – Jasmine Birtles, Jane Mack
  (£12.99, Boxtree)
The Motley Fool UK Investment Guide – David Berger and James
  Castle (£12.99, Boxtree)
The Money Diet – Martin Lewis (£7.99, Vermilion)
Think Yourself Rich – Sharon Maxwell-Magnus (£9.99, Vermilion)
Your Money Or Your Life – Alvin Hall (£6.99, Coronet)
You Can Be A Movie Extra – Rob Martin (£6.99, Titan Books)
Daily Mail Tax Guide – Jane Vass (£9.99, Profile Books)
The Daily Telegraph Tax Guide – David Genders (£6.99, Pan)

Useful websites

www.fool.co.uk – great website for all things financial (and
everything else if you look on the discussion boards) from the
Motley Fool

www.moneysavingexpert.com – top money-saving tips from
Martin Lewis

www.moneysupermarket.com, **www.moneyextra.co.uk**,
www.moneyfacts.co.uk – websites where you can research and
buy the best rated financial products

www.dti.gov.uk – the official site of the Department of Trade and Industry

www.inlandrevenue.gov.uk – the Inland Revenue's very helpful site

www.dwp.gov.uk – information on pensions and benefits on this site from the Department of Work and Pensions

www.businesslink.gov.uk – the website for the government-funded Business Link

www.simpleliving.net — a website for anyone who's interested in a simpler, cheaper, less materialistic way of living

www.studentfreestuff.com – a website full of freebies for students

www.garage.com helps entrepreneurs and investors build great businesses

www.nvst.com Private Equity Network, a web-enabled meeting place for investors, advisers, and entrepreneurs

www.startupzone.com/ www.inc.com/ small business planning and advice

www.shell-livewire.org – sponsored by Shell, helps 16- to 30-year-old people start up and develop their businesses

www.princes-trust.org.uk – aged 18 to 30 and unemployed or 'underemployed' in the UK? Get a grant or low-interest loan from the Princes Trust to help you start up your business

www.fsb.org.uk – Federation of Small Businesses. They represent the interests of small business people across the UK. They offer discounted schemes for insurance, medical care, financial services, Internet design and banking

www.homeworking.com – an excellent website full of all kinds of information for people wanting to work from home or set up their own business

www.byots.co.uk – lots of help and information on business management

www.dti.gov.uk – government support and initiative for business and commerce. Particularly check out www.dti.gov.uk/support where you will find all the different types of support on offer

www.businessadviceonline.org – partially funds the Business Links in England and works with the many other government and local schemes

http://bcuk.smallbiz.uk.com – Business Clubs UK

The Professional Contractors Group Limited – www.pgc.org.uk, 0845 125 9899, Lakeside House, 1 Furzeground Way, Stockley Park East, Uxbridge UB11 1BD

Enterprise agencies:

www.nfea.com – National Federation of Enterprise Agencies covers England with 82 separate enterprise agencies divided into nine areas

www.scottish-enterprise.com – Scottish Enterprise companies cover south-west Scotland with 13 area enterprise companies

www.hie.co.uk – Highland and Islands Enterprise covers the Scottish Highlands of the North-west; based in Inverness, they have ten local enterprise companies

www.businessconnect.org.uk – Business Connect Wales has four area Business Connect agencies, each with their own branches, amounting to 43 offices across Wales

www.investni.com – Local Enterprise Development Unit with two area enterprise offices

Business suppport networks:

www.businesslink.org – Business Links cover various regions with 84 hub offices

www.sbgateway.com – Small Business Gateway has 13 regions with 54 area offices

www.bis.uk.com – Business Information Source Network is part of the Highlands and Islands Enterprise service

www.businessconnect.org.uk – Business Connect Wales provides this service combined with its enterprise role; it has four area Business Connect agencies

www.investni.com – Economic Development Network works with the Local Enterprise Development Units, local government and the Training and Employment Agency to provide business development advice

Business development agencies:

www.englishpartnerships.co.uk – English Partnerships is 'the national force for regeneration and development in England'

www.wda.co.uk – the Welsh Development Agency was formed in 1976 and is now part of the new National Assembly for Wales

www.scotland.gov.uk/who/elld – the Enterprise and Lifelong Learning Department is part of the Scottish executive and drives Scottish economic development

www.detini.gov.uk – the Department of Economic Development works with the UK Department of Trade and Industry and the Department of Employment to represent the interests of the Northern Irish economy

Chambers of Commerce – these have had a bit of a shake-up in the UK, but you can look at www.chamberonline.co.uk/, 'British Chambers of Commerce', to find your local UK chamber using a map of the UK